Improvisation in Drama

ANTHONY FROST and RALPH YARROW

MACMILLAN

First published 1990 by
THE MACMILLAN PRESS LTD
Houndmills, Basingstoke, Hampshire RG21 2XS
and London
Companies and representatives
throughout the world

ISBN 0–333–38820–8 hardcover
ISBN 0–333–38821–6 paperback

A catalogue record for this book is available
from the British Library.

13   12   11   10   9   8   7   6   5
03   02   01   00   99   98   97   96   95

Printed in Hong Kong

Contents

List of Plates   vii
General Editor's Preface   viii
Acknowledgements   ix

Introduction   1
  Definitions   1
  Early history: shamans, clowns and actors   4

PART I   WHO? MAJOR PRACTITIONERS OF IMPROVISATION

1 Improvisation in Traditional Drama   **13**
  Introduction – the principle of improvisation   13
  Overview   14
  Precursors: Stanislavsky and Meyerhold   15
  Jacques Copeau   20
  Le Théâtre du Soleil   30
  Improvisation and 'traditional' theatre training   31
  Mike Leigh   37
  Further thoughts on play-construction using
    improvisation   42
  New York Giants versus Chicago Bears   45

2 Improvisation in Alternative Drama   **55**
  Roddy Maude-Roxby/Theatre Machine   55
  Jacques Lecoq and the semiotics of clowning   61
  Dario Fo and Franca Rame   73

3 Beyond Drama – 'Paratheatre'   **83**
  Jerzy Grotowski   83

PART II   WHAT? THE PRACTICE OF IMPROVISATION: IMPROVISATION EXERCISES

Introduction   95
4 Preparation   **97**
  Relaxation   97
  Games   97
  Balance and 'body/think'   98
  Space and movement   100
  Concentration and attention   101
  Impulses and directions   103

5   **Working Together**   **105**
    Trust and respect   105
    Making a machine   106
    Showing and telling   107
    Entrances and exits   108
    Meetings and greetings   109
    Blocking   110

6   **Moving Towards Performance**   **112**
    Senses   112
    Tenses   113
    Status   114
    Masks   116
    Masks – another view   121

7   **Applied Improvisation Work**   **126**
    Who/where/what   126
    Objectives and resistances   127
    Point of concentration (focus)   128
    Memory   129
    'Set'   130
    Character   131
    Narrative   134

PART III   WHY? THE MEANINGS OF IMPROVISATION:
           TOWARDS A POETICS

Introduction   143
8   **Enriching the Communication of Meaning**   **144**
    Implications of psychodrama and paratheatrical
       approaches   144
    The censor's nightmare   146
    La disponibilité   151
    Transformation   155

9   **Meaning and Performance**   **165**
    Some aspects of meaning in performance   165
    Texts, signs and meaning   166
    Co-creativity   169
    Gremlin's Theatre   175
    New combinations   179

    Notes   182
    Bibliography   199
    Index   206

List of Plates

1. I Gelati in Commedia masks (photograph courtesy of I Gelati)
2. Copeau's *Comédie Nouvelle*: Saint-Denis as Knie, Suzanne Bing as La Célestine, Dasté as César (photograph courtesy of Et. Bordas, from J. Lecoq (ed.), *Le Théâtre du Geste*, 1988)
3. Jacques Lecoq in neutral mask (photograph courtesy of Patrick Lecoq)
4. Lecoq teaching at his Paris school (photograph courtesy of Et. Bordas, from J. Lecoq (ed.), *Le Théâtre du Geste*, 1988)
5. 'The fight in the dark', from *The 1984 Game*, University of East Anglia, 1983 (photograph courtesy of Anthony Frost)
6. Free improvisation with Roddy Maude-Roxby (Theatre Machine) (photograph courtesy of Jo Rice)
7. Théâtre de Complicité in *Please Please Please* (photograph courtesy of Théâtre de Complicité)
8. 'Croquet': Ric Morgan and Roddy Maude-Roxby (Theatre Machine) 1981 (photograph courtesy of Bernard Phillips)

General Editor's Preface

In the past ten years, Theatre Studies has experienced remarkable international growth, students seeing in its marriage of the practical and the intellectual a creative and rewarding discipline. Some countries are now opening school and degree programmes in Theatre Studies for the first time; others are having to accommodate to the fact that a popular subject attracting large numbers of highly motivated students has to be given greater attention than hitherto. The professional theatre itself is changing, as graduates of degree and diploma programmes make their way through the 'fringe' into established theatre companies, film and television.

Two changes in attitudes have occurred as a result: first, that the relationship between teachers and practitioners has significantly improved, not least because many more people now have experience of both; secondly, that the widespread academic suspicion about theatre as a subject for study has at least been squarely faced, if not fully discredited. Yet there is still much to be done to translate the practical and educational achievements of the past decade into coherent theory, and this series is intended as a contribution to that task. Its contributors are chosen for their combination of professional and didactic skills, and are drawn from a wide range of countries, languages and styles in order to give some impression of the subject in its international perspective.

This series offers no single programme or ideology; yet all its authors have in common the sense of being in a period of transition and debate out of which the theory and practice of theatre cannot but emerge in a new form.

University of East Anglia   JULIAN HILTON

Acknowledgements

Thanks to a variety of editorial hands at Baker-Mahaffy and Macmillan, and in particular to our colleague and General Editor, Julian Hilton, for his encouragement and most valuable comments. We also owe a considerable debt of gratitude to performers we have talked to and worked with, especially Jacques Lecoq, Roddy Maude-Roxby (Theatre Machine), James MacDonald and Malcolm Tulip (I Gelati), Simon McBurney and Clive Mendus (Théâtre de Complicité), Rena Mirecka (Teatr Laboratorium), and our friend and colleague Franc Chamberlain (who has also read and commented on part of the book). Thanks also to several generations of UEA drama students; and to those from whom we have learned or continue to learn in other contexts: Nicholas Brooke, Douglas Brown, Max Flisher, Tony Gash, Tony Hall, Clive Barker, David Hirst, Amanda Frost and Jackie Yarrow.

For Simric and Kielan Yarrow

and
for William Frost and
in memoriam
Kathleen Frost

Introduction

There are people who prefer to say 'Yes', and there are
people who prefer to say 'No'. Those who say 'Yes' are
rewarded by the adventures they have, and those who
say 'No' are rewarded by the safety they attain. There
are far more 'No' sayers around than 'Yes' sayers, but
you can train one type to behave like the other.

Keith Johnstone, *Impro* (1981)

Definitions

Improvisation: the skill of using bodies, space, all human
resources, to generate a coherent physical expression of an
idea, a situation, a character (even, perhaps, a text); to do
this spontaneously, in response to the immediate stimuli of
one's environment, and to do it *à l'improviste*: as though taken
by surprise, without preconceptions.

Improvisation is fundamental to all drama. All performance
uses the body of the actor, giving space and form to an idea,
situation, character or text in the moment of creation. It does not
matter that the play has been rehearsed for a month, with every
move, every nuance of speech learned and practised. In the act
of performance the actor becomes an improviser. The audience
laughs, and he times the next line differently. He hears the lines
of his fellow performers as if for the first time, each time, and
responds to them, for the first time. He keeps within the learned
framework of the play; he does not make up new lines, or alter
the play's outcome in any drastic way. Yet, the actor improvises;
and the relationship between formal 'acting' and 'improvising'
is so intricate that we might say that each *includes* the other.
Improvisation is a part of the nature of acting, certainly. But,
more importantly, acting is only one part of the creative process
of improvising.

1

Improvisation is physical response, including the verbal. It is immediate and organic articulation; not just response, but a paradigm for the way humans reflect (or create) what happens. Where improvisation is most effective, most spontaneous, least 'blocked' by taboo, habit or shyness, it comes close to a condition of integration with the environment or context. And consequently (simultaneously) expresses that context in the most appropriate shape, making it recognisable to others, 'realising' it as act.

In that sense, improvisation may come close to pure 'creativity' – or perhaps more accurately to creative organisation, the way in which we respond to and give shape to our world. The process is the same whenever we make a new arrangement of the information we have, and produce a recipe, a theory or a poem. The difference with doing it *à l'improviste*, or *all'improvviso*, is that the attention is focused on the precise moment when things take shape. As well as being the most exciting moment, this is also the most risky: what emerges may be miraculous or messy – or a panic retreat into habit or cliché.

Some teachers of juggling begin by giving the pupil three balls and getting the student to throw them up in the air. The tendency is to clutch reflexively, to tighten up, to panic and to try desperately to catch the balls. The teacher will smile, shake his or her head, and make the beginner throw the balls again, this time making no effort to catch. When the balls hit the ground the teacher will nod, 'That's *supposed* to happen.' The right to fail, to make a hash of it, is affirmed from the beginning. The student learns to get out of the life-conditioned reflex of trying to 'make it happen'. Then the teacher gives the relaxed student one ball to be thrown gently from hand to hand. Then two, helping the student to overcome the convulsive clutching which prevents the second ball from being thrown up as the first descends. 'Don't try to catch it, concentrate on throwing, on *emptying* the hand – make it ready to receive the descending ball.' Finally, as the gentle rhythm of juggling is learned, the third ball is easy to master. The hardest thing to learn is not 'how to juggle', but how to let the balls drop.[1]

It is the same with improvisation. The hardest thing to learn is that failure doesn't matter. It doesn't have to be brilliant every time – it can't be. What happens is what happens; is what you have created; is what you have to work with. What matters is to listen, to watch, to add to what is happening rather than subtract from it – and to avoid the reflex of trying to make it into something you think it *ought* to be, rather than letting it become what it *can* be.

Learning how to improvise may, therefore, be rather more than just getting used to 'botching things up', or doing something 'on the spur of the moment'. It may even be something like a skill for living. Not just doing anything in the moment, but learning how to make use of as much of ourselves and as much of the 'context' as possible; learning how to fill the moment.

What happens in a 'theatre' or other 'performance space' is important in the context of the world 'outside'. They exist in some sort of dialectical relationship with each other, rather than in separate compartments. Just as theatre may not merely mirror society, but acts as a force within it which changes its shape, so too improvisation of various kinds has often changed the shape and direction of theatre; and being 'innovative' or 'improvisatory' may be something that is more necessary for all aspects of human relationship than is often acknowledged. Habit is the great enemy of evolution. Is the kind of thing that happens in improvisation similar to the processes by which, for instance, a biological structure evolves to new levels of order? It might well be, for improvisation is about order, and about adaptation, and about truthfully responding to changing circumstances, and about generating meaning out of contextual accidents. It is about failing, and about not minding failure. It is about trying again, and about enjoying the process without straining to get a known result. It is about creation.

This book is the first, we believe, to offer a unified view of a very important field, dramatic improvisation. It brings together a number of studies, of individual practitioners, of techniques and of theories. It is, for example, the first attempt in English to fully assess the significance of the teaching work of Jacques Lecoq. It analyses the contributions to twentieth-century theatre made by such diverse talents as Jacques Copeau, Mike Leigh and Dario Fo, and relates them via the differing uses each has made of improvisation. It explains the significance of the various exercises offered by impro teachers and relates them to a larger view of drama. It offers a taxonomy of such exercises which is, we hope, as useful to the scholar as to the drama student or acting coach. It is the first to relate hitherto unvalued, unscripted and unrecorded performance to the major preoccupations of twentieth-century literary and dramatic theory; a poetics of improvisation.

In writing it, we have attempted to integrate a number of different perspectives – the historical, the critical, the practical and the theoretical; and improvisation is seen as a larger process which intersects the smaller field of drama at certain key points (speaking both historically and figuratively) to their mutual enrichment. For reasons of space and clarity, we concentrate primarily on those nodes of intersection in the twentieth century. Our subject is 'Improvisation in Drama' rather than the immensity of improvisation in its pure state. But in any exploration it is necessary to seek out the boundaries of one's field, and to look over the fences into adjacent pastures. Thus we have alluded to activities other than drama which make use of improvisation, and we have tried also to look at the more liminal or marginal reaches of the subject in terms of, for example, shamanism and what Grotowski calls 'Paratheatre'.

Early history: shamans, clowns and actors

Improvisation, both within and without drama, is not a new phenomenon. It has a long and noble history which, for reasons of space, can only be briefly summarised here.

That history begins with the shadowy figure of the *shaman*. The term properly denotes a man or woman who, through trance, is believed to be able to penetrate the spirit world at will and return safely, bringing tales, spirits and curative medicinal powers from the other side. Initiated, inspired and intoxicated (with dance, or with drink, or with the ivy-derived narcotic used by the worshippers of Dionysos) the shaman's ecstatic state of transformation is universally recognised.[2] He gives up his body, letting it become a theatre for the gods to appear in. The shaman pre-dates the priest (whose organised, codified and ceremonial form of religion, symbolic rather than manifest, no longer requires the ecstatic personal vision of the mystic; and rather distrusts it) just as he pre-dates the actor. He is, as Huizinga[3] would describe him, the origin of the *vatic* poet; god-smitten and *entheos* (literally 'enthused', meaning 'to have a god within'). He is the *hypokrités*, the answerer or interpreter of his people.

And he is a performer: doctor and priest, story-teller and clown. As both the repositor and the creator of his people's mythology and cosmology, he is the 'bringer of tales' from that other world. He is a healer, a 'clever-man', a conjuror, in part a charlatan; but he is also the one who can journey to that other world where his people's legendary store is kept. The shaman it is who can supply the shared narrative with its mythopoetic power and who – when at last drama is born – is able to perform it. He can contact and *make visible* the 'double', the other side of our nature, the spiritual or inner self. It is this shamanistic function of manifesting those forces which are believed to operate on the dark side of human consciousness to which Artaud refers to in *The Theatre and its Double* as 'active metaphysics'.[4]

The shaman is a prototype of the poet, the priest and the actor. The poet's function is to give utterance to that which others cannot say. The priest's function is to mediate with the supernatural, between man and not-man. The actor's function is to express, through his body, a second, virtual reality and to make that imagined reality manifest. The vatic utterances give birth to poetry; the spirit medium function of the shaman develops into the codified priesthood; the presentational magic evolves into the craft of the clown. He is the sacred actor, the holy fool.

But the comic genius is not confined to ritual or to trance. The clown is a universally loved and admired figure; historically encompassing far more than just a painted face and funny costume:

> it represents a vision of the world that both intellectual and so-called primitive cultures have valued highly, a sense of the comic meaningful to children and adults alike, and a dynamic form of acting based on startling technique and inspired improvisation.[5]

Clowning often begins within a sacred or religious context, burlesquing sacred ritual *within* the ritual.[6] Often, too, the clown represents the regressive element, acting out childish or adolescent fantasies of sexuality and scatology which adulthood represses (which is also a feature of later *commedia*, and one which early scholarship deliberately underplayed).[7] But the clown soon escapes from the confines of the sacred. His true origin is in the play instinct itself, and the pleasure he provides is too valuable to be restricted to a holy day.[8]

The theatre clown is universal. He appears, for example, in the Sanskrit drama of India, as the slow-witted servant Vidusaka (whose name means 'one given to abuse'). His partner is Vita, a witty parasite character who invariably gets the better of him. Vidusaka is typically a bald dwarf, with red eyes, and protruding teeth. He, and the other clownish figures of the *Mahabharata* and the *Ramayana*, speak Prakrit rather than the upper-caste Sanskrit, the language of gods and kings. Yet Vidusaka himself is of the highest caste. There are no clowns in the original epics; and in the written stage texts the clowns' roles are small, Yet, on stage, where mime and improvisation can predominate over script, the roles naturally expand and acquire an indispensable theatrical life entirely their own – as Hamlet knew.[9]

John Towsen makes the important point that the clown's ability to improvise has allowed him to become (for example, in modern Asian drama) a privileged political satirist, outside the confines of the censor.[10] That political role has been there throughout the history of clowning: its chief exponent in Western drama today is, perhaps, Dario Fo.

Clowns were known among the ancient Greeks, too, where they were called, among other things, *planoi*.[11] One history of the actor begins (according to Aristotle, who well understood that the improviser antedates the tragedian[12]) along the Isthmus (between Athens and Corinth) in the town of Megara. The *polis* of Megara had a developed tradition of secular drama from about 581 BC, when it became a democracy (seventy or so years before Athens). This tradition is known as the Dorian *Mime*. Probably its performances were crude, parodic and improvised. The masked performers were not possessed by the god; their burlesque provided a balancing, humanising version of the sacred events.

The *deikeliktai*, meaning perhaps 'those who put on plays', the little companies of masked actors popular among the Dorian Greeks, also specialised in tiny farces on everyday subjects; the stealing of apples, or the arrival of a quack doctor (an echo of shamanic healing, perhaps, now itself subject to the parodic impulse). They were also known, most significantly, as *autokabdaloi*, which means 'buffoons' and 'improvisers'.[13] Their performances probably included obscenities, acrobatics, juggling. At the heart of the performance lay both the burlesqueing – the relativising – of sacred myth, and the celebration of the human body.

Just as the shaman's virtuosity can include tricks, and the great festivals contain within themselves elements of celebration, pure fun, games and spectacle, so the parodic impulse coexists with the religious; the profane is intermingled with the sacred. In just this fashion, two thousand years later in Western Europe, the little devils who run amok through the spectators at the Mystery plays, with gunpowder squibs 'in their hands, ears and arses',[14] represent an enduring sense of fun and love of spectacle. The spirit of *carnival* is a powerful and enduring force.

The mime *humanises* the drama. In counterbalance to the demonic he offers the *corporeal*. He is, after all, a physical being; nothing godlike about him! He has a body which likes to stuff its face with food, to shit, to fuck. He is constantly reminding us of our humanity. His costume grotesquely extends his body: a big nose, belly, phallus.[15] His jokes are crude, certainly, even gross. He can reduce Herakles the demi-god to a mere glutton, Dionysos to a drunkard, the sacramental to the excremental.

The mime took many forms in many countries. From the Saxon *scop* and Middle English *gleeman* (and sexy 'glee-maiden' sometimes), to the German *minnesinger*, the French *jongleur* and *trouvère*, the Russian *skomorokhi*, and the Italian *giullare* their talents ranged from juggling, rope-walking and animal training to minstrelsy and acting. What links them is the way all clowns work with their audiences. Their style is always open and presentational; highly 'theatrical' theatre. Sometimes the mime comes indoors and works for a private patron; more often, the mime's master is the crowd, and his theatre, the street. There are rules for working with a crowd, as any modern 'busker' can testify. The clown has to make contact swiftly. He has to keep our attention in the noise and bustle of a street. That dictates the size and scale of his gestures. Watching good street-entertainers is the first step towards understanding the power of *commedia*.

Commedia dell'arte means (approximately) the comedy 'of the professional actors', (the *comici dell'arte*); in contrast to the *commedia erudita* (or the *commedia sostenuta*), the 'erudite', written plays created by the courtly amateurs of the theatre in sixteenth- and seventeenth-century Italy. There was also a mixed form, and the same troupes nearly always played in all three styles.

Sometimes the companies were highly renowned and could afford permanent bases; at the other extreme, the poorer players were attached to, for example, the Venetian *mountebanks*, using their clowning skills to draw crowds in the streets to whom a quack doctor (again a shamanistic echo) could peddle his nostrums. Each mountebank employed a *zanni*, a zany clown to pull in and please the crowd by his clever improvisations. The clown would pretend to mock his master, providing a parallel to the master–slave comedies of the ancient world, and a bridge to the farcical master–servant relationship of Pantalone (or Dottore) and Zanni (Arlecchino, or Brighella) in the Italian Comedy.

Perrucci's description of *commedia all'improvviso*, in his *Dell'arte rappresentiva, premeditata, e dall'improvviso* (1699),[16] provides a very salutary qualification of what professionally improvised drama is really like. These actors, remember (like their ancestors the mimes, and the Dorian *deikeliktai* before them), are dependent upon the successful reception of their work for their living. And professionals, even professional improvisers, leave very little to chance. *Commedia is* improvisational, but it is rehearsed and practised improvisation. The actors wear stock masks, each performer as familiar with his mask as with his own skin. It is *commedia a soggetto*, on a subject, or on a scenario (*canovaccio*), known and prepared in advance. As well as the agreed *soggetto*, the performers could fall back on fairly standardised routines called *lazzi*, pieces of rehearsed comic business, accompanied by *battute* (standardised repartee) and *concetti* (premeditated rhetorical passages). The *lazzi* and *concetti* would be mastered by all the members of a troupe as part of their training, regardless of which mask they commonly wore.

A manager or a senior actor would function as the play's 'director' and would rehearse (*concertare*) the scenario. According to Perrucci,[17] the *concertatore*'s job was to create the scenario, or to choose and read the scenario to the actors, making sure they understood the plot and the characters in it, and he would plant the *lazzi* and attend to the practical details such as props. The *concertatore* would, therefore, control the framework within which the actors improvised.

The *commedia all'improvviso* dominated the European stage for three hundred years, spawning local imitations in many countries, and influencing many major playwrights; among them, Shakespeare, Molière, Marivaux, Gozzi and Goldoni. Nor are its techniques forgotten. They are still with us in, for example, the work of actors from the Lecoq school, and in the plays and more especially the live performances of Dario Fo. Fo is an expert on *commedia*, performing the *lazzo* of 'The Fly' with consummate skill. It is part of the tradition out of which he has come (he stresses the lineage of the *pre-commedia* actors, the *giullari*) and his written plays are full of wonderfully undisciplined theatricality – where the lively theatrical energy of the mime-improviser bursts through the restraints of the politically conscious text.

Improvisation does not vanish – for improvisation is at the heart of all theatre – but the tradition of improvised play-making disappears with the development of the enclosed, plush and decorous theatre space during the eighteenth century. The rise of the function of the director, too, contributes to the disappearance of the tradition. No longer just the stage or company manager, or one of the actors; no longer just the organiser of rehearsals, the *concertatore*, but an *auteur* in his own right; the director's vision of the performance has often promoted a style of work in which improvised creativity *on stage* is not valued, and taught rather than communally worked out or improvised moves, gestures, deliveries become the order of the day.

Our own time has seen the resurgence of improvisation. Initially confined to the rehearsal room and the classroom, it is now breaking out once again. It is ultimately irrepressible, for it is central to both the function and the condition of the actor, and its re-emergence marks a revaluing of the actor in our cultural society.

But improvisation in our own era is different from that which precedes it. While there are courses which return to the original shamanistic transformation and psychological healing (via improvised Mask work and psychodrama), and another that returns to the commedic, or mimic tradition, our age has also discovered new and unsuspected values in improvised drama.

Part I

Who? Major Practitioners of Improvisation

Chapter 1

Improvisation in Traditional Drama

Introduction – the principle of improvisation

Improvisation is not just a style or an acting technique; it is a dynamic *principle* operating in many different spheres; an independent and transformative way of being and doing.

The twentieth century has seen an explosion of experiments which have embraced the principle of 'improvisation'. Music, for example, has been transformed by the various forms of jazz: technical proficiency has been allied to improvisation to create a practically inexhaustible synthesis. In modern dance, Isadora Duncan and Martha Graham, in different ways, opened up a wealth of new, plastic possibilities for the expressive body. The former immediately and spontaneously danced the truth of what she felt. The latter broke down the rigid formulae of classical ballet and replaced them with a language that responded to the world around as well as within the dancer. Graham wrote: 'There is a necessity for movement when words are not adequate. The basis of all dancing is something deep within you.'[1] (The main subject of our book is, of course, improvisation in drama, and in this section we shall be looking at the uses – and the users – of this principle in the drama of the twentieth century. But we shall also be stepping outside the field of artistic creation, for the same principle is being borrowed from drama and used in innovative ways in other endeavours.)

Overview

All theatrical performance ideally strives for a rigorous authenticity. The lines of development we will be discussing in this section lead in three principal directions, but each ultimately demands the same degree of commitment, and each is concerned – though from different angles – with an exploration of 'self' and 'reality' for performers and/or audience. This concern is basic to theatre and its relationship to human capacity and to the meaning of individual and communal acts; it links practice – outlined in the exercises and techniques given in Part II – with the historical and theoretical perspectives of Part III.

Improvisation is used in three major contexts. It feeds firstly into what we might call traditional theatre training, as a preparation for performance and a way of tuning up the performers. We can place this in the (Stanislavskian) tradition of 'character' preparation, or, to put it another way, as a method of schooling the actor to project the 'reality' of the character; a process which involves the development of imaginative skills so that the body can experience and express appropriate emotional states: discovering in oneself the self or being of 'another' and presenting it.

We discuss the use of improvisation in actor training below; this line of work tends – though not exclusively or rigidly – towards the naturalistic, the documentary, even the socio-political, with a relatively clearly defined concept of 'character' as the focus of deterministic forces: what D. H. Lawrence called the 'old stable ego of personality' clings to this and inhabits the structure and content of the 'well-made play'. Perhaps the most extreme development occurs in the improvisation-for-performance work of Mike Leigh, where a scripted text arises from improvisation fleshed out by 'sociological' research. (Though observing from life, we should note, is common to virtually all actor training, the uses that, say, the Bristol Old Vic Theatre School and the Ecole Jacques Lecoq put it to may, however, be interestingly different.)

The second tradition (or perhaps anti-tradition) rests on a more radical acknowledgement of the fragmentation of nineteenth-century notions of a consistent personality. The comic and the satiric vein, often allied to improvisation, challenges assumptions about stable social personality and 'bourgeois' respectability; taken to extremes, it undercuts political, religious and philosophical myths about the coherence of individual identity and its consonance within a system of stratified order and significance. The work of Jarry, Artaud and Beckett, for instance, extends and foregrounds this destabilisation; it also requires a more radically physical and improvisatory approach to acting, and it is not surprising that alongside this eventually scripted and accepted form of theatre, work on and with improvisation should have continued to develop almost as a form in and for itself. Improvisation of this kind both serves as an exploratory form of theatre and – here we move into the third, 'para-theatrical' context – also locates the issue of self and reality in spheres other than the narrowly theatrical.

The more radical modes of improvisation both accept the consequences of the disintegration of the existential self and attempt to use them positively. Grotowski's actors learn to 'disarm', to arrive at a condition without the protective masks of the familiar or the comfortable escapes of dramatic cliché. The work focuses not on the reality of the character but on that of the *performer*; where it emerges as public theatre, it is the inventiveness and authenticity of the performers in their relationship with the spectators which is foregrounded, as opposed to the presentation of a narrative. Here improvisation and performance are seen as part of a developmental process which can thus extend beyond theatre into, for example, psychotherapy or education.

We can, therefore, clearly identify three main strands which delineate twentieth-century improvisation: (a) the *application* of improvisation to the purposes of the traditional play; (b) the use of *pure* improvisation in the creation of an 'alternative' kind of theatrical experience; and (c) the extension of improvisatory principles *beyond* the theatre itself.

Precursors: Stanislavsky and Meyerhold

We might assume that Constantin Stanislavsky (1863–1938) was the originator of the modern use of improvisation, at least as a rehearsal and training device. Many of the scenes described in his books, *An Actor Prepares*, *Building a Character* and *Creating a Role*, in which the director 'Tortsov' guides his young protégés through the processes of self-discovery, are improvisatory in nature. But these books are the product of Stanislavsky's later years, after a heart-attack had forced him to give up acting. They do not necessarily relate to his own theatrical

practice, particularly in the early days of the Moscow Art
Theatre.

Stanislavsky did use a form of 'proto-improvisation', a kind
of imaginative projection of oneself into a role, and began to
suggest to his actors (a) that they might do this together, as a
group, away from the pressures of actual rehearsals; and (b) that
they do it continually, *outside the theatre*, while practising simple
physical activities. The concentration required led them towards
group outings, boating or mushroom picking, away from the bustle
of 'normal' town life, so that the actors could slowly become
immersed in their characters. But Stanislavsky seems not to have
developed this strand of his work.

The custom of the time was for the director (whose craft, it
must be remembered, was still a fledgling one) to write down,
to pre-compose, the *mise-en-scène* in its minutest details, and
then to train the actors to carry it out. The technique was
derived from Ludwig Chronegk's practice with the Duke of
Saxe-Meiningen's company (which had paid its second visit to
Moscow in 1890 – Stanislavsky saw every performance). This was
certainly Stanislavsky's way of working on the famous production
of *The Seagull* (which established the reputation of the Moscow
Art Theatre in 1898) and on most of the subsequent productions
up until at least 1906: in all his famous early productions for
the Moscow Art Theatre, from *The Seagull*, via Gorky's *The
Lower Depths* in 1902, to beyond *The Cherry Orchard* in 1904,
Stanislavsky had little recourse to any systematised production
method, let alone one which included improvisation.

It took a long time for Stanislavsky to come to the central
conclusions of his early work: that a director should be interested
in the actor's process rather than trying to dictate a result; that
an actor should blend himself with the character he plays; that
when playing a villain one should look for his good side; that (as
Schepkin had said) it was not important that one played 'well' or
'ill' – what mattered was to play truthfully. But Stanislavsky was
also, at this time, overimpressed by the externals of naturalism; by
a scenic naturalism which gave the illusion that genuine emotions
were being played out within it, and also by the autocratic example
of Chronegk. Only later in his work, after the famous vacation in
Finland in 1906, would he consciously transfer the emphasis to the
inner life of the character: in effect, the creation of the Stanislavsky
'System'.

And it was not until 1911, when Stanislavsky founded the First Studio of the MAT, that improvisation became in any way central to the practical work (and even later before it became part of the theory). According to Paul Gray, improvisation was first introduced by Stanislavsky's trusted friend and associate Leopold Antonovich Sulerzhitsky, whom Stanislavsky had put in charge of the Studio's developmental work.[2] Improvisation immediately became the rage among the younger generation of actors and actresses who made up the First Studio; and was equally powerfully resisted by the older generation. For Olga Knipper, Ivan Moskvin – even for Nemirovich-Danchenko himself – there seemed nothing practically useful in the Studio's work at first. But for Yevgeni Vakhtangov, Mikhail Chekhov, Maria Ouspenskaya and Richard Boleslavsky, Sulerzhitsky's technique was a liberation.

Mikhail Chekhov, for example, nephew of the playwright and perhaps the greatest actor of his generation, was also a gifted improviser, developing Stanislavskian naturalism into the realms of the abstract, and stressing the creative force of the actor's imagination. In his own work after leaving Russia in 1928, at Dartington in England and in America, Mikhail Chekhov would stress improvisation, in performance, between the members of a creative ensemble. Improvisation, for him, should always be based on a specific *ground* (such as, for example, the Stanislavskian 'objective', or 'significance', which is a way of making every action into 'a little gem in itself'). Even in Russia he was noted for the brilliance and variety of his invention: 'It was like a game between him and his audience. It was hard on his less-gifted fellow actors, but it brought them along too when they found the freedom that improvising gives.'[3]

It was really only in the last phase of his work, when he had ceased to act and when the translator Elizabeth Reynolds Hapgood had prevailed upon him to write down his way of working, that Stanislavsky himself began to consider seriously the techniques of improvisation, making the students work on scenes entirely without a text.

As David Magarshack points out, Stanislavsky had never really applied this purely theoretical idea to prove its efficacy in practice. It would be his successors who would elevate this experimental way of working into a central tenet of 'The Method'. Stanislavsky's work has led directly to that of modern America (both the 'Method', and the 'New York School' of improvisation discussed below) and to the plays of Mike Leigh, in which the *sine qua non* of performance is the truthful depiction of naturalistic character. His influence on the theatre of the twentieth century is still immense, but the naturalistic theatre's development of applied improvisation is due to his successors and emulators rather than to Stanislavsky directly.

Similarly, although Meyerhold pioneered experimental physical work with actors (culminating in the famous bio-mechanics) and was fascinated by *commedia*, popular theatre and mask, he did not develop this into exploration of the *actor*'s creativity.

The modern 'alternative' examination of improvisation begins (if it has to have a beginning) with Vsevolod Meyerhold (1874–1940). He had been one of the MAT's leading actors during the early, autocratic stage, but had left Moscow in 1902. He returned in 1905, having worked as a director in the provinces (where his own style had largely followed Stanislavsky's). Stanislavsky invited him back to join the MAT Studio Theatre project. It was in working on Maeterlinck's *La Mort de Tintagiles* and Hauptmann's *Schluck und Jau* that his basic disagreement with the MAT's 'realistic' concept of theatre became apparent. A conflict between himself and Stanislavsky ensued, and the Studio Theatre was closed before it had opened. Meyerhold went to work at the Komisarzhevskaya Theatre in St Petersburg and later at the Imperial theatre, the Alexandrinsky. Throughout their later careers Meyerhold and Stanislavsky stood on opposite sides of an ideological divide. For Stanislavsky, especially as his work developed, the actor was the focus of theatre. For Meyerhold, the focus was the director's art. The division between them was a formal one, and it should not obscure the great respect each had for the other. Meyerhold was both Stanislavsky's protégé, originally trained and nurtured by him, and his artistic *alter ego* who dared to explore avenues that remained closed to the conservative MAT.

In 1910 Meyerhold opened the 'Interlude House' at the former Skazka Theatre at 33 Galernaya Street, St Petersburg, to explore aspects of popular and street theatre and, especially, *commedia dell'arte*. He adapted Arthur Schnitzler's pantomime *The Veil of Pierrette*, turning it into his own *Columbine's Scarf* – turning the cloying sweetness of the Harlequinade back into the powerful nightmarish grotesquerie of E. T. A. Hoffmann.

Because he was working at the conservative Imperial Alexandrinsky Theatre at the time, he was asked by the management to conduct his experimental work under a pseudonym.

At the suggestion of the composer and poet, Mikhail Kuzmin, he took the name of 'Doctor Dappertutto', a character from E. T. A. Hoffmann's *Adventure on New Year's Eve*. Doctor Dappertutto was a real-life manifestation of the mask, a ubiquitous Doppelgänger who assumed responsibility for all Meyerhold's experiments in the eccentric and the supernatural for the rest of his time at the Imperial theatres.[4]

Although the Interlude House was shortlived, the Dappertutto experiments continued for many years. Meyerhold's fascination with *commedia dell'arte* had a number of levels. Firstly, he was fascinated by the theatre of masks. Where Stanislavsky's theatre was exploring the 'inner truth' of character, Meyerhold glimpsed the equally profound 'exterior truth' of the mask. He was also fascinated by the figure of the *cabotin* (which he regarded in a very much more positive light than Copeau later did). The figure of the itinerant, poor, professional actor, descended from the classical *mimus*, via the Russian *skomorokhi* (Russian equivalent of the *jongleur*) and *balaganschik* ('fairground booth-player') no less than the Italian *comici dell'arte*, attracted him powerfully.

Secondly, his awareness of *commedia dell'arte* was conditioned by his acquaintance with a number of later European sources: the drawings of Callot, with their grotesque and malicious, sexual and scatological figures; the *fiabe* of Carlo Gozzi, with their deliberate room for the actors' improvisations, their poetic, magical delicacy; the plays of Goldoni, with their developing interest in psychological realism and their literary grace; and, finally, the works of the Romantic E. T. A. Hoffmann, with their masked and transformed mysticism, their fascination with reality and its double.[5]

Revolutionary though this work may seem, the fascination was primarily an intellectual, literary, aesthetic affair. Secondarily, Meyerhold was engaged with the actor's physical skills: the extraordinary plasticity of the street-entertainer would ultimately become the basis of the scientific bio-mechanics with which his name is associated. Only thirdly, we believe, was Meyerhold interested in the *actor's* independent creativity. He returned to the idea of the *commedia dell'arte* scenario, set in advance by the *concertatore*, or laid out by a master dramatist like Goldoni or Gozzi. Meyerhold was the archetypal *metteur-en-scène*, in his way every bit as much an autocratic director as Chronegk. The idea of the actor as creator would come not from Russia but from France.

The first person to investigate improvisation as *the* means to explore the nature of acting, the first man to grasp the full significance of this way of working, was Jacques Copeau. In Limon, in 1916, he wrote:

> It is an art which I don't know, and I am going to look into its history. But I see, I feel, I understand that this art must be restored, reborn, revised; that it alone will bring a living theatre – the theatre of players.[6]

Jacques Copeau

Albert Camus said: 'In the history of the French theatre there are two periods: before and after Copeau.'[7] This judgement might be extended to the history of improvisation, for it was Copeau (1879–1949) who truly began the modern tradition. John Rudlin, in the Preface to his book on Copeau, enumerates the many debts which the modern theatre owes to Copeau's teaching and practice:

> In no particular order: drama games; improvisation; animal mimicry; ensemble playing; writers-in-residence; *commedia dell'arte* revival; mime; mask-work; repertoire rather than repertory; community theatre; theatre as communion.[8]

Copeau was not the first to use improvisation as a rehearsal and training technique: Stanislavsky, we have seen, used it at the Moscow Art Theatre Studio; Taïrov had employed it at the Kamerny, too (as part of the 'Synthetic Theatre' – derived from Marinetti's Futurist experiments). But Copeau, at Le Vieux-Colombier and in his teaching, was the first really to base a system of exploratory work upon it, and the impact of his decision is still reverberating.

Jacques Copeau was a drama critic before he became a theatre man – in fact, he was thirty-four when he began to direct. He was part of the reaction against the realism of Antoine's Théâtre Libre (though he knew and admired Antoine and regarded Stanislavsky as a source of creative inspiration), against the false rhetorical style of the Comédie Française, and against the crassness of boulevard theatre. He read and in many ways admired Craig and Appia, but disagreed with their proposed alternatives. Instead, in 1913, he published his own 'manifesto' – his *Essai de Rénovation Dramatique* – and founded his own theatre in the rue du Vieux-Colombier in Paris.

In the beginning, Copeau did not so much have a vision of a future theatre, as a certainty that such a theatre would be possible – if only the right conditions were fulfilled. His manifesto ended with the now-famous plea, '*Pour l'ouvre nouvelle qu'on nous laisse un tréteau nu!*' (For the new work, just leave us bare boards!),[9] and almost his first act, practical and symbolic, was to empty the stage of the old music-hall building. He ended the 'tyranny of the technician', leaving the stage open and free for the actor to perform and (just as importantly) to rehearse on. By 1921, he had stripped away the proscenium arch and replaced it with an open, multi-levelled end-stage.[10] His nephew and protégé, Michel Saint-Denis, later wrote:

> As I remember that stage, precise images of the plays I saw on it come to my mind . . . each play seemed to leave traces of its pattern on the stage floor, each design unique, different from every other. . . . That bare stage and the way in which it was equipped did away with naturalistic illusion.[11]

Yet, with a minimum of technical means, Copeau's actors achieved a remarkable degree of realism when they wanted to – even astounding Antoine with Charles Vildrac's *Le Pacquebot S.S. Tenacity* (1920), in which a few tables, chairs and bottles were enough to create the ambience of a seamen's café in a harbour.

As a director, Copeau was renowned both for his fidelity to the text, and for his ability to train and develop actors. He believed in the 'organic' approach, coming to discern what it was that the written text demanded of the actor. He could choreograph scenes brilliantly, but the result rarely gave the impression of having been imposed from without. He sought out the 'musicality' of the text and, having found it, could then rehearse it in a disciplined and precise manner.

He came to improvisation in an interesting way. Copeau believed in ensemble acting. He believed deeply in truth on the stage. But he also believed in liberating the physical and vocal creativity of the actor. Acting in Paris in 1920 was still dominated by two highly contrasted schools: broadly, the classical (exemplified by the Comédie Française) and the naturalistic (Antoine's Théâtre Libre). The 'classicists' overelaborated the text, using it as a vehicle for displays of virtuosity. The 'naturalists' stripped away the beauty of the text, 'deflating' it (in Saint-Denis's terms) and losing touch with the actor's essential theatricality.

And so this great lover of the text resolved, for a time, to take away the text from his actors – to withhold it from them – in order to force them to rediscover the essentials of the craft of acting. He had no real idea, at first, of how to achieve his aims. It is possible that he was as 'thrown' by the withdrawal of the script as his students. But he had intuition and remarkable teaching skills (complemented by those of Suzanne Bing, his best actress), and he was a great risk-taker. He knew where the work should start, that was enough:

> Therefore in his teaching Copeau temporarily withdrew the use of texts and made the study of the expressiveness of the body – Improvisation – his point of departure. He led all the work in an empiric fashion, guided by experience, observation and experiment. With the support of his collaborators in various fields, he invented exercises with many progressions and developments.[12]

Copeau developed a hierarchy running from immobility and silence through movement to sound and finally to words and text.[13] This underpinned much of his work, particularly with Mask, which Copeau regarded as of great importance; here Copeau states:

> The departure point of expressivity: the state of rest, of calm, of relaxation, of silence, or of simplicity . . . this affects spoken interpretation as well as playing an action. . . . An actor must know how to be silent, to listen, to respond, to stay still, to begin an action, to develop it, and to return to silence and immobility.[14]

This is the first expression of the central concept of *neutrality* to which we shall return in Parts II and III.

The scenic innovations represent one aspect of Copeau's

genius. The other was his ability to teach actors. Many of his early collaborators later went on to become teachers of drama in their own right, especially Suzanne Bing, Charles Dullin, Louis Jouvet and, of course, Michel Saint-Denis. Their influence upon drama, in France and beyond, is incalculable. Suzanne Bing taught drama games, animal mimicry, mask-work and mime (she taught Etienne Decroux, who later taught Marcel Marceau). Dullin founded L'Atelier, where Decroux also taught. Among their pupils were Jean-Louis Barrault and, briefly, Antonin Artaud. Both Jean Dasté and Barrault contributed to the teaching of Jacques Lecoq. Jouvet, Copeau's greatest actor in the early days, founded a company at the Théâtre des Champs-Élysées and later became a professor at the Paris Conservatoire, as well as a resident director of the Comédie Française. Michel Saint-Denis (about whose Compagnie des Quinze we shall have more to say later) was responsible for founding no less than five major drama schools, two in London, others in Strasbourg, New York and Montreal, and Jerzy Grotowski has referred to Saint-Denis as 'my spiritual father'.

Already in 1913, Copeau had dreamed of a new type of theatre school alongside the Vieux-Colombier theatre. He felt that actors were 'the enemy of the theatre'. More precisely, the enemy was *cabotinage* – we might translate it as 'ham' but it also implies a kind of clinging to habits of thought and action. The *cabotin* is fundamentally uncomfortable on the stage: he looks for things to do, for 'business' to hide behind. Rudlin describes it well: 'The stage is an Eden where actors constantly appeal for something to hide their nakedness. What Copeau now sought was an appropriateness that would not clothe the actor's bareness, but celebrate it.'[15]

Jacques Lecoq – a spiritual descendant of Copeau – teaches clowning at his Paris school. The centre of this work is learning how to be at home on the stage – even when the clown has nothing to fall back on except himself, his audience and what can be created between them in the moment of performance. Sending the clown out to amuse an audience, armed with absolutely nothing (no 'gags', no jokes, no script, perhaps not even speech) is a way of 'de-cabotinising' the student actor.

By 1916, Copeau had sketched out the prospectus of his ideal training establishment, and the School itself opened its doors in 1921. The prospectus is worth describing.

1   *Rhythmic gymnastics*, based on the eurhythmics of Jacques-
     Dalcroze. (Later Copeau was to revise his opinion of this
     type of work.)
2   *Gymnastic technique.* This included breathing exercises
     as well as sport, fencing, athletics. The aim was total
     possession by the actor of his physical resources. Copeau
     based much of this work on Georges Hébert's *L'Education
     Physique de l'entrainement complet par la méthode naturelle*
     – a series of books that revolutionised the French system of
     physical education. Copeau used Hébert's methods as ways
     of developing the *play instinct* through physical ability and
     instinctive action.
3   *Acrobatics and feats of dexterity.* To give the actor suppleness
     as well as strength. Ideally these skills should be taught by a
     clown, and would be of great use in comedy and farce work.
     (Copeau was impressed by circus clowns, and he invited the
     Fratellini Brothers to teach at the school.)
4   *Dance*
5   *Singing*
6   *Musical training.* The actors were to be taught at least
     the basic skills of playing various instruments.
7   *General instruction.* For two hours a day, the children of
     the school (for Copeau believed that the future would lie
     with those brought up under this method rather than those
     retrained in it) would have academic studies. The adults
     would develop their cultural awareness through seminars
     and by conversation with artists and writers.
8   *Games.* Copeau and Suzanne Bing were perhaps the first
     drama teachers to recognise the value of *games* work (which
     will be discussed further in Part II). They recognised that
     children learn through play, and that the responses of play
     are natural and authentic. Copeau speaks here not of a sys-
     tem but of an 'experiential education', using the child's own
     natural means of learning. He writes 'Somewhere along the
     line of improvised play, playful improvisation, improvised
     drama, real drama, new and fresh, will appear before us.
     And these children, whose teachers we think we are, will,
     without doubt, be ours one day.'
9   *Reading out loud.* Copeau was a brilliant reader. He felt it
     was vital to inculcate in his students the ability to respond to

a text immediately and fully; to be able to vocalise a text at sight required a quickness and flexibility of mind as well as voice, enabling the actor to express the author's intentions fully and instantly.

10   *Recital of poetry.*
11   *Study of the repertoire* (which, of course, meant mainly the French classical repertoire).
12   *Improvisation* (see below)[16]

To this list Copeau added mask and mime work and (after a discussion with Craig) study of the technical crafts of the theatre. The Vieux-Colombier School operated from 1921 to 1924. Much of what is envisaged in this prospectus could not immediately be realised, but there was enough success eventually to move Copeau to close the theatre in order to concentrate on the laboratory work of training.

On improvisation, Copeau wrote in that same 1916 prospectus:

Improvisation is an art that has to be learned. . . . The art of improvising is not just a gift. It is acquired and perfected by study. . . . And that is why, not just content to have recourse to improvisation as an exercise towards the renovation of classical comedy, we will push the experiment further and try to give re-birth to a genre: the New Improvised Comedy, with modern characters and modern subjects.[17]

What Copeau envisaged in *la comédie nouvelle* was a twentieth-century revitalisation of the energy of *commedia dell'arte*. He understood that simply to re-create *commedia* was of no use: the masks, situations, *lazzi* of the Italian comedy belonged inextricably to their own time. Academic reconstruction was only of use as an aid to the generation of a New Improvised Comedy (as Rudlin translates it) – a new form for the present.

Copeau conceived of a company entirely devoted to such work. Each actor would develop and play one specific role, just as the performers of *commedia* had. At first, Copeau himself would be the well-spring of the work, providing scenarios and training. But, gradually, the new characters – the new Masks – would become independent of him:

Choose from the company the six or eight actors most appropriate to such an enterprise, the ones with the most go in them, the most self-confident, and the best assorted ensemble – who would henceforth dedicate themselves almost entirely to improvisation. A genuine brotherhood: the *farceurs* of the Vieux-Colombier. Each actor would light upon a single character from this new *commedia*. He would make it his own property. He would feed it. Fatten it from the substance of his own being, identify with it, think of it at all times, live with it, giving things to it, not only from his own personality, external mannerisms and physical peculiarities, but also from his own ways of feeling, of thinking, his temperament, his outlook, his experience, letting it profit from his reading, as well as growing and changing with him.[18]

The attempts to put this dream of a twentieth-century *commedia* into practice were, unfortunately, beset by apparently insuperable difficulties. Where could he find such a troupe, willing to make the act of dedication he envisaged? What sort of character types would so vividly encapsulate the preoccupations of the twentieth century as Arlecchino, Pantalone and Pulcinella had those of the sixteenth? What should the scenarios be about? Copeau didn't know – but he was willing to find out.

There were willing actors, too, among them Jean Dasté, Aman Maistre, Suzanne Bing, Jean Villard, Léon Chancerel, Auguste Boverio, Copeau's children Pascal and Marie-Hélène and his nephew Michel Saint-Denis. In 1924 Copeau relinquished the Vieux-Colombier and withdrew with a dedicated group of actors (affectionately nicknamed *les Copiaux* by the locals) to Pernand-Vergelesses, a village near Beaune in Burgundy. There, for the next five years, he based hiis work in an old *cuverie*, a converted barn.

The work was developmental, ranging from the austere discipline of Noh drama, singing, dance, mime and acrobatics, to comic improvisation, *commedia* work and, later, character improvisations with and without masks. Shows were devised for the region (for example, a play based on the labour of the vineyard worker, performed before two-thousand such workers in the village of Nuits Saint-Georges after the wine harvest).

Our comic improvisations were instantly accepted by this audience. Because there was never any barrier between players and audiences, the spectators sensed how much they influenced the actors, how they could affect their performances, indeed, how at times they could lift the actors to a rare degree of exhilaration.[19]

Throughout his work, from 1916 onwards, Copeau had been making notes towards the creation of *la comédie nouvelle*. Not it was possible to attempt it with the Copiaux. They worked in 1925 on classical *commedia*: Jean Dasté (Copeau's son-in-law) played Arlequin; Copeau himself played Pantalon; Jean Villard worked on Pedrolino and Léon Chancerel on the Doctor. The group did evolve new, personalised characters, too. Chancerel evolved the Mask of 'Sebastien Congré' ('archivist, timid paleographer, molly-coddled and ridiculous'). Jean Dasté created 'César' ('an old "quacker" with a keen nose for business'). Suzanne Bing created 'Célestine'. Boverio invented 'Lord Quick' (a 'thoughtless, fat old man, who delighted in recalling his entire past life, both literary and worldly'). Michel Saint-Denis created the Masks of 'Jean Bourgignon' and 'Oscar Knie' ('a violent character who made great demands on him and became a parasite on his own personality' and who both hated and was inseparable from 'César'[20]).

There were successes and failures with this work. One problem was that virtually all the Masks created were male. Perhaps Copeau had implicitly envisaged a masculine monasticism in the 'brotherhood' ideal; perhaps (as Dasté was to argue) the 'trance-like' state of improvisation and Mask work requires great strength and is more easily undertaken in a sustained way by men. A greater problem was that the Masks created did not have the universality of their *commedia* ancestors. Among the many successes, though, must be the 1926 production of *L'Illusion* at Pernand-Vergelesses – which the Copiaux later toured around Europe – and the 1928 *La Danse de la Ville et des Champs* (which featured, among other things, the sojourn of the city dweller 'Oscar Knie' in the countryside).

The Burgundy period with *les Copiaux* came to an end in 1929. The ensemble had reached a point where, in Copeau's opinion, it needed to return to the mainstream of French theatre – though without him.

We could act, dance, sing, improvise in all kinds of ways, and, when necessary, write our own dialogue. . . .[We had] become an ensemble with a fertile imagination and the technical means to represent in our work many aspects and facets of the world. What we were lacking was, no doubt, a few more actors and, above all, a writer.[21]

Copeau encouraged the group to return to Paris. He himself was quite seriously ill and planned to retire and devote himself to writing (although in the 1930s and early 1940s he undertook a number of practical directing projects). He had recently embraced Catholicism and wanted to devote himself to the creation of a mystical drama, to explore the nature of 'theatre-as-communion' (for example, in his collaborations with Paul Claudel). He undertook a number of large-scale religious works in which many of the principles evolved through the Vieux-Colombier were brought to a different level. Before parting from *les Copiaux*, however, he introduced the group to the young playwright André Obey. Michel Saint-Denis reformed *les Copiaux* into the Compagnie des Quinze and the work moved onto a different level.

Devoted to physical expression still, the Compagnie des Quinze none the less wanted to work with a writer. Basing themselves again at the rebuilt Vieux-Colombier, they continued to improvise,[22] but now in collaboration with Obey. Together, they continued to evolve theatrical languages (including *grummelotage*, a mixture of real words, mime and silent improvisation derived from the study of *commedia* and popular theatre). It was a creative tension between text and improvisation, with the constant danger that one would overwhelm the other. Plays such as *Noah*, *Le Viol de Lucrèce* and *Don Juan*, however, showed that the collaboration could succeed brilliantly.

From 1931 to 1934 the Compagnie des Quinze took Europe by storm. In Paris, though, the Vieux-Colombier was still regarded as an 'art house', distrusted by the traditionalists and (perhaps) not radical enough for the modernists. The company tried to repeat Copeau's experiments by retreating again to the country – this time to Aix-en-Provence. Within six months the company had disbanded, defeated by financial pressures and the strain of communal living.

But Copeau's vision of *le tréteau nu* had been realised. The experiments of the years 1920–34 had demonstrated that a way back to the simple power of the medieval trestle-stage was possible, that community drama based on improvisation could succeed where the sophisticated classics had failed, and had proved beyond doubt that improvisation itself could form the basis of a system of training that could reinvigorate and revitalise the whole craft of acting.

Some of the principal elements of Copeau's theory and practice can be summarised as follows:

1   Much of Copeau's work was directed not immediately towards performance, but towards *readiness for performance*, as an underlying educational and developmental goal for himself and his actors.
2   The company learned (with lots of ups and downs) about working for each other, functioning – even living – as a group (with, ideally, no emphasis on 'stars').
3   Copeau himself learned as he went along; his directing included large elements of responsiveness, intuition and adaptation. The principles of change and involvement in a process were more important than the need to conclude or arrive at a finished product.
4   Improvisation operated within the context of games, mime and Mask work, *commedia* and so on, and could develop along with any of these towards new forms of theatre. Copeau started by using text-related improvisations but later developed a freer and more eclectic use of text in the search for *comédie nouvelle*.
5   Copeau's subsequent concern with theatre-as-communion can be seen retrospectively to illuminate much of his career, from sincere and passionate critic of sterility, via the function of *patron* of a group enterprise culminating in community-rooted performance, to identification of theatre as a shared creative act with para-theatrical significance for individual and society.

Like many others who take improvisation seriously, there is a slightly Messianic flavour to Copeau's life and work (Grotowski is clearly similar). There is a British (and academic) tendency to raise eyebrows at this degree of commitment, but without the energy it harnesses, little – especially in terms of motivating actors – would get done.

It is no exaggeration to say that practically every major

initiative in modern theatre can trace its lineage back to Copeau in some degree. His influence is subtle and often very tenuous, but it persists. He worked at some time with virtually every major figure in the French theatre of his day, and his students and collaborators have spread that influence to succeeding generations. The Theatre Guild and the Group Theatre in America acknowledged his influence. Most of the major British actors of the late 1930s onwards worked with Saint-Denis. And, most important, Copeau's initiatives still permeate (often without conscious realisation) drama training at all levels.[23]

Le Théâtre du Soleil

The tradition of Meyerhold and Copeau reaches its clearest contemporary development in the work of Ariane Mnouchkine's Paris collective. The Théâtre du Soleil was formed in 1964 as a workers' co-operative by members of the Association Théâtrale des Etudiants de Paris (ATEP, founded 1959) who included Ariane Mnouchkine, who had already worked in university theatre in England.

At first the company's work was naturalistic, even explicitly Stanislavskian:

> In 1969 the company mounted *Les Clowns*, a production which was their first real attempt at group creation – the result of an investigation of the circus as a form of popular theatre, intended to break away from the constraints of socialist realism and what the company referred to as *psychologisme*.[24]

This was followed in 1970 by perhaps their most famous piece, *1789*, 'a group creation based on improvisations'.

1789 was premiered in Milan at Strehler's Piccolo Teatro, then performed at their now famous base, the Cartoucherie, until 1974. By this time, the group had established their commitment both to popular theatre forms, and to collective, improvised creation around a powerful political statement.

Mnouchkine (who is happy to be thought of as the artistic 'midwife' rather than director of the group) works almost entirely through improvisation. She provides visual materials, imaginative prompts, research materials; and the work grows out of lengthy discussion and careful repetition.

In working on their next project, *L'Age d'or*, the company

(partially) succeeded in doing what Copeau dreamed of, creating a contemporary form of *commedia* that could speak to the twentieth century. Not *la comédie nouvelle* exactly, for the actors of the Théâtre du Soleil had no intention of developing their Masks for the rest of their careers. But to the extent that the work addressed contemporary themes (exploitation, poverty, sexual politics) and did so via the reinvention of *commedia dell'arte* (without attempting any historicist reconstruction of it) Copeau's vision was fulfilled.

In the resultant play, Pantalone becomes a real-estate promoter; Abdullah-Harlequin a cheap construction worker who is bribed to work on a high scaffold in a fierce wind. He dances his death fall to Verdi's 'Requiem'. Pantalone tries to stop the show, tries to cover up the scandal.

Like Copeau's own company, the Théâtre du Soleil went on retreat into the countryside, contrasting the reactions of the villagers of the Cévennes with those of the Parisian critics. Unlike the latter, the villagers simply accepted the work in its totality, making no distinction between the formal elements and the political content. The Théâtre du Soleil's discoveries about the creative relationship between a community theatre and its patrons via improvisation exactly parallels those of Copeau and Saint-Denis:

> The actors improvised every day in various village meeting places, both outdoors and indoors, around themes proposed by the people, who were very receptive to the masks, costumes and physical movements of the performers, as well as to the accuracy of what was expressed about their lives.[25]

Mnouchkine and her company read Copeau for the first time (as his *Registres* were being published) in 1974, during the rehearsals for *L'Age d'or*. But their inspiration also goes right back to Meyerhold's early conception of a reborn theatre of the *cabotin* and the *balaganschik* – and includes Meyerhold's political as well as theatrical fervour.

Improvisation and 'traditional' theatre training

The decision of the Compagnie des Quinze to work with a writer seems in retrospect an almost symbolic act, representing a shift of emphasis – a movement from improvised back towards scripted drama. The collaboration of Saint-Denis's troupe with André Obey seems to symbolise a particular reaccommodation of the script-based play.

Of course, neither Copeau nor Saint-Denis had ever had any desire to abandon the written play permanently. *L'Illusion* and *La Danse de la Ville et des Champs* were both plays with scripts (the former adapted by Copeau himself, the latter compiled by Jean Villard-Gilles and Michel Saint-Denis). What was important about Copeau's experimentation was the creation of a new type of *performer*, out of which a new type of drama might, one day, emerge. It was a way of renovating the classical drama from within, rather than an abandonment of it. As Rudlin puts it: 'Actors of *parts* are sustained by a dramatic illusion of which they are part; performers of *plays* by a nothing-to-hide, open contact with the spectator.'[26]

The relationship with Obey was a step towards that new openness; a true collaboration of creative performers with a sensitive and gifted playwright rather than a resubmission of the actors to the text. The collaboration showed that there was, indeed, a new way to create plays.

But, as a symbol, the return to Paris from Pernand-Vergelesses restores our sense of perspective on Copeau's work. The dream of a New Improvised Comedy was still a long way off.

In the Burgundian search for *la comédie nouvelle* we may discern the quest for a totally improvised theatre; in the return to the Vieux-Colombier with Obey we may see the reincorporation of improvisation into the traditional forms of play-making. Improvisation becomes just one of the many means of theatre, valuable certainly as a process which develops the actor, and which the actor and writer may use explicitly to develop the final play, but no longer the primary method of creativity.

And that is what, basically, improvisation has remained for the traditional theatre. The pressures of time, the constraints of economic resources, the fear of failure, have all combined to restrict the spread of impro work in 'mainstream' theatre. Rehearsal time is too short (especially in England, where four weeks may see a play from first read-through to first night) to allow much scope for 'experimental' work around the text. Money is scarce, even in the subsidised sector, and theatre is seen, after all, as a commodity – even the Arts Council of Great Britain talks not of 'productions' (the produce of human labour and artistic endeavour) but of 'product' (a commodity to be sold). There is a fear that audiences will not buy a product which does not look 'finished'. Audiences expect, do they not, to see *results* on the stage, not *processes*, no matter how fascinating?

Neither the National Theatre (which has offered workshops on improvisation) nor the Royal Shakespeare Company, nor any of the major subsidised repertory theatres has ever mounted a fully improvised show. (Plays created by improvisatory means are a different matter.)

Is it a failure, then, of nerve? Or does it go deeper? Is it, perhaps, a failure of improvisation itself to attract such skilled theatre workers? Why are actors and directors so resistant?

One answer may lie in the *training* of such people. Actors and directors have been taught to regard improvisation only for its developmental value in actor training, and for its occasional usefulness in the rehearsal situation. Virtually all modern drama schools, in varying degrees, use improvisation (just as they might use games, mask work, mime and so on) in the training of actors. In this they follow, consciously or unconsciously, the precepts of Michel Saint-Denis. After the collapse of the Compagnie des Quinze, he was responsible for the development of no less than five major drama schools. He set up the London Theatre Studio in Islington in 1935 with George Devine and Glen Byam Shaw. It lasted until the outbreak of war in 1939.

Saint-Denis's influence upon men like George Devine (the creator of the English Stage Company at the Royal Court twenty years later, and himself a great teacher, especially of mask work) was enormous and beneficial. But he had come to see the actor's role as an interpretative one, which is strange when one considers the stress on the creative role in his earlier work:

When I use the word actor, I actually have two sorts in mind: the kind who works with a text and the kind who works without one. When his work is based on a text, I think of him as the actor/interpreter; when he acts without a text, I call him the actor/improviser. Naturally, at the highest levels of our art these two breeds of actor tend to merge.[27]

The search would be for the performer who could more successfully interpret a text than evolve one; and many of the students were, indeed, professional actors, already fixed in their habits of work and thought.

Saint-Denis's principle for training was to 'stimulate the initiative and invention of the future interpreter by making him pass through the experiences of the actor-creator'.[28]

Accordingly, the training programme was primarily based on improvisation work. But now Saint-Denis added:

> a carefully selected group of Stanislavsky's exercises: those which would not lead our actors to an excessively subjective concentration which might prove detrimental in acting a classical role.[29]

Saint-Denis's experiences at the LTS (and later in teaching or planning for the Old Vic Theatre School, 1947–52; L'Ecole Supérieure d'Art Dramatique, Strasbourg, 1952–7; the National Theatre School of Canada, 1960; and the Julliard School Drama Division, New York, from 1968) laid down what we might call the 'invisible curriculum' of most drama schools in Europe and America with regard to improvisation.

His own *ideal* four-year curriculum – which he describes in *Training for the Theatre*[30] – is very clear on the relationship of improvised work to formal rehearsal of plays. The first year is largely improvisatory, with no public performances. This is the 'Discovery Year'. Mask work, observation, transformation and solo and group non-verbal improvisation are stressed. So far so good. But in the last term of the second ('Transformation Year') we find that the Improvisation work is to cease to give more time to the Interpretational work – specifically a Chekhov play. In the third ('Interpretation') year, Improvisation work is suspended altogether (except for two weeks in the middle term on preparatory exercises in the Restoration style). He splits his curriculum throughout into two groupings: 'Technique' and 'Imagination'. Both Improvisation and Interpretation come under 'Imagination'. By the middle of the course, then, the imagination is entirely given over to interpretative rather than purely creative work. Improvisation has become the servant of interpretation. In the final ('Performing') year there is 'no improvisation work, unless something special is needed for the rehearsal projects for the repertory season or unless there is opportunity to offer a unique master class'.[31]

The drama school curriculum is clearly designed to 'produce' actors and, in their final year, present them to potential employers in a series of public 'coming out ceremonies'. Improvisation in this context is one of the tools by which 'an actor prepares' for the job.

There is nothing fundamentally wrong with Saint-Denis's plans for training actors, and this is by no means an attack on his intended curriculum. But we can see, here, how most Western drama schools have tended to utilise improvisation in training. Every school is different, naturally. English schools do not have the luxury of four years' work and have to cram everything into three years (or, in the case of postgraduate acting courses, one year). Each school will have its own philosophy of training. Some will stress the Stanislavskian approach to characterisation more than others. Some will concentrate more upon technique than upon imaginative development. Some will endeavour to keep the creative work running alongside the repertory of productions. But in virtually all cases, as *production work* begins to become the priority improvisation gets relegated to the 'back burner'. The business of a drama school is to turn out actors capable of working in the prevailing conditions of modern theatre, after all; and improvisation is seen as less conducive to that end than, say, stage combat training.

Improvisation is used, of course, in rehearsal work for productions (if the director is willing to allocate space and time for it). But it is subservient to the search for the 'inner life'; it is a tool used for 'creating a believable character', which (despite the theories of Brecht and others) is still seen as the fundamental task of the actor.

The two main uses of improvisation in traditional drama (including drama training), then, are (a) to do with the exploration of a character's inner nature and the accommodation of that nature to the actor's own; and (b) the further exploration of character within situations which extend beyond those contained within the play.

The director may set up an improvised situation in order to let the actors discover what they themselves, as human beings, might do or feel in such circumstances. The actors gain insight into the circumstances which the characters in the play have to contend with, and their responses become more authentic as a result. The actors can draw upon their own vicarious experiences at difficult moments in the performance.

Or it may be that an actor will use 'improvs' to explore his assumed character in situations outside those explored in the play. An actor may ask, 'What is my character like when he is alone? when he is with his friends? his boss?' Out of this kind of work the actor may build up a wealth of small, circumstantial details – how his or her character walks, talks, drinks, handles props. In performance these details will inform his or her playing and lend it credibility. It will be nearer the truth since it depends upon experiential discovery via the body of the actor rather than upon imposed externals.

In developing the 'reality of character', Stanislavsky was concerned with 'inner truth': the performer needs to develop emotional and physical resources which clearly are his or her own, even though they are used to invite empathy with (or in Brecht's view, to signal) some specific or typical behaviour patterns which constitute a fictitious character to be 'read' by the spectators. Saint-Denis paraphrases it thus: 'It is only from within himself (i.e. the actor), and through physical actions inspired by or drawn from his own inner resources, that the character can be realised.'[32]

This realisation has to be coherent, not a matter of bits and pieces stuck on (a collage of a style of walking, a tone of voice, an accent); even Brecht, who was not concerned with all-round characterisation, demanded a complete *Gestus*. Saint-Denis sees it emerging from an alternation between this 'subjective' work on oneself and a more 'objective' understanding, via the text, of the role. Balance between 'reality of self' and 'reality of role' is an important basis *either* for mainstream acting or for more exploratory and ultimately extra-theatrical work. The essentials of improvisation can underpin both strands, and it is only the difference of focus which separates them. Ultimately, theatre is a way of 'knowing ourselves' better, and improvisation energises that process, whatever channel it may take.

There is, however, one area in which improvisation and what we are here calling the 'traditional' theatre have formed a new and experimental liaison. In the field of play-creation a new synthesis has recently taken place. It brings together the concern for detailed and truthful characterisation as the basis of acting, the idea of the actor as part-creator of the work, the methods of improvisation and the traditional crafts of the playwright. The focus of this synthesis is the playwright and director, Mike Leigh.

Mike Leigh

Mike Leigh, the son of a doctor, was born in Salford in 1943,[33] and grew up 'as a middle-class kid in a working-class area',[34] which gave him an ambivalent but deeply perceptive view of class relationships.

Leigh's training at RADA included virtually no improvisation work. Improvisation was simply not a part of actor training at that time, even though innovative theatre directors such as Joan Littlewood and even film directors such as John Cassavetes were using the technique quite commonly. RADA, like most other drama schools in Britain in the late 1950s and early 1960s, clung to a traditional view of the stage, largely untouched by the changes being wrought by the 'new wave' of dramatists in the wake of *Look Back in Anger*, and the Berliner Ensemble's visit to London – or even, at that stage, by the ideas of drama teachers such as Michel Saint-Denis. The actor was seen entirely as an interpreter rather than as a creative artist.

Leaving RADA in 1962, Leigh worked as an assistant stage-manager and bit-part actor in films before enrolling in the pre-diploma course at Camberwell Art School. Here he experienced a realisation which was to prove crucial. Sitting one day in the life-drawing class:

> I suddenly realised what it had been that we hadn't experienced as actors. In the life drawing class there were a dozen or fifteen kids and everyone was making a serious and original investigation into a real experience. Nobody was doing a second-hand rendering of something. I began to think that acting could be creative in the same way that any artist is.[35]

After Camberwell, Leigh went on to study Theatre Design at the Central School of Arts and Crafts. He also studied for a period at the London Film School. After training, he worked for a time as an actor, director and designer. He directed the first production of his friend David Halliwell's play *Little Malcolm and his Struggle Against the Eunuchs*. The production was difficult, and the company that Leigh and Halliwell had set up, Dramagraph, sank without trace, leaving Leigh with doubts about his directing abilities. It also left him with a desire to write his own plays.

Leigh was impressed by Beckett's ability to make his audience share his characters' time, to concentrate on the moment of performance itself, and Peter Hall's work at the Royal Shakespeare Company, which allowed Brechtian values to creep into the English theatre. Hall also brought Saint-Denis and Peter Brook into the RSC, and Leigh saw much of the work being produced by them. Most interesting for us is Leigh's response to Peter Brook's 1964 RSC production of Weiss's *Marat-Sade*, in which the actors were asked to base their characterisations upon actual case-histories of mental patients. When some of the rehearsals were broadcast on BBC Television's *Omnibus* arts programme, Leigh thought, 'If they can do all that, why don't they take it a stage further and make up a play?'[36]

And so Leigh himself began, at the Midland Arts Centre for Young People in Birmingham, to make up plays with young amateurs. The first of these, *The Box Play*, taught him a number of valuable lessons. Although the play was highly successful – it was fun to see and to perform, and its subject matter (a family of six living in a cage-like box in the middle of the stage) worked well as 'cartoon' – Leigh wasn't satisfied with it. He regarded it as 'force-bred' (the inexperienced actors had to be coached throughout the improvisations) and his own experience of working this way was limited. He created parts for all the people who came to the rehearsals, and he describes the methods as being fairly arbitrary ('you're the dog; you're the dad; you're the mum – improvise'). Leigh felt that the work in this play and in subsequent workshops was too shallow, simply stringing together rather superficially theatrical ideas.

His second play, *My Parents Have Gone to Carlisle* (1966), established some of the basic principles which have guided his work ever since. The improvisations were kept private (to avoid the actors trying to 'perform' before they were ready). The play started from an event (a teenage party) to which the players could relate personally. The actors were encouraged to build up biographical details about their characters, and improvisation extended beyond the immediate situation of the play to look at those characters in other contexts. He drew the final play out of the 'real events' of the improvisations.

There remained the problem of the play's final organisation. The improvisations were realistic and truthful, but not very communicative. The natural tendency of such sensitive exploratory work without an audience is to be 'introspective and inaudible'. There is nothing wrong in this: the work is for the *actors'* benefit. But the transition from private to public had to be made, and Leigh felt the need to impose his own sense of order. He shaped the final play out of the actors' work, but in order to do so he often had to work against the 'naturalism' of the rehearsals.

In 1967, Leigh joined the RSC as an assistant director. This allowed him to work with professional actors on *NENAA*. Here he realised that:

> if an improvised play was really to be a totally organic entity, genuinely evolved from characters and relationships, then I had been wrong in starting rehearsals . . . by stating plot or theme and then 'filling it in'. . . . I saw that we must start off with a collection of totally unrelated characters (each one the specific creation of its actor) and then go through a process in which I must cause them to meet each other and build a network of real relationships; the play would have to be drawn from the results.[37]

In some ways this type of work can be related to Copeau's experiments in the 1920s (though it merely unconsciously echoes them). The idea of a play evolving out of characters created by the actors is not so far from the ideals of *la comédie nouvelle*; though instead of *masks*, which the actors would develop throughout their lives, we have naturalistic *characters* evolved for the duration of a play's work period.

Leigh began rehearsals for *NENAA* by providing a series of receptacles, objects such as 'boxes, suitcases, egg-cups, a bucket, a coffin', and getting the actors to build characters suggested by one of the objects. This is analogous to mask work, responding to an object which gives the actor a starting point for improvisation. But, in Leigh's 'pre-rehearsals', where the actors work singly (and privately) with the director, the object (as in Stanislavsky's work) is to create the 'inner lives' as well as the external physical mannerisms of the characters. The job was then to structure situations in which the characters thus created could meet and, in the second, 'structuring' phase of the rehearsal process, interact. Finally, an overall situation had to evolve which would contain the action that developed between the characters. Leigh found a structuring principle in the following statement:

> What we are in life may be conditioned by what we do or the role circumstances force us to play, but this is not necessarily the case, and we would remain our inherent selves irrespective of job or role.[38]

This acknowledges that 'inner truth' is more powerful than crudely deterministic manipulation, and is implicitly in accord with much improvisation theory.

In other words, Leigh found that once the characters had been devised he could suggest (or accept suggestions) that the basic situation in which that character was operating be changed. The 'Italian barber' (played by Peter Rocca) in *NENAA* asked if his character could become a café proprietor. Leigh realised that he could. Naturalistically, Luigi became an 'ex-barber' who now ran a café. Practically, this allowed the company to evolve a setting which would contain the action of the play. 'Gerald' (played by Gerald McNally), a Tyneside filing clerk who dreamed of founding a North-East New Arts Association – the NENAA of the title – went to work in Luigi's King's Cross café and the rest of the play took shape from that.

Between 1965 and 1969 Leigh created nine plays based on improvisational work. Until then (says Paul Clements in his book on Leigh, *The Improvised Play*) he still believed he would become a solitary playwright. It took him a long time fully to understand that working via improvisation was a way of being a dramatist.

Mike Leigh *is* a playwright; all the more so, perhaps, in that his plays are wrought rather than written. He is a writer of plays in the other sense too; though his plays are written *on* and *with* his actors. The early choices are all his. He asks his actors to make lists of potential characters, but they may never know what has attracted him, what possibilities he has glimpsed for future developments, or why he has chosen one character for them to work on rather than another. The process (which Leigh has subsequently devised) of keeping the actors apart from one another until the characters have been formed is directly analogous to the mental compartmentalisation of the more traditional writer of scripts. One level of the play is very privately developed and, while the actors are never puppets, they never really have access to that level of the composition. When they are brought together and begin to interact, many of the fundamental choices will already have been made. The possibilities will have been narrowed down. The future pattern will not be predictable but its shapes will have been conditioned by Leigh.

The plays themselves are 'traditional' in two senses: first, in that Leigh has said he is not interested in 'happenings' and they are therefore not improvised in performance (although one knows that the depth of characterisation is such that, if anything accidental were to happen during performance, the actors would be able to accept and incorporate it *in character*); second, in that the result is always a tightly crafted and (usually, apparently) naturalistic drama.

In Leigh's best-known works (the play and film *Bleak Moments*, 1970–1, the film *High Hopes*, 1989, and his published plays *Abigail's Party*, 1977, and *Goose Pimples*, 1981) this is quite obvious – as the 'finished' and 'published' versions of the original performances make clear. The publication of the playscripts of these works, which were 'evolved from scratch entirely by rehearsal through improvisation',[39] reaffirms Leigh's status as a 'traditional' playwright. The plays can be (and are) performed by actors other than their original creators without recourse to further improvisation. But it in no way detracts from them to realise this, nor does it detract in the slightest from the efforts of the original performers which went into their creation. It is simply to acknowledge and value that *process*, while recognising that the *result* is a 'play' in the mainstream theatre's sense of the word.

Mike Leigh's influence has spread during the last ten or fifteen years. Actors and actresses he has worked with have gone on to direct in their own right (Les Blair was in *The Box Play* right at the beginning; Mike Bradwell, the founder of Hull Truck, played Norman in *Bleak Moments*; Sheila Kelley was in *Babies Grow Old*, *Nuts in May*, *Ecstasy* and *Home Sweet Home*). Sara Pia Anderson and Phil Young are other deviser-directors who have essayed play creation in the improvised style after Leigh.

Paul Clements, however, makes the very telling point that it was not until after Phil Young's *Crystal Clear* in 1982 (televised by the BBC in 1988) that any major drama critic explicitly acknowledged that:

improvised plays are just as much plays as any other kind. . . .
Indeed the tendency with improvised plays appears to be
towards a much higher degree of accuracy in characterisation
than with the average pre-conceived authorial script.[40]

And the general critical tendency is still to regard the improvised
play as somehow too 'loose', too 'unfinished', perhaps as not 'a
real play' at all.

Leigh's works are certainly 'real plays'. They are created
experientially. They are based upon observation. They are
authentic, carefully crafted and detailed examinations of character
and social environment. They are drawn from life – 'serious and
original investigations into real experiences', the crucial discovery
of the Camberwell art classes applied to the theatre – but they are
also shaped and purposive events, poetic and symbolic statements
about the ways in which human beings live and relate and fail.
Leigh and those who have collaborated with or learned from him
have shown that improvisation need no longer be just a rehearsal
device of the drama schools. With Leigh's plays, improvisation has
become the source and means of dramatic creation itself.

Further thoughts on play-construction using improvisation

'Improvisation' does not exclude the devising of pattern –
or movements or words. It may be a kind of spatial collective writing or creative participation: a group working on an
idea, or individuals contributing different (sometimes thoroughly
researched) parts to a communal effort. As such it can form part
of a working method for groups in education or in creative writing
courses.

This kind of work is at the basis of most of Mike Leigh's
plays. But what it is going towards is the production, for actors
and audience, of something that on the one hand feels 'authentic'
and on the other hand is centred around a kind of liveliness, a
sense that something *present* is happening. The success of the
performance has less to do with adherence to a conventional
notion of 'realism' than with an imaginative entering into ways
of speaking and moving which *transmit* that sense of reality. And
that is achieved through hard work, research, practice, rehearsal:
traditional enough methods, yet ones which can also be used to
set up (and in any really dynamic performance always do set up)

a situation in which the actors are *ready to cope with anything*. They are fully there, in context: they are not 'pretending'.

How do you learn this? Essentially in the same way that any real learning takes place – by doing it. That is to say, by making it an active exploration by all aspects of mind and body: intellect, discrimination, decision making, response, sensitivity, motor skills and so on. 'Working through' something – provided it is all active working, and not falling back on habits and clichés of speech and behaviour – is a way of setting up feedback loops by which action can evolve to more and more appropriate forms.

So Leigh runs scenes many times, building them up from what he and his actors discover in the process. The 'director' is in the first instance a kind of sounding-board, finding out what seems to the actors to work; only secondarily is he involved in selecting or editing, and then in reorganising, what has been a collective input. And this stage, too, can be fed back to the actors – as many directors from Brecht to Brook have done – as part of an evolving process of 'rehearsal', by which the play itself is moved through successive phases *as it is materialised*. That is to say, it does not pre-exist as an abstraction, or even as an idealised text: its physical coming-into-being interacts with and produces the script, which may only be 'finalised' at a late stage.[41] For Leigh's television plays it has to be formalised, due to demands of running-time, camera angles and so on: but a stage performance can be more flexible. Some 'fringe' companies not only construct plays in similar ways, incorporating improvisation in their research and development, but can afford to leave more room for it in the public performance (for example, National Revue Co., who frequently invite direct audience participation in games, or Théâtre de Complicité, whose precise sense of timing of elaborate mime or semi-vocalised sequences allows for changes of direction depending on response).

This, to an extent, gives the lie to Clements's remark that 'Leigh is not experimental at all in any self-conscious sense'[42] and the gloss that his innovation has to do with content rather than form. It also suggests that Leigh's activities transcend the somewhat narrow (Marxist-derived) view of class and social determinism which his plays tend to deal in. This restriction may in fact be a useful kind of focusing in terms of coming up with a finished product, but the process of arriving at it suggests different virtues too.

Incorporating the actors' research – both academic/investigative (going out and taking notes) and physical (finding out what it feels like to walk or talk like that kind of person) – into the performance means on one level involving them in the choices from which the play evolves, and on another level making them both discover and generate the 'sub-text' or underlying motivation for each character or event. They are involved in an *existential* (how to find the resources in their own experience), *psychological* (how to motivate), and *semiological* (how to present in words and actions) commitment to the development of character and incident.

So in their 'improvising' the actors are exercising basic and important skills which go far beyond just falling back on humorous parody of clichéd behaviour; they are involved in precise creative performance. And they are also involved *together*: each person's discoveries have to be modified to fit with those of the other actors – a process that serves to deepen the 'collective reality'. This result is not incompatible with Leigh's political position referred to above, nor, for instance, with some of Brecht's methods of working with actors, but it also goes beyond this into aspects of group process and individual self-actualisation. The focus is, both individually and collectively, on the *why* rather than just the *what*. It's a way of getting into how people feel in particular situations and how they express that in words and actions; and that's why Leigh's plays work.

Because of the actors' involvement, their personal investment of interest and their share in the result, the process is fascinating and fun: qualities which are usually found in good improvisation. And the collective commitment supports this, as well as serving an 'anti-star' (and anti-director) system, which again is in accord with the political assumptions behind Leigh's work. The anti-dictatorial approach has implications for the use of improvisation in education and psychotherapy, too: things you do for yourself usually make more impact. Furthermore, there are implications for the structure (financial and political) of commercial theatre which parallel some of the features of the carnival/fringe tradition.

Leigh is also careful 'to avoid closing down his options too soon'.[43] By keeping alive as many possibilities as the actors can cope with, Leigh is in effect signalling the way all improvisation tends to gather at the point of bifurcation where all creative directions remain open. Even in working towards what will eventually be quite a tightly scripted and prepared piece, it is important to retain this flexibility for as long as possible: you never know what may later be able to be combined into the finished article. As Jean-Louis Barrault has it, 'theatre is . . . the art of the present moment';[44] it is vital to keep that moment as highly charged with subsequent developments as possible.

Finally, Leigh refuses to 'work it all out for the audience':[45] if there is work for them to do they will have much more invested in the performance and will contribute to it. This again highlights a fundamental requirement of improvised theatre, which, because it locates its effectiveness precisely in the moment of interchange between one word/action and the next, between one actor and his or her partner(s), and between actors and audience, necessarily demands an active condition of all those who figure in the 'receiver' role at any given instant. Improvisation, both generally and in Leigh's theatrical and political practice, is about waking us up rather than lulling us to sleep.

New York Giants vs Chicago Bears

The development of improvisational drama in America is complex, and falls quite outside the pattern we have described so far, which is primarily European. True, the use of *applied* improvisation derives ultimately from Europe. But it has become so thoroughly neutralised as to have become distinctively American. And there is also a genuine native tradition quite distinct from anything we have met so far in this study.

For convenience (and because there *is* a geographical as well as metaphorical distinction to be made) we can categorise the former, naturalised tradition as the 'New York' school, while the latter, native impro is associated with the 'second city', Chicago.

Michel Saint-Denis (through his influence on the drama school curriculum, especially at the New York Julliard School) undoubtedly added a great deal to American actor training, as he did to that of Europe. But the use of improvisation in American acting pre-dates Saint-Denis, stems more directly from the Russian rather than the French tradition, and is inextricably bound up with the development of American written drama.

Richard Boleslavsky (born Boleslaw Srzednicki in Poland, 1889, and educated in Russia) had trained at the Moscow Art Theatre since 1906. Like Mikhail Chekhov, he had been a leading member

of the First Studio under Sulerzhitsky, directing the first production there (Heijerman's *The Good Hope*) in 1911 and remaining
a member of Stanislavsky's company until 1920. Finding himself
increasingly at odds with post-revolutionary Russia, Boleslavsky
fled, first to Warsaw, and thence in 1922 to New York, where he
worked as a director for an *émigré* revue company.

In 1923, following the celebrated tour of the Moscow Art
Theatre to America, there was enough interest in Stanislavskian
acting techniques for Boleslavsky to be asked to run a Laboratory
Theatre on Russian rehearsal techniques. He was soon joined by
Maria Ouspenskaya, one of the MAT's actresses (who had studied
with Sulerzhitsky since 1908, and joined the First Studio also in
1911) who had chosen to leave the Russian company and remain
in New York after the tour. The new venture was christened the
American Laboratory Theatre, usually known as the Lab.

> There were three aspects of the total training: (1) development
> of the actor's body and voice, which Boleslavsky called the
> outer means of expression; (2) refinement of the inner means
> of expression which enabled the actor to live through – in
> his imagination – the situations conceived by a playwright;
> and (3) enlargement of the actor's intellectual and cultural
> awareness.[46]

The first aspect was done by specialists in ballet, interpretive
dance, eurhythmics, fencing, mime, voice, speech and make-up.
The third aspect was taught by specialist teachers in theatre
history, art, music, literature and 'ideas of Western culture'.
Boleslavsky and Ouspenskaya particularly specialised in the
second aspect, and the work was derived from Stanislavskian
practice, which was totally unknown in America until this time.

The aim was to train an ensemble for three years before letting
them perform publicly, though this ideal was eventually compro-
mised. As the repertory theatre of the Lab took up more of
Boleslavsky's time, so Ouspenskaya took most of the responsibility
for teaching. Her classes centred on small group improvisations,
one-minute plays and character work. Her improvisations, often
animal or object characterisations, stressed observation but also
tried to use improvisation to explore aspects of characterisation
alien to the actor's own personality – something the MAT had

resisted. Her work was closer to Stanislavskian practice in its use of given circumstances:

> Improvised situations, such as waiting at a train station, were often complicated by varying the given circumstances suddenly to force the student to adjust and react flexibly to different situations while remaining true to the basic *données* of his character. During improvisations students were urged to connect with each other – to become sensitive to one another's subtlest changes in attitude or behaviour.[47]

This is the core of the New York style: derived from Stanislavsky but with subtle differences, used in the development of characterisation, and basically a system which functions *intra-actively* – between the actors in the scene. The Chicago system, as we shall see, derives from a different, not originally theatrical tradition, and stresses *inter-action* between the performers and the audience. The New York style, like its Russian original, strives to keep its intentions 'upstage of the footlights', inside the scene. The Chicago style crosses the boundary into the auditorium, both ways.

The Lab, which Boleslavsky ran from 1923 to 1929, was profoundly influential. Among its approximately 500 members were Stella Adler, Ruth Nelson, Eunice Stoddard, who studied acting; the critic Francis Fergusson (who was Boleslavsky's assistant for a while); and Harold Clurman and Lee Strasberg, who studied directing and whose ideas – developed from Boleslavsky's teaching rather than directly from Stanislavsky (who had yet to publish) – would profoundly affect the development of American acting, writing and drama teaching via first the Group Theatre and later the Actors' Studio. Boleslavsky left the Laboratory Theatre in 1929, and spent the remainder of his life working as a director in Hollywood, where he died in 1937.

Ouspenskaya founded her own school in 1932 and then, in 1936, she too went to Hollywood, where she died in a fire in 1949. Her work is the bridge between Stanislavsky's understanding of the improvisational *étude*, based on the given circumstances of the play, and the simplified, naturalised version of his work that would later typify the work of the Actors' Studio in New York under Lee Strasberg.

As well as the usual repertoire of improvisation exercises,

Strasberg developed Stanislavsky's notion of 'public solitude' into
the 'Private Moment exercise' in which the participants explore
themselves, and work on their own blockages. Pretending that the
audience is not present, the performer does something that she
or he would normally do if they were alone. Strasberg stressed
the danger of this exercise for emotionally disturbed actors, since
the introspective exercise can act as a negative reaffirmation of the
original problem. Just as damagingly, the Private Moment at the
Studio was not private enough; it was shared with others. Laurence
Olivier was present on one notorious occasion when two actors
– one male, one female – briefly attired, powdered each other
with talc, oblivious to the onlookers, for half-an-hour. Obviously,
baldly described like this (as it was) the method sounds appallingly
self-indulgent. Yet the mistake is not in the doing of the exercise,
but in the breakdown of its privacy. Not what were they doing; but
what were *we* doing there?

This was the New York style carried to an extreme: theatre
is *never* a Private Moment. It is the most public of all the arts.
A feeling of exclusion makes the spectator angrier than anything
else in theatre can. Strasberg attempted to overcome the tension
generated by the presence of onlookers which blocks the release
of the actor's emotional flow. Following Stanislavsky, he offers
the actor a way to find his or her still centre while on stage under
stress – 'public solitude'.[48] The audience *can* be perceived, though,
as threatening the fragility of the actor's mood, and the response
is to turn inwards, to close out the spectator. It is something of
great value in therapy, of great value in rehearsal (for example,
Mike Leigh's intensive private work with individual actors) – and
of no use at all in public performance. It denies performance. At its
worst, the Method could lead to that denial; at its best, it produced
electrifying public acting. Strasberg sensed the blockages in actors
– indeed, perhaps the Actors' Studio began to attract blocked
actors to it, craving liberation in personal psychodrama. In the
exercises, that release could be obtained, and creativity made to
flow. In the public presentation of the exercise, an irreconcilable
– and therefore risible – contradiction became manifest. And the
baby was washed away with the bathwater. This was a confusion
that the Chicago school carefully avoided from its inception.

The first theatre in Chicago was opened in 1847, and the city
has been a theatrical centre since the turn of the century. In 1912
the British playwright Maurice Browne and his actress wife Ellen

Van Volkenberg opened the Chicago Little Theatre (following the example of the Boston Toy Theatre of the previous year). It was in the vanguard of what came to be known as the 'little theatre movement' that quickly engulfed America:

> The influence of the new movement . . . was also felt abroad. Browne claims that Jacques Copeau told him he had found inspiration for the Théâtre du Vieux-Colombier from accounts of the Chicago experiment.[49]

Be that as it may, Chicago was and is still the source of a uniquely American dramatic energy, and the Chicago style of improvisation has its roots in the work of a number of different people, some of whom had little or nothing directly to do with the theatre.

Neva L. Boyd was a teacher, sociologist and educational theorist. In 1911 she organised the Chicago Training School for Playground Workers. From 1914 to 1920 she was Director of the Department of Recreation in the Chicago School of Civics and Philanthropy. Then, in 1921, she founded the Recreational Training School at Chicago's Hull House. From 1924 to 1927 she had Viola Spolin as a student living in her house. Spolin writes:

> I received from her an extraordinary training in the use of games, storytelling, folk dance, and dramatics as tools for stimulating creative expression in both children and adults, through self-discovery and personal experiencing. The effects of her inspiration never left me for a single day.[50]

From 1927 until she retired in 1941 Boyd worked as a sociologist on the faculty of Northwestern University (at Evanston, Illinois), teaching play theory, leadership and group organisation. After retiring she became a consultant to the Activity Therapy Program of the Illinois Department of Welfare, working in the State School system. She continued to teach, and to use play in teaching, virtually until her death in 1963.

Essentially, Neva Boyd's work was similar to Caldwell Cook's 'Play Way' (at the Perse School in Cambridge at about the same time[51]). In the Foreword to a collection of children's games published in 1945 she writes:

The educational value for so-called normal children of games dynamically played is unquestioned; their therapeutic value for hospitalised children has been demonstrated beyond doubt; their use as therapy in the treatment of mental patients has proved effective; and their corrective value in the re-education of problem youth has been repeatedly demonstrated in schools and custodial institutions.[52]

While the book in question deliberately does little more than list and describe about 300 children's games, Boyd is in no doubt about the sociological, physiological and psychological bases of games theory. Jean Piaget and Margaret Lowenfeld would, in various ways, continue to develop the educational and psychological theory: the dramatic use of games was to be developed chiefly by Viola Spolin and her pupils in America, and Naftali Yavin, Albert Hunt and Clive Barker in England.

Viola Spolin, having been trained by Boyd, began as a teacher and drama supervisor on the Chicago WPA (Works Progress Administration) Recreational Project during the New Deal years, developing a 'non-verbal, non-psychological approach'[53] to help train students to use drama in community work – a remarkably advanced project for its time.

Her greatest single contribution was the development and systematisation of Boyd's insights about the use of games. Working with illiterate immigrants and their children, she devised many non-verbal improvisations. Also Spolin, working primarily with children and amateur adults, was the first deliberately to open up improvisational work to include audience-suggested material. This would, in later years, become a feature of what we are calling the 'Chicago style'. Spolin, like Roddy Maude-Roxby, uses the term 'player' in preference to 'actor' with regard to this kind of developmental work. The method (which grows out of Neva Boyd's work, parallels Suzanne Bing's, and which anticipates Clive Barker's) centres on games; so much so that her definition of the term 'Improvisation' begins 'Playing the game'.[54]

In 1946 Spolin moved to California where, with her assistant Robert Martin, she ran the Young Actors' Company in Hollywood until 1955. It was during the eleven-year period of this group that Spolin began to write down her work; but the final draft would have to wait until he was able to return to Chicago for a visit in

1959. Her book, *Improvisation for the Theatre*, first published in 1963, was the first to attempt to codify and to teach improvisational acting. It was reprinted in 1987, evidence perhaps that interest in impro is growing around the world?

The final draft of Spolin's book had to wait until she was given the opportunity to observe at first hand the workings of America's first fully professional improvisational theatres. The central figure in the creation of both, back in Chicago, was her own son, Paul Sills.

Sills entered the University of Chicago as a student in 1948. Many gifted actors were attracted to the artistic environment blossoming around the University during the immediate post-war years; among the best known would be Edward Asner, Fritz Weaver and Mike Nichols, while Elaine May and David Shepherd were among the many performers informally associated with the University Theatre.

Paul Sills joined the University Theatre group; then, in 1953, he was instrumental in setting up the Playwrights' Theatre Club which, as its name implies, was intended to produce the works of great playwrights. Twenty-five plays were produced in two years, a lot of them Shakespearean or modern classics. The Playwrights' Theatre Club lasted until 1955, when Sills teamed up with David Shepherd to found the first performance group solely dedicated to improvised work: The Compass.

Shepherd's original idea was for a theatre derived (in inspiration) from the *commedia dell'arte*. Both he and Paul Sills were heavily influenced by the theories of Bertolt Brecht (Sills later studied briefly in East Germany and ran classes in Brechtian theory and practice). Shepherd wanted Compass to be a working class theatre for culturally deprived groups in industrial centres of America, such as Gary, Indiana. In the end it was decided that Chicago University had its own cultural deprivation problem, and Compass settled in Hyde Park. The Chicago school adopted Brecht as its mentor, much as the New York school had appropriated Stanislavsky. Compass and its many successors derived their cabaret style from Brechtian 'Smoking Theatre'. Compass's political aspirations, though, were shortlived. An early associate, Andrew Duncan, describes the Compass clientele as 'lumpen-bourgeoisie',[55] and Shepherd himself quickly became frustrated that the group seemed more concerned about fighting their Jewish intellectual parents than about fighting McCarthyism.

From the start it was agreed that Compass was to have no playwright, and no scripted play: its work would be based upon scenarios which could be hung up backstage like the 'platt' in an Elizabethan theatre. The first Compass production was *The Game of Hurt*, from a scenario devised and directed by Paul Sills. Like the *commedia*, this wasn't imagined as totally free improvisation:

> The original idea was to have a scenario which was – as we fondly imagined – the *Commedia dell'arte* idea. We wrote a story out, usually eight to twelve scenes written out on a sheet of paper, and we'd follow through the scenes by rehearsing.[56]

In addition to the main piece, the group also performed short 'Living Magazine' pieces (of a rather more superficial sort than the 'Living Newspapers' developed by the Federal Theatre Project in the 1930s) and, most significantly considering Paul Sills's early training in his mother's TIE work, *audience requests*.

The audience request, or the immediate incorporation of suggestions from the audience, is the most distinctive feature of the Chicago style. Mike Nichols and Elaine May, for example, astounded audiences and critics in 1960 by their virtuosity in using audience-determined material. (John Monteith and Suzanne Rand do exactly the same kind of act today, and this style now also forms the basis for the popular radio and television improvisation game, *Whose Line Is It Anyway?*) In particular, the audience request characterises Sills's next venture, the famed Second City, established (by Sills, Bernie Sahlins and Howard Alk) in 1959 and still, thirty years later, an important breeding ground for all that is best in American acting. A New York spin-off of Compass, Ted Flicker's The Premise (which would later be involved in a row with the British censor), tended to concentrate mostly on one-line jokes, but Second City, under Sills's guidance, allowed 'long, complicated scenes, whole plays, to evolve . . . whole scenaria, all sorts of parodies and operas and musical versions',[57] while Alan Myerson's spin-off troupe, The Committee (1963–73) would develop a yet more serious, politically involved type of improvised theatre in San Francisco.

The Second City format involves the presentation of a main show (which has been built up and rehearsed over a number of months). This is then followed by audience suggestions which the players are allowed to think about and discuss for a short while. Or they may do 'spot improvs' – suggestions acted on immediately, without reflection – which are treated by actors and audience alike as virtuoso feats (when they work). At regular intervals, the best of the resultant material is then selected out, discussed, refined, rehearsed, and will form part of the next main show.

The 'Chicago style' (obviously no longer confined to that city) bifurcates into comic strip performance (typified by Shelley Berman, Joan Rivers, the late John Belushi, Dan Aykroyd, Gilda Radner), and quiet, totally credible naturalism (Barbara Harris, Alan Arkin, Alan Alda, Betty Thomas). The division has always been present in American acting, to some extent, with the conflicting Broadway paradigms of the musical and naturalistic drama. But the conflict was also part of Second City's make-up.

In its early days, many of the actors were university intellectuals, excited by the boundaries of their new form. But there were also those for whom improvisation was only a means of generating and developing performance material; they saw it as a form of play – or rather revue – construction. Impro was a product of the great period of satirical comedy, the era of Lenny Bruce and Mort Sahl. Second City became increasingly a prisoner of its own success. Young talent was attracted to the theatre not so much because it was the home of improvised drama, but because it was an excellent platform from which to launch a career in comedy or, increasingly, in television. Clever caricatures began to replace the more thoughtful 'people scenes' of the early shows.

Paul Sills left Second City in 1967; co-founder Bernie Sahlins took over and ran the company until 1984, when he, in turn, sold his interest to Andrew Alexander, the producer of the Toronto Second City. Sills and Viola Spolin opened The Game Theatre, which was followed in the early 1970s by Sills's highly successful Story Theatre. The Game Theatre was centred primarily on Viola's exercises. Leaving revue behind, the idea was to have the *audience* play the impro games, becoming their own performers. The technique of Story Theatre was related to impro though it usually used pre-existing narrative and textual material. Sills moved to Los Angeles and set up a small company under the title Sills and Company, which continues to play the theatre games devised by his mother from Neva Boyd's work. The company includes his daughter Rachel, a fourth-generation improviser. In 1986 the company mounted a five-month off-Broadway tour, which was widely acclaimed by the New York critics.

For David Shepherd, the original conception had been political, derived from Brecht. He has since continued to experiment with proletarian theatre forms. Currently, he is the mastermind behind the growth of 'theatre sports' – 'Impro Olympics' – in the USA and Canada.

But for Paul Sills and Viola Spolin, the work passes (like Grotowski's) beyond the borders of the theatre, into the para-theatrical world of self-discovery and self-actualisation, the creation of 'free space' in man.

> All the people who have worked with improvisational theater know that there's a free space they can come back to and they like to come back to. . . . I'm not interested in improvisational theater *per se*. I'm interested in the establishment of those free spaces where people can do their own work, and I'm interested in the forms which begin to emerge in these free spaces.[58]

The basic difference between the New York and Chicago styles is that the giants of the New York theatre world confined improvisation, seeing it only as a rehearsal tool or play-writing device. The actor was confined, too; like Saint-Denis they imagined the actor to be primarily the interpreter (in Greek, *hypokrités*) of a written script. Paul Sills is the inheritor of another tradition. An irascible and difficult director, by all accounts, and occasionally uncommunicative, he is none the less inspired by the *idea* of communication. In Chicago, improvisation games were a way of communicating between people, especially those disadvantaged and without a social voice, long before they were borrowed by the stage.

Chapter 2

Improvisation in Alternative Drama

Roddy Maude-Roxby/Theatre Machine

I think the most important moment in improvisation
is when you don't know what will happen next.

Roddy Maude-Roxby

The genesis of Theatre Machine is outlined by Keith Johnstone in
his book *Impro*. The company was actually formed at Montreal's
EXPO 67 by Johnstone, as director, and four actors: Ben Benison,
Roddy Maude-Roxby, Ric Morgan and John Muirhead. Primarily
interested in comedy improvised in performance, the group had
worked together at the Royal Court Theatre, London, in the
mid-1960s. They had given lecture-demonstrations to schools and
teacher training colleges (educationalists were already becoming
aware of the value of their techniques in teaching).

There followed a period in which THEATRE MACHINE
established its improvisatory style with audiences at home
and abroad and also produced scripted and unscripted plays:
Clowning, *Brixham Regatta*, *Robinson Crusoe*, *Arabian Nights*,
and the Sir and Perkins plays *The Martian*, *Time Machine* and
Moby Dick.

With the departure of their director in '71 THEATRE
MACHINE's four actors formed a performance group, self-
reliant, without a director, designer or author, these roles being
taken on 'in the moment' during the performance.[1]

55

The company has remained loosely organised since then, the four actors following separate careers and coming together to become 'Theatre Machine' at will. Technically speaking, the company has disbanded but the organisation is *so* loose that a mere technicality like that doesn't prevent the occasional Theatre Machine event or tour:[2] the 'company' was recently challenged – by Keith Johnstone from his current base in Canada – to take part in an 'Impro-Olympics' contest![3] They are also active in various spheres. Roddy Maude-Roxby, for instance, in addition to performing, runs workshops and works in the community in both theatrical and 'paratheatrical' capacities. Like Johnstone and Grotowski, the 'educational' or developmental aspect emerges from the practice of theatre activities.

Theatre Machine emerged from work at the Royal Court Theatre with George Devine, who was closely associated with Michel Saint-Denis, as well as from Johnstone's own input. It has been the only professional company to present performances which are 'totally' improvised; not only does its work link with the use of improvisation in traditional theatre – if of an 'experimental' kind, given the Royal Court's emphasis on new writing for the theatre[4] – but it also marks a limit which even 'fringe' productions rarely approach.

Johnstone joined the English Stage Company as a writer in 1956 (the year of Osborne's *Look Back in Anger* – but also the year in which Lecoq founded his School in Paris) and was a leading member of the Writer's Group, a practical workshop created by Devine and run primarily by William Gaskill, which developed the talents of, *inter alia*, John Arden and Edward Bond.

Terry Browne, in *Playwrights' Theatre*, describes the training work done at the Court's Studio. In 1963, at the Jeanetta Cochrane Theatre, they mounted a term on Comedy. Devine taught 'comic tricks'; Claude Chagrin – an early Lecoq graduate – taught mime; Gaskill taught comic improvisation and comic mask work (much of which he had learned from Devine – and hence from Saint-Denis); Johnstone taught narrative and the fairy-tale. In 1963 Johnstone took this group over and, in 1965, with the group that was to become Theatre Machine, he presented the Christmas show called *Clowning*:

> *Clowning* was an improvised show: there was no written script of any kind – though there was an extremely loose structure – and

all the actors changed parts for different performances. . . . The improvisational work which led to and made up *Clowning* ante-dated the other apparently related *avant-garde* movements in the fringe theatre, such as the Living Theatre; but *Clowning* is very different in kind: although certainly related to the *Commedia dell'arte*, its more immediate inspiration is the English music hall tradition. Indeed, the use of improvisation is the only point of contact with the Living Theatre, for *Clowning* and the Theatre Machine are essentially concerned with making people laugh.[5]

Clowning had to be presented officially as a *lecture* – because of the Lord Chamberlain's inability to pass improvisational work. We nowadays tend to forget the dead hand of official censorship, which was not abolished in Britain until 1968.

William Gaskill, Johnstone's colleague at the Court, has said of him:

All his work has been to encourage the rediscovery of the imaginative response in the adult; the refinding of the power of the child's creativity. Blake is his prophet and Edward Bond his pupil.[6]

With reference to Theatre Machine, it is necessary to define what 'total' improvisation means in this context. It does not mean a completely random and chaotic show. Rather it is a compilation of a number of *lazzi*-type ingredients: the performers have 'up their sleeves', as it were, a number of characters – some with appropriate masks or bits of costume – or fragments of sketches. Some sections may be quite familiar to them or quite fully rehearsed. But everything is open to change. In the rehearsal process a scene, a dialogue, a song, may start to go well, and it may be included in the running order for the performance. But 'on the night' it may come out quite different, as one of the participants develops it in another direction, or it may be cut short and left as a kind of embryonic possibility. The detail of each performance is never finalised, although the approximate shape of the overall sequence necessarily has to be known in advance for obvious practical reasons.

THEATRE MACHINE is improvised performance. If you don't know the show is improvised, or don't believe it can be, then the bits that work well will seem obviously rehearsed. The bits that flop you will think 'obviously not rehearsed' – you'll think those are the 'improvised' bits and you'll wonder why they improvise, if it doesn't work.[7]

Theatre Machine point out that, of course, a lot of rehearsed, scripted theatre doesn't work too well either. Theatre managements often take three performances to be convinced that each show is truly improvised.

> On the second night they would ask why didn't we do the famous scene of the night before? Particularly if it had been mentioned by the critics – or why had we 'saved' such and such a scene for the second night? The next night they ask why don't we rehearse the best scenes and do them as a show?[8]

They provide the answer:

> THEATRE MACHINE has throw-away form, it is disposable theatre, ideas and memories get re-cycled and the best is really best because it comes out of the moment; and sometimes you were just ahead of them.[9]

This idea of 'throw-away' theatre captures the very essence of improvised drama. The term is also used by Dario Fo and Franca Rame (*un teatro da bruciare*), although in their politicised context, theatre is used, and then disposed of, in the same way as a newspaper is burnt once it has served its purpose of informing the reader. Theatre Machine's 'disposibility' is simply an acceptance and a celebration of the central fact of performance – the ephemeral act of co-creation between actor and spectator 'in the moment'.

Theatre Machine's method of working depends on very close mutual support by all performers. Timing is one important example: if something threatens to flag, for instance, the actors on stage are dependent on one of their colleagues taking the responsibility of entering and changing the direction. They must all be highly sensitive to each other and to what is happening, totally 'present' and alert, prepared to support each other and not 'block'. Whatever happens has to be accepted as right and used in the on-the-spot construction of a scene. The actors are at their most vulnerable.

Here we can see in operation many of the issues central to Johnstone's approach to improvisation and basic to Copeau's and Saint-Denis's adoption of it as fundamental to actor training. The links with Grotowski are clear also. Theatre Machine push the demands to the limit because there is nowhere to hide on stage: ultimately, all acting is about being able to take full responsibility for yourself and for your colleagues. In this light it is clear that improvisation is valuable both as individual training and as a way of enhancing ensemble work. There is perhaps no more direct way of experiencing our mutual responsibility, and ultimately that is both a psychological and a political realisation.

One of the key elements of Jacques Lecoq's training[10] is the emphasis on *play*; using and enjoying the moment and what it brings. Maude-Roxby uses the term 'players' in preference to 'actors' in his improvisation work. This is part of a deliberate strategy, accompanied by a relaxed and apparently non-directive manner, to help participants to feel at ease. 'Playing' suggests a game in which everyone can take part, and in which there are more rewards than penalties; it takes the heat off the rather threatening nakedness of improvisatory situations. Maude-Roxby often says that his sessions are about 'not acting', a maxim which is related to Lecoq's work on clowning.[11] The basis of clowning is the ability to feel OK about being yourself and making a fool of yourself. It necessarily includes a passage through vulnerability, but it can't afford to get stuck in it. So, too, 'play' admits the possibility of making mistakes, or rather implies that it doesn't matter, allowing the chance for what we might think of as 'mistakes' (if we are thinking about 'giving a good performance') to be re-evaluated as possibilities of new directions. Everything in Maude-Roxby's work can lead anywhere, so there is no *a priori* categorisation of right and wrong. Rightness is more a question of *attitude*, not of what you do but of how you do it, whether you are prepared to play with what comes along. 'Play' in this context also has the idea of interplay, of the development of the range of the possible.

Many of the exercises Maude-Roxby uses are similar to things discussed below in the section on techniques. It's his way of using them that is particularly interesting. He seems to be open to the developing sense of structure, seeking an organic form which emerges through the activity. Collecting objects, talking about them, evolving a narrative; finding different ways of moving and building a 'scene' around their interrelationships; developing from one person/object/position to more and more complex collages or combinations, with or without speech; arranging a collection of bodies or masked players. All of these work off not knowing what will happen, building in the unexpected, allowing it to become an unforced part of a construction or meaning which emerges as part of a (group) process.

This kind of work also gives free rein to fantasy – allowing it to bypass cliché – by linking it to physical events which don't have a specific, predetermined meaning. The shape which the body adopts, or the function of an object, are not interpreted as fixed notations in a set code, as they might be in naturalistic performance. There, for instance, a chair tends to be a specific sign in a particular context – it denotes economic or social status – or a bodily position is evidence of a particular psychological state (head drooping, shoulders dropped, hands clasped = powerlessness, depression and so on). In impro situations, the chair could become an umbrella, a bicycle, the horns of a bull; the pose could suggest a child being told off, a person sheltering from a storm and dying to go to the loo, praying and so on. The sign ceases to *denote* and becomes the possibility of infinite *connotation*; it opens out to the play of significance.

Absence of specific meaning allows anything to be imagined – but not in a total void, because the physical event ensures a physical memory-trace. The impulse to meaning is generated in conjunction with the physical event, as the body moves and relates to itself, to other bodies or objects: the pattern of meaning evolves as a succession of such relationships and assessments. So this kind of activity is doing at least three important things at once: showing that signs are arbitrary, helping us to play with them, and getting us to experience that we make meanings with the body as well as with the mind. It is also a mediation between structure and freedom, between memory and imagination, between the given and the created.

It might not at first sight be obvious that improvisation has at least as much to teach about semiotics and structuralism as do learned tomes full of complicated terminology; nor do we claim that theatre practitioners such as Maude-Roxby consciously intend it to do so. (Most of Theatre Machine's work is just *fun*, comic, unselfconscious and totally absurd: 'meaning' is never sought after – it occurs in the joint experience of the performance but much of the work has no great 'significance' beyond the simple pleasure of making new and unexpected combinations – a group of hippopotamuses knitting pullovers from barbed wire; a hero swallowed by a monster finding renewed life as an heroic turd. Absurdity is celebrated, not in any nihilistic way, but because it is the triumphant liberation of the confined imagination.) But if these and other ways of talking about how we give meaning to our lives make any sense, they must be understandable in terms of actual physical events: we must be able to *do* them as well as *think* them.

Theatre, of course, is about *physicalising* the sense-giving act. Structuralist analysis has highlighted sense-giving as a central human activity, and indicated how different codes of meaning and kinds of discourse are elaborated and given privileged status in different usages. Structuralists tend to view the symbolic and the mythological as processes of *encoding* but, as useful as this is, it to some extent ignores the role of the body. If symbolism, as Susanne Langer suggests,[12] is about giving form to *feeling*, theatre may help to underline the equality of the mental and the physical in this process, and improvisation work particularly acknowledges that mind and body have to be treated in tandem.

Jacques Lecoq and the semiotics of clowning

Jacques Lecoq (born 1921) began by teaching physical education and sport, and with rehabilitation work among the disabled. He became an actor in Grenoble just after the end of World War Two. Lecoq learned improvisation from Claude Martin, a pupil of Dullin, and worked with the Association Travail et Culture (TEC), who gave shows based on improvisation and organised spectacles for 10–15,000 people after the Liberation (echoes here of Fo and Piscator). He joined the Compagnie des Comédiens, and here he discovered *le jeu du masque* and became interested in movement training for the actor. In 1947 he worked at Education par le Jeu Dramatique (EPJD), a Paris school for actors, which had been founded by Barrault, Roger Blin, Jean Dasté and others. In 1948 he went to Italy, where he was to stay for eight years. In Padua, he produced his first plays at the University Theatre, and he claims to have discovered '*le jeu de la Commedia dell'arte*' in the markets of the town: '*Commedia* has nothing to do with those little Italian troupes who export precious entertainments. It's about misery, a world where life's a luxury. . . . If you're thinking of *commedia*, forget about Italy.'[13]

In 1951, Lecoq created the Theatre School of the Piccolo Teatro in Milan. The Piccolo Teatro (della Città) di Milano was the first permanent theatre to be opened in Italy after the war. Founded in 1947 by the avant-garde directors and drama critics Paolo Grassi and Giorgio Strehler, it was fast becoming the leading national playhouse. Here Lecoq worked as both director and teacher and here, too, he developed his speciality in mime and dramatic choreography. It has been said of him that he combined the mime of Decroux with *commedia* to form his own synthesis. In working as a choreographer on a production of a Greek tragedy at Syracuse, Lecoq discovered the power of choric work; but he also gained experience of a vast number of other theatrical styles, assisting on Strehler's early productions of Brecht, and choreographing the young Dario Fo and Franca Rame in revue-work.

In 1956 he returned to Paris to found his own Ecole Internationale de Mime et de Théâtre. Since then, Lecoq has collaborated with the Théâtre Nationale Populaire, the Comédie Française, the Schiller Theater – even the RSC. Since 1969, Lecoq has also been a professor at the University of Paris VI, directing a Laboratory devoted to the study of movement and dramatic architecture. He has performed his demonstration piece *Tout Bouge* ('Everything Moves') in many countries.[14]

Lecoq's Paris school has given rise to some of the most important developments in performance style to have occurred during the last three decades. He originally had an interest in movement in sport, and this physical perspective has remained at the basis of his work. He worked with Michel Saint-Denis and Jean Dasté, at first in Grenoble and later in Paris, and thus has direct links with the tradition of Copeau. He represents, however, an important modification and development of what Copeau began, both in terms of approach and of the organisation of a coherent curriculum.

The overall aim of Lecoq's work is to: 'découvrir les règles du jeu théâtral par une pratique de l'improvisation tactile à tous les niveaux (du réalisme à l'abstraction)',[15] which might be glossed as: to discover the essentials of play and interplay in theatrical performance by the practice of improvisation using the whole range of tactile possibility at all levels (from realism to symbolic condensation). The significance of 'règles du jeu théâtral' and 'improvisation tactile' – key phrases in Lecoq's method – will be touched on further in what follows.

Four things figure prominently in most of Lecoq's courses: (a) the establishment of the 'neutral body', including use of the neutral mask; (b) the concept of 'play'; (c) observation and research, both of 'realistic' detail and of rhythm and movement; (d) the *auto-cours*, or 'do-it-yourself', work, in teams or groups towards producing various kinds of performance.

The structure of the courses themselves typically involves work which can be classified into three areas: (a) basics of dramatic performance; (b) the play of styles; and (c) movement and plasticity in terms of the architecture of space.

These areas can be further broken down, and we will discuss them below. Lecoq's written outlines often express things in groups of three (the 'rhythme ternaire', beloved of French stylists; for example, he gives three modes of action and three kinds of gesture); in addition to unconscious linguistic assimilation, this represents the sense of physical rhythm which is an important facet of much of Lecoq's work. Running through Lecoq's presentation of his work is a metaphorical complex related to the activation of space in performance; starting from 'la récolte de rhythmes moteurs' (a gathering or harvesting of fundamental rhythmic impulses, dynamic rhythm, or the basic rhythms of life), going on to suggest that moods and emotional tones can be identified according to the orientation taken by the body in space (melodrama is 'oblique', as is jealousy, whilst pride elevates and shame seeks to lower itself), and finally engaging with 'l'architecture invisible du drame'.

Lecoq breaks down movement and gesture structurally, using anthropological and physiological criteria (based on Jousse's *Anthropologie du geste* and his own early physical training work). For him, 'l'homme pense avec tout son corps',[16] and these criteria enable him to offer his students a way of analysing and reproducing the dynamics of action.

There may well be interesting parallels here with, for instance, the work of Laban[17] and the approach to movement teaching in other schools; or indeed with more abstract evaluations of the significance of a *poétique de l'espace* in the work of literary critics like Maurice Blanchot. But what we are concerned with here is the relationship to improvisation.

Impro work is a central part of Lecoq's courses: a typical four-hour session will contain one hour movement, an hour-and-a-half improvisation and an hour-and-a-half *auto-cours* work in groups, which aims to use the results of the first two areas in building up group presentations.[18] So there is a very close fusion of movement and improvisation in developing the 'play' of performance. And perhaps nowhere else do we find such a precise intellectual and practical structure to movement work in the context of improvisation. For Lecoq, theatre is an 'acte essentiellement physique', and it must thus deploy its range of meanings through the movement of bodies in space. Every organism has spatial coefficients of position and direction; each mood or style may also operate like an organism in this sense. Lecoq's method is directed towards the identification and physical assimilation of these relationships, so that they come to form a 'vocabulary' on which the performer may call as appropriate. Lecoq calls it the 'saisie du réel qui se joue dans notre corps'.[19] Perhaps the nearest equivalent is the lengthy and complex physical training undergone by students of Indian forms such as *Kathakali* to acquire a richly detailed gestural vocabulary and the extraordinary bodily plasticity necessary to articulate this. Lecoq's work, tough though it is, is not quite as rigorous as that, and it is directed towards a somewhat different end.[20] But in both cases the skill and energy required to produce 'poetry in space' is made available through intense physical preparation.

It is thus in this context that we need to see Lecoq's use of improvisation, and the way in which the concept of 'play' is central to it. Lecoq uses the term to signify the energy that is shared between performers on stage and in rehearsal – the ball that the game is played with – which is why for him improvisation is very much a matter of physical activation. 'Play' also means the *inter*-play of this activity, emphasising the relationships which spark off or create new combinations: people, movements, moods or styles meet and collide, giving rise to different possibilities. Structuralism's 'play of the signifier' is relevant here, suggesting the idea of verbal play and inventiveness. Other appropriate shades of meaning include the hint of 'bringing into play', and the sense of 'possible movement or scope' as in the degree of play in a bicycle chain, for instance. This picks up another useful angle, namely the balance between freedom and restraint; 'play' here indicates a fruitful tension within reasonably precise limits.

All of these usages are underpinned by the sense that 'play' is a salient feature of mankind's capacity for the production of symbolic form, signalled primarily in Schiller's *Aesthetic Letters* and in Huizinga's *Homo Ludens*. Thus it also implies *playfulness* – the pleasure derived from discoveries in the moment of creativity. As a further gloss we might think of Marivaux's nicely ambiguous title *Le Jeu de l'Amour et du Hasard*, where 'jeu' signifies at least the following: (a) capriciousness; (b) interplay; (c) something amusing or diverting; (d) the playing of a game or competitive match; (e) a stage entertainment. This plurality of possibility is central to the improvisatory mode.[21]

Thus for Lecoq 'play' is very much a question of developing the physical articulation of mimetic possibility; for him 'mime' signifies all the resources available to the actor including his use of text,[22] and the function of improvisation is to set those resources in play. Therefore, the outcome is in and through performance, that necessarily improvisatory moment when imagination composes new shapes and makes active the knowledge that resides in the body.

'Le style est un esprit de jeu', says one of his course descriptions ('style is a way of playing/a sense of play/a kind of playfulness'): the body of the actor has to be 'disponible' (open, available, ready – see Part III) to engage in different styles which demand that he or she be capable of 'changer l'espace, la vitesse et la matière de son jeu' – that is, to transform the various coefficients of performance, whose 'content' (*matière*) then becomes something quite different. The 'spirit' of play which emerges is precisely the ability to *activate* a particular configuration, to enter the game of its structuring: an acute mental and physical condition permitting creation to occur: 'provoquant (l')imagination à inventer des langages'.

Lecoq uses the *masque neutre* as the first and fundamental stage in the development of this condition; through it he aims at a physical condition ('état neutre'; 'état de disponibilité silencieuse'; 'masque du calme') which is at the basis of dynamic extension in space (*l'espace*), time (*vitesse, rhythmes moteurs*) and matter (*animaux, éléments, matières, couleurs, lumières*).[23]

His work then proceeds via the *larval mask*, which offers nascent expressive states, towards an incorporation of the 'passions' in melodrama and *commedia*. For him, improvisation is less about psychological liberation (though that is, as it were,

taken for granted) than a matter of building up resources of
physical awareness about how people move, how the body
develops certain attitudes when it is in certain modes, about
the acquisition of precise mimicry which can then be activated in
the construction of scenarios, at first more realistically imitative,
then involving more elaborately imaginative forms.

For Lecoq, knowledge comes about *through movement*: so 'he
attempts to return the mime to the precognitive state, freeing him
to gather a new set of sensory impressions in a neutralised state of
naiveté'.[24] He works (via the neutral mask) towards what he calls
mime de fond, the 'gestural rendering of the essence of reality'.[25]
This reflects an Artaudian belief in the ability to discover a
pre-verbal level where, after passing through the *silence de fond*
– the first phase of his work, Lecoq says, is about forgetting[26] –
one may begin to: 'find the gesture of the word, the actions for
the verbs in the profound silence in which they were born'.[27]

Anthropologically and anatomically, movement precedes language, and Lecoq seeks to return students to that situation where
they discover emotion and meaning through gesture: the *mime de
fond* is also the *mime du début* – of the beginnings of all knowing
and all articulation.

The *disponibilité* Lecoq seeks is a situation of balance which
can draw upon an extensive range of possible movement and
action which has been internalised in the preparatory work. Thus,
though the resonances of the term are not entirely different from
those conveyed by André Gide and other French writers (that is,
a kind of spontaneous openness to 'nature', to instinct, to the life
of the senses, and a state of 'being ready for anything that comes
along'), the emphasis here is less romantically effusive and much
more centred upon precise corporeal preparedness. Performance
cannot afford to be approximate, even though it may respond to
the demands of the moment or adapt to the feedback messages
it is receiving from the audience. We can, perhaps, point to a
salient difference here between the technical precision of Lecoq's
work and the 'purer' and 'rougher' – though no less skilled –
improvisation of Johnstone and Maude-Roxby.

Here as elsewhere, then, 'neutrality', of mask and of the whole
body, is not a kind of blankness; it is highly charged. The body has
a wide range of available resources; neutrality engenders a state
in which they are ready to go into play, but not programmed to
operate in a predetermined way. The 'waking up' exercise often

used by Lecoq and others in neutral mask-work[28] indicates the desired condition: it's rather as if the whole body were 'full of eyes within' and they are all opening to an unfamiliar world.[29] The coefficients of action have to be drawn anew. But if it works, this kind of alertness as the basis of performance can produce inventive and delightful play.

Lecoq uses the Clown to illustrate this. (The Clown is the 'esprit de jeu' *par excellence*: Lecoq says that clowns operate 'at a point where all is blunder' – where the unexpected is the rule, therefore.) The semiotics of clowning rate a closer look in this context.[30]

A clown emerges from behind a screen. He wears a red nose, but otherwise has no props. He looks at us. And for some reason we laugh. He looks at us again, pleased to see us. We laugh louder. He takes delight in our laughter, and that pleases us too. The clown has done nothing – except *notice* us. And yet we are laughing. He had told no jokes. He has performed no 'routine' to amuse us. So why have we laughed?

That red nose? Partly; this tiny mask (no less than, say, the great whole-body mask of the Indian *Kootiyattam*) will activate in the viewer the tripartite semiotic awareness described by Charles Sanders Peirce: it is iconic, indexical and symbolic.[31]

It is iconic. It enlarges and distorts the nose, makes the face appear open and round, and its redness pulls our eyes to the clown's face. It could be a grotesque deformity, but we can see that it isn't. It's artificial, obviously a mask. It looks stupid, and the clown is happy to wear it. *Ergo*, the clown is happy to appear stupid. He doesn't mind. He is not afraid of making a fool of himself. He is vulnerable, and happy to be so. His face is a disarming icon of happy stupidity.

It is indexical. It draws attention to the eyes and mouth, the expressive parts of the face, pointing that expression and at the same time defamiliarising it. When the clown looks, the nose enlarges the gesture, telling us that the look is *significant*. The nose magnifies the movements of the face, alerting the spectator, informing him that the gesture is being presented, is on display, is to be watched.

And it is symbolic, certainly. We have learned to associate the red nose with the art of clowning, and so we have certain co-ordinates of expectation, which we want to have fulfilled. The very entrance of that nose arouses in us the expectation of laughter

to come, predisposing us to judge the clown's actions in a certain
way, making us willing to laugh at the slightest provocation. So,
indeed, the red nose is a part of the reason for our laughter.

But only a part; for the true clown doesn't need the false nose.
He could have made his entrance without it, looked at us, and
we would still have laughed. Why? Was it the look? It must have
been; the clown did nothing else. Ah, but he did. He *entered*. But
all performers have to enter. So they do, but the clown's entrance
is unique. It has only one purpose, to make us (sooner rather than
later) start to laugh. The clown comes into our space and makes us
laugh. The fact that the clown was *aware* of our presence was vital.
In this instance the clown actively acknowledged us and directed
what he was doing in an obvious way towards us. He made *contact*
with us directly and openly. If he had entered and not been aware
of us we might have felt excluded from his performance (unless he
made us aware that his *not* noticing was deliberate, for example, by
starting some action as if he were alone and then being suddenly
startled by our presence). So the clown has included us in his
game; right from the start we are implicated in whatever he is
doing. He is doing it for us; and with us, too, for whatever we
do will influence what he does next. If we laugh he may repeat
the action. If we don't laugh he will almost certainly repeat it,
insisting that it is important, magnifying its significance until its
very triviality becomes the occasion of our mirth.

Was it the timing of the look? Of course – but what *is*
timing? What governs it? The answer is: *we* do. If the object is to
surprise us, then the look has to take us by surprise: that governs its
rhythm. A slow look won't surprise anyone. Its speed is dictated by
its intention towards us. And, just as crucially, by what it reveals to
us about our partner up there on the stage, the clown. That rhythm
tells us about the nature of this particular clown, and establishes his
relationship to us. Some clowns are slower or quicker than others.
Some like to slow us down, in order to catch us out with a sudden
movement later; others like to bombard us with images and ideas,
insisting that we move mentally as fast as they do physically. And
the rhythm tells us, also, about how the clown is feeling. If he is
uncomfortable, if he is not happy to *just be there*, with us, then
his rhythms will be fractionally off. We will know, subliminally,
and we won't laugh.

The clown plays. The clown plays the realities of what and

where and with whom he finds himself to be. He cannot know these realities in advance, for so much of it depends upon us, the audience, that it cannot be pre-planned. Everything is *new* to the clown. Of course, the clown always has 'an act' up his sleeve, a sure-fire set of gags and jokes and routines. But in good clowning he may never have to use them. He can keep the pre-planned material in reserve until the *true* clowning ceases to be effective. A good example might be Jack Benny's violin; or Victor Borge's piano. How long does it take before either of them actually *plays* the musical instrument? And when they do, the playing is certain to be interrupted by the more important 'play'.

The clown has to 'find the play' in the immediate context. The work is hard and, especially in the early stages, fraught with fear of what Lecoq calls *la tasse* (the 'cup') – in other words, catastrophic failure.

The clown emerges from the screen. Nothing happens. Why? He didn't see us. He claims he did. Yes, he looked at us, but he didn't *see* us. Try it again. He fails again. Why? This time he *acted* noticing us, and we weren't impressed. He tries a funny walk. But we have seen funny walks before. He gets desperate; we get bored. He gets bored, and afraid. But he can't go until he has made us laugh. What can he do? He looks at us, and suddenly we see the reality behind that look. We respond to its truth. The clown has told us something about himself, revealed something. That is interesting, and we perk up. He senses that and, latching onto it, enlarges it. He begins to play truthfully. He is bored and afraid, so he begins to *play* his boredom. He yawns unexpectedly, and suddenly we do laugh. Now he's got something to work from. If he's good, he will develop from that tiny response and build on it. He will try a few simple things. He may try, for example, imaginary weight-lifting. We do not laugh. He doesn't back away from the idea. Instead, he magnifies it greatly, as if telling us how really marvellous it is. He does it again, even bigger and then, just as suddenly, he reincorporates the thing we found funny, the yawn. He quotes it, comments on it. He *plays* being bored with weight-lifting. And we laugh once more.

Clowning is one of the purest forms of improvisation. None of the things the clown does are ever guaranteed. Everything is on the brink of *la tasse* – because everything is real. The successful clown plays *his* clown:

> For several years now, the clown has taken on a great import-
> ance; not in the sense of the traditional circus, which is dead,
> but as a part of the search for what is laughable and ridiculous
> in man. . . . We put the emphasis on the rediscovery of our
> own individual clown – the one that has grown up within us,
> and which society does not allow us to express.[32]

He finds the things about himself that are funny, and plays
on them; not in the sense that he calls attention to his physical
peculiarities, but in that he understands his own 'rhythms', his
own ways of being, and magnifies these for his audience, happy
to be vulnerable and honest about himself.

This exercise calls upon the student to leave aside habits
of performance and find what is genuine in the moment.[33] It
asks the student to be truthful about himself. It asks that he
be happy to go on, unarmed (in Grotowski's sense), expectant,
open to the context in which he finds himself. Once, if ever, that
condition has been discovered – through trials and many errors
– the clown is ready to develop a more studied 'act'; which he
should be equally happy to abandon as he begins to work with
his partner, the audience.

Neutrality, play, rhythm; and the offering of himself, fraught at
any moment with not just the possibility, but almost the necessity,
of failing and looking silly: the clown incorporates all of these in
the 'encounter'[34] with the audience, and always underscores the
frailty and the miracle of creation. At any moment his act is on
the verge of dying, and yet somehow he rescues it, and another
fragile construction of gesture or words is launched.

Samuel Beckett evokes such a world constantly created from the
brink of failure, which is the condition of clown and improviser.
Undertaking this training exercise, having to enter on command
without anything to do but entertain an audience, without preparation, without props, without a character, without a script,
without rehearsal, is uncannily like the situation of Vladimir and
Estragon in *Waiting for Godot*, desperately passing the buck from
one to the other with 'Your turn to play'.

Beckett perfectly understands the condition of the clown,
and that of the improviser.[35] The final words of his novel *The
Unnamable* express, though in the context of the writer rather
than the actor, the fear of self-revelation, of being *true*, of finally
encountering oneself:

it will be I, you must go on, I can't go on, you must go on, I'll go on, you must say words, as long as there are any, until they find me, until they say me, strange pain, strange sin, you must go on, perhaps it's done already, perhaps they have said me already, perhaps they have carried me to the threshold of my story, before the door that opens on my story, that would surprise me, if it opens it will be I, it will be the silence, where I am, I don't know, I'll never know, in the silence you don't know, you must go on, I can't go on, I'll go on.[36]

Beckett's world is like Lecoq's in its utter absence of self-pity (the protagonists are totally 'unheroic' and going on is the only thing they can do). And in both cases the attitude overrides any tendency to dwell on the 'blocks'. 'Where I am', in a neutral mask or a red nose, is 'the silence you don't know'. If you let that silence go on, it stops being a silence in which you don't know, and becomes an introverted embarrassment crowded with self-accusations, justifications and excuses jostling each other into impotence and leaving you rooted to the spot. What Beckett and Lecoq emphasise is the need to act (speak, write) *immediately* from the silence, from the unknowing. In doing that you acknowledge it and put your trust in it; you follow Tristram Shandy in getting out the first word and trusting to Almighty God for the next; you validate the silence as a temporary collecting-point ('threshold of my story') which can be activated to produce the next sequence of moves. For Lecoq, the actor is not an interpreter but an 'author who needs to discover his own style'.

Precision of observation and practical work enables Lecoq's graduates to acquire the resources which ensure that the silence is full, an extensive physical vocabulary ready to draw on. (Lecoq again: 'the only possible starting point for this work will be various references recognised in the body'.) Improvisatory invention is then the activation of these resources at appropriate moments so that they emerge in new sequences. The 'text' (*parole*) of iconic and symbolic signs which they generate is derived, of course, from an existing 'language'; but it is also something which is never exactly the same, because it is rooted in the psychological and physical state of the actor and produced through that. Generation of 'text' is always reconstruction; the *jeu de styles* in Lecoq's training gives rise to an ability to construct and reconstruct form.

His work has spawned many exciting companies and solo

performers whose style reflects his concern with plasticity and physical precision. Among them are *Théâtre de Complicité*, whose work relies on exact observation and subsequent stylisation of movement and mood, sharpened by the interplay between idiosyncratic rhythms developed by each performer. From this they construct a texture of emotional situations inscribed in time and space as shape and rhythm and counterpointed by expressive *grummelotage*: their show entitled *A Minute Too Late* deploys their impeccable timing via a series of reflections on attitudes to death – and is itself a comment on the improviser's art. In contrast, Footsbarn Theatre's inventiveness has led to a manipulation or restructuring of Shakespearean texts.

Lecoq trainees have produced shows based on a variety of mime styles and movement, using a range of masks and exploring to the full the possibilities of 'physical' theatre. All of Lecoq's protégés are different; and all of them work in differing fields of theatre. Ariane Mnouchkine, Stephen Berkoff, Peter Brook and Dario Fo have all learned from and with Lecoq. The British group I Gelati has made a speciality of *commedia* work, yet their most recent project, for example, was a five-actor version of Brecht's *The Good Person of Szechwan*. The American Avner the Eccentric presents shows which are a mixture of circus skills and clowning. Moving Picture Mime Show gained their greatest successes using 'larval' mask-work and mime. Footsbarn are most noted for their vigorously physical reinterpretations of Shakespeare.

What links these very disparate groups and individuals – apart from time spent with Lecoq in Paris – is not that they all follow Lecoq's precepts. They don't. In the end, like all students, they take from their training the things that have impressed them most; and, like all creators, they use the things thats serve their own artistic needs and discard the rest.

What links them, then, is not a stylistic unity. Each group has its own artistic integrity. Each is making its own vision of a future theatre. They are not all, by any means, devoted to improvisational work: yet all of them share a common theatrical vocabulary, and that internalised repertoire of physical and imaginative skills which marks the successful Lecoq graduate.

In over thirty years Lecoq claims to have taught 3,000 students from more than sixty countries, and many of them are well known in Europe and the USA. They return occasionally to Paris, and Lecoq acknowledges with a certain pride the existence of a kind of 'mafia' of his graduates. Certainly they recognise and value each other's work, and attribute much of its success to their training.

Lecoq himself has, in addition to his early contacts with ex-Copiaux, worked with Dario Fo, Jean Vilar and Giorgio Strehler; given workshops outside Paris (including one for the RSC in London); and edited and contributed to a collection of essays on gestural language.[37] He clearly occupies a major position in the history, theory and practice of improvisation in theatre, particularly in terms of the growing importance of clearly conceived and precisely executed physical expression. In his work, improvisation and mime become ways of developing highly focused capacities for generating richly iconic texts which articulate an extensive internalised vocabulary of gesture, shape, rhythm and sequence in continually inventive patterns and structures.

For Lecoq, the occasional resurgence of the improvisatory (that is, the *mime de fond*, for him) marks periods of redefinition when theatre returns to its roots. From here it can emerge, as does his own work and that of his students, in new forms, and it does so because his training most centrally focuses on: 'pitting the student face to face with himself in a state of perpetual discovery'.[38]

Dario Fo and Franca Rame

In order to grasp what is we find so impressive about the improvisational style that stems from Lecoq's work, a concrete example would help; something to demonstrate to the critical reader what it means to embody the principles we have been discussing, some work that consciously stems from and uses exactly the techniques we have described. If such an example is needed, then it must be the work of Dario Fo and Franca Rame.

But English-speaking audiences have a multiply distorted view of Fo and his (now separated) wife Franca Rame's work. It is necessary to clarify those distortions – recognise them as such, at least – before proceeding to look at what the Fos' real achievements are.

1 The first problem or distortion lies in the fact that we only know a very small and highly selective fraction of their work. This is now happily changing, with increasingly available translations and productions of their plays. Fo is currently Europe's most popular playwright, with more productions in more languages than anyone else. Still, it is true that most people outside Italy associate the Fos with a limited number of works: *Can't Pay? Won't Pay!*, *Accidental Death of an Anarchist* and *Female Parts*.

2 Secondly, the plays do not have the political bite that they do in Italy. English audiences do not always realise just how strong the Fos' political commitments are. The English versions, divorced from their original context, often seem cleverly satirical – but sometimes merely whimsical. There are, of course, parallels between political injustice or governmental corruption in Britain and Italy, but the translations are usually unable to tap them or, if they do, the result seems contrived and artificial.

3 A third distortion is that non-Italian speaking audiences primarily regard Fo as a playwright. Fo is not present to them in the theatre, any more than Shakespeare is. All they have of him are the plays which bear his name (though, as suggested below, they are as much the work of the translators and adaptors as Fo's). In Italy both Fo and Rame have long been celebrated as performers of their own works rather than as writers.

Dario Fo does not write plays – in the sense of consciously seeking to write enduring dramatic works.[39] That the plays do endure, and are so enjoyable even in translation, is testimony to the skill with which they are first created and then shaped through a series of encounters/transactions with their audiences. But Fo's primary aim is to create:

> a throwaway theatre [*un teatro da bruciare*], a theatre which won't go down in bourgeois history, but which is useful, like a newspaper article, a debate or a political action.[40]

Like Theatre Machine, Fo and Rame produce disposable drama. But theirs is not disposable in the consumerist sense. It is a theatre 'to burn', like a newspaper when its purpose has been served. They are plays of the situation, activist responses to a social and political context. Their usual techniques are farcical, and their structures are often very loose – looser than would be the case if they were crafted only at the typewriter rather than in the theatre. The 'play', for Fo and Rame, is not finished when its author stops typing – in fact, it has only just begun its process of being wrought. It will be rehearsed with fellow theatre-workers, and will change and develop throughout that period, as with traditional plays.

But then the next, perhaps most important, phase begins. The play is offered to an audience, and will continue to change and develop in response to that audience's reactions during and after the performances. Fo's Italian audiences – occasionally of a size more usually associated in England with football crowds than studio theatregoers – are his active collaborators in the creation of his plays. Sometimes they have had to undergo police searches before being admitted to the playhouse because of Fo's 'subversive' political status. *Mistero buffo*, for example:

> has always relied on improvisation, since the audience is involved in it and doesn't play a passive part, since it imposes its rhythms, and provokes off-the-cuff lines. This type of theatre is recreated from performance to performance, and is always different, and never repetitive.[41]

Fo often tries out his plays as public readings and regards the discussions and suggestions from the audience as the 'third act' of the play.

Fo is much more than a playwright. He is a director, teacher, stage designer, student of architectural and theatrical history, song-writer; most importantly, he is a political activist and a theatre performer.

4 Finally, the act of translation itself means that the play becomes a fixed script. It loses its improvisational relationship to the audience. Stuart Hood writes:

> Franca Rame and Dario Fo work within a tradition of improvisation which means the texts of their plays are difficult to 'fix'; they change according to the changing political situation, according to the different audiences. They are like living organisms but within them there is a hard skeletal framework of radical criticism of our society and of relationships within it.[42]

Accidental Death of an Anarchist, for example, was first produced at the same time that Inspector Calabresi, implicated in the 'defenestration' of the anarchist Giuseppe Pinelli (and who was himself assassinated in 1972), brought a libel suit against the

left-wing paper *Lotta Continua*. These court hearings were the
immediate context against which the play was first received.
The play was constantly updated, and each night included a
report on the day's proceedings in the case. *Mistero buffo* is
re-created from performance to performance. Again, Franca
Rame speaks of developing her one-woman show with audiences
in the same way,[43] rather than having a fixed, received script
to which her performance nightly adheres. When the play is
translated (a) to another country, (b) to another language, (c) to
a different political context, and (d) to another performer – all
that Rame has gained experientially is lost. The play may become
by default a fixed 'text' to be rehearsed and performed, in a way
completely alien to its original conception as a living relationship
to a contemporary theatrical and social context.

Yet, despite these inevitable distortions, Fo and Rame's
reputation is growing. Enough of the spirit and theatrical power
of their work remains to excite audiences and performers all over
Europe and America.

Dario Fo was born in 1926 in San Giano, near Lake Maggiore
in Lombardy. His father, Felice, was a staunch socialist, and a
keen amateur actor. As a child, Fo would repeat the tales of
the local story-tellers to his brother and sister, and at the age of
seven built a puppet theatre with which to act out stories. He also
studied and imitated the gestures and techniques of the *fabulatori*
(descendants of the medieval *giullari*), and came to be regarded
by the locals as an expert. Tony Mitchell points out how large a
part first-person story-telling plays in almost all of Fo's plays,[44] and
Fo himself regards the techniques of the *fabulatori* as 'a structural
storehouse', a point of reference for all his later work.

Fo sees the *comici dell'arte* as professional (which the title
implies) 'court jesters' taken up and given official recognition by
the ruling classes; while the *giullari* 'are essentially pre-*commedia*,
the popular, unofficial mouthpieces of the peasant population'.[45]
Attempts to relate the farcical and comic elements in Fo's work
to the *commedia* tradition miss the mark. His work goes back, he
believes, to an earlier tradition of itinerant comedy, that deriving
directly from the *mimes*. Writing to the director of the Washington
production of *Accidental Death*, Fo declared:

Don't call my play a comedy. I call it farce. In current

language, farce is understood as vulgar, trivial, facile, very simple. In truth, this is a cliché of Official Culture. What they call comedy today has lost the rebellious strain of ancient times. What is provocative and rebellious is farce. The establishment goes for comedy, the people for farce.[46]

Fo is an authority on *commedia* technique. He is perfectly aware of the tradition of Ruzzante, Cherea and the *comici dell'arte*, and he consciously uses techniques (such as *Grammelot*, an onomatopoeic theatre language[47]) derived from *commedia* theatrical practice. But he always tries to relate the origins of those techniques to their social context. For example, *Grammelot* originates in the attempt to avoid censorship, and in the enforced exile among foreign audiences of persecuted troops. Fo believes it antedates the *comici*, who reinvented it.

He is not concerned to resurrect long-dead traditions for their own sake: rather, the *commedia* techniques develop the quality of *souplesse*, and help the actor to discover physical ways of relating to his audience. The mobility of Fo's face is not suppressed, for example, by the Mask of *il Magnifico* – it has to work harder, though, to animate the Mask. And the tradition of physical comedy which mingles setpiece *lazzi* with improvised *canovacci* and direct asides to the audience obviously does relate to Fo's own performance style.

Giorgio Strehler, still a major figure in European theatre although almost totally unknown in Britain, was a powerful early influence on Fo. Strehler pioneered the plays of Brecht in Italy, and although Fo later came to disagree with Strehler's style of theatre, his Piccolo Teatro was the crucible in which Fo's own style was formed. In 1952 – after having successfully worked in radio, where he developed his powerful vocal skills – Fo formed a revue company, known as I Dritti, with the actors Franco Parenti and Giustino Durano. Together they wrote, directed and acted in a revue called *A Finger in the Eye* (*Il dito nell'Occhio*) which they staged at the Piccolo Teatro.

This piece was highly significant in many ways. It broke new ground theatrically: it belonged to the tradition of *avanspettacolo* – popular variety entertainments between film showings – but was zanier, more satirical and more political. Fo designed the sets and costumes. Franca Rame was in the cast (they married two years later). Strehler did the lighting. But, most important, it

introduced Fo to a French associate of Strehler. The choreography
for *A Finger in the Eye* was done by Jacques Lecoq.
  Lecoq taught Dario Fo

  a considerable amount of mimic and vocal technique to shape
  his spontaneous improvisations. Lecoq trained Fo to use his
  physical defects (long arms and legs, uncoordinated body and
  flat feet) to advantage rather than hiding them, instructing him
  in the different forms of laughter, while also introducing him
  to *Grammelot* and character transformation, ingredients which
  were to come into their own in *Mistero buffo*.[48]

Fo, a natural improviser, none the less needed to learn the
theatrical skills of performance. Lecoq taught him how to find
'his' clown, his personal comic style. One might say that, although
their encounter took place before the school was founded, Fo is
the most distinguished alumnus of L'Ecole Jacques Lecoq. Their
acquaintance has continued since then (despite various disagree-
ments), with Fo giving special classes to Lecoq's students.
  Franca Rame has also taught Dario Fo: she, too, is a
gifted improviser, coming from a touring theatre family (Teatro
Famiglia Rame) with a repertoire of popular farces.[49] She shares
in the traditions of the *fabulatori* and the *giullari* – perhaps even
the *cabotin*. David Hirst reveals[50] that her attitude to improvisation is that of all strolling professionals: nothing is left to chance!
She records her performances and makes detailed notes of which
ideas and jokes worked and which did not. Her (and hence Fo's)
style returns to the kind of improvisation that rests, like that of
the *commedia*, on solidly prepared and rehearsed foundations.
  In 1959 she and Fo struck out on their own with their
Compagnia Fo–Rame. In the mid-1960s, after working in the film
industry and in television, Fo began the serious research into the
history of popular culture and medieval theatre that would take
performance shape as *Mistero buffo*, while also experimenting
with dramatic styles and forms. He and Franca had come to
believe – even before the political upheavals of 1968 – that
the conventional bourgeois theatrical framework within which
they had been operating was too restrictive: its ability to absorb
the Fos' increasingly more committed political invective (Rame
joined the PCI in 1967) and envelope it in a context of 'harmless'
entertainment meant that a break was necessary.

Fo and Rame were at the height of their popularity when, in 1968, they decided to abandon working for *le théâtre digestif* – bourgeois entertainment – in order to dedicate their talents towards 'the struggle for radical change in Italian society'.[51] They are politically to the left of the PCI: their break with it led to the setting up of La Comune as their base in Milan. They have suffered personally for their convictions: Fo was, very briefly, jailed in Sardinia in 1973, and in the same year Rame was abducted, beaten up and raped by members of a Fascist organisation. They have been accused of supporting terrorism. Until recently, despite the growing popularity of their plays in the United States, they were refused entrance visas.

Politics lie at the centre of all their work, and they conceive of theatre as direct intervention in, rather than detached comment on, political life. That abrasive, urgent struggle is rarely so visible in English versions of their plays, even when presented by left-wing groups. Sexual politics are central to Rame's self-expression, too. She is at the forefront of the women's movement in Italy, and her monologues are performed by actresses across Europe and America. Now that she has separated from Fo, one expects her to develop further her own independent career as a feminist writer and performer.

The piece that exemplifies the style they have evolved together, and which ties together many historical threads, is Fo's long solo *Mistero buffo* ('comical mystery play'), a dramatisation of a collection of medieval texts deriving from the strolling secular performers and street-entertainers of Europe. It is a *bouffonerie* – a grotesque spectacle – a carnival version/inversion of sacred events mingled with *lazzi, canovacci, grummelotage* and mime – all bound together by Fo's modern *discorsi*, which contextualise the pieces and serve as prologues and discussion prompters.

Fo performs it on a bare stage, without lighting effects, dressed in black trousers and a black sweater. He usually has a microphone slung around his neck, because he performs in large spaces: sports stadiums, public squares and large halls.

Mistero buffo is not a static text: it has undergone innumerable revisions, and several versions. The play continues to be created every time it is performed. The pieces Fo performs as *Mistero buffo* now are not necessarily the same as those he performed in 1969. This develops the idea that even a scripted play is different from night to night into a principle of construction.

It is as if one man has created and performed an entire medieval cycle, an epic conception. It is the conception which makes these pieces into a *play* – rather than a series of clever sketches. The pieces cohere around the idea of undercutting the repressive structures of church and state; by taking an officially accepted form and casting it back into the language of the peasant, he reveals what is grotesque in those structures themselves.[52]

The peasant language of *Mistero buffo* is described by Fo as 'fifteenth-century Padano' – a mixture of Po valley dialects, adapted, modernised, made up – alongside *Grammelot*. In fact, it is the 'pure' language of the physical performer, whatever his era. It will be reinvented to suit the needs of any period. It relies on the actor's body, on his ability to produce and mimic sounds, and on onomatopoeia.

The piece with which Fo usually opens *Mistero buffo* is called 'Zanni's Grammelot' ('Il Grammelot dello Zanni'). Zanni, the prototypical *commedia* character, is here played without a mask (although in an *Arena* documentary Fo demonstrates how to play the traditional *lazzo* on which it is based in a mask).[53] It is based on the theme of peasant starvation but, typical of Fo (and his sources), the subject is treated as bitter farce: Zanni is so hungry he imagines he is eating himself. He then dreams of an enormous feast. Finally, waking, he catches and eats a fly. Each detail of the scenario is physically portrayed with great virtuosity, accompanied by the onomatopoeic sounds of cooking, eating and digesting.

The pieces are introduced by *discorsi* in which Fo - using the familiar *tu* form – addresses the audience directly, explaining, scene-getting, expanding and improvising.

'La Nascita del Giullare' ('The Origin of the Giullare') is a central text in *Mistero buffo*. It derives from a twelfth-century Sicilian text, stemming originally from the Orient. A serf, abused by a landowner, helps a stranger who turns out to be Christ. Christ gives the peasant 'a new language' with which to attack the overlords through mockery: 'So the mission of the *giullare* is political rather than religious, despite its sacred origins, and his message is the subversive mockery of the ruling class.'[54]

Dario Fo's vision of the birth and mission of the *giullare* takes us back to the very origins and purpose of the alternative comedian, and adds a political dimension. The *giullare*: 'originates from the people and takes their anger in order to give it back to them, mediating it with the grotesque, and with rationality, so that the people can become aware of their own condition.'[55]

The only weapon of the oppressed is satire; the technique is one which mingles traditional skills (as the performer specialises) with improvisation - a response to the immediate context which must include the audience. When one remembers, say, the references to the system of tithes in the Wakefield *Mactatio Abel*, are we not dealing with a similar impulse?

Fo's intended audience is the industrial working class, just as the *giullari* played to the rural peasantry. In Italy, he achieves this aim, playing in occupied factories as often as in 'art houses'. He listens to that audience both during and after the show. Listening during the show means responding to their laughter, shaping and reshaping the text, breaking the frame to incorporate topical or local allusions. Listening afterwards, in the 'Third Act', means incorporating political and social, as well as dramatic, criticism. He has been attacked by the Church for blasphemy in the way he inverts Gospel narrative to reveal the Church's underlying message of political servitude; and he has been attacked politically from all sides. For the terrorists he is too moderate, for the PCI he is too militant, for some other political dramatists (like John McGrath)[56] his style is too disorganised to be politically effective, and for the conservatives (in art as well as politics) he is simply unspeakable. But:

> When I relate the origin of the *giullare* in *Mistero buffo*, I'm able to tell the story in a convincing way because I believe in it, I believe in the mission which the *giullare* originally chose for himself as the jester of the people. I also believe in it because I've experienced what it means to be the jester of the bourgeoisie.[57]

Dario Fo, the politicised clown, inheritor of the traditions of the *giullari* and the *comici dell'arte*, stands as the embodiment of the improvisational style of performance and audience relationship that grows from Lecoq's work. That relationship and that style are crystallised in Fo's use of the familiar *tu*. From the moment the clown enters, his relationship with the audience *is* a familiar one. What Lecoq's work centres on – above and beyond the acquisition of technique – is the necessity of *complicité*. The linguistic familiarity is more than just a cliché. The improviser's relationship to the audience (in Martin Buber's terms) is that of 'I and Thou', not 'I and It', because in this style of work more explicitly than in any other the performer and his audience create the piece *together*.

Chapter 3

Beyond Drama – Paratheatre

Jerzy Grotowski

Jerzy Grotowski (born 1933) came into contact early in his career with the work of Stanislavski (at the Polish State Theatre School in Cracow, and at GITIS in Moscow, where he did a one-year directing course, learning also about Meyerhold and Vakhtangov). Visiting France in 1957, he learned of the works of Jean Vilar, his teacher Dullin and Marcel Marceau (a pupil of Decroux, who was taught by Suzanne Bing). Thus, he was open to the traditions of Stanislavsky, Meyerhold and Copeau, in addition to those of Polish writers and directors (for example, Witkiewicz, Slowacki and director Juliusz Osterwa, who founded one of the first theatre *communities*, similar to Copeau's and Stanislavsky's experiments and prefiguring those of Grotowski himself[1]).

In 1959 Grotowski became the director of 'the only professional experimental theatre in Poland'. The 'Theatre of the Thirteen Rows' had a small company, dedicated to ensemble work from the outset. It began in Opole with nine actors, three of whom were to remain to form the nucleus of the later Teatr Laboratorium group. These were the actress Rena Mirecka (fresh from the Cracow Theatre School), and the actors Zygmunt Molik (also from the Cracow School before working with the rival company in Opole), and Antoni Jaholkowski. In

1961, these three were joined by Zbigniew Cynkutis and Ryszard Cieślak. (Stanislaw Scierski joined in 1964; the Venezuelan actress Elizabeth Albahaca joined in the late 1960s). This group – together with Ludwik Flaszen as Literary Director – have been the co-creators of most of Grotowski's work ever since. In January 1965 the company transferred its activities to Wroclaw, where it nominally remained until its final dissolution in January 1984, after twenty-five years of performance, teaching and research.

Jennifer Kumiega describes the theatrical situation in Poland at the time as being largely dominated by the director, and (as with Western theatre) by literature.[2] Right from the beginning (and despite his increasing status as *auteur*) Grotowski wanted to re-establish the primacy of the actor, and of communication via the actor's body:

> To create theatre we must go beyond literature; theatre starts where the word ceases. The fact that a theatrical language cannot be a language of words, but its own language, constructed from its own substance – it's a radical step for theatre, but Artaud had already realised this in his dreams.[3]

The company moved gradually towards this goal, both through discussion with the 'Friends of the Theatre of the Thirteen Rows' and through performances such as Mayakovsky's *Mystery-Bouffe*, a stage version of *Shakuntala* (on which Grotowski began his collaboration with the designer Jerzy Gurawski), and *Dziady* ('Forefather's Eve', with words by Mickiewicz). This production saw the beginning of Grotowski's relationship with Eugenio Barba, later to found Odin Teatret, who came to see one of the performances, stayed on as Grotowski's assistant for two years and was largely responsible for popularising his work outside Poland. Then followed the major productions which established the Theatre Laboratory as an internationally respected group of theatrical pioneers: *Kordian*, *Akropolis*, *Faust*, *The Hamlet Study*, *The Constant Prince* and *Apocalypsis cum Figuris*.

These early productions laid the foundations for Grotowski's theatre. Jennifer Kumiega discusses four main areas of development during this period:

(i) the emergence of the principle of 'poor theatre'; (ii) the attitude to, and treatment of, literature and text; (iii) spatial construction and relationships (environmental theatre); and (iv) the actor–spectator relationship.[4]

These are the four main planks on which Grotowski's early work rests. In 'poor theatre', the actor's body is the primary resource. Everything else can be dispensed with: text, costume, lighting and so on, are revealed as 'accidents' rather than 'essentials' in the act of performance. The actor can be and do anything and everything. (For instance, if a mask is needed, then the actor's own facial muscles can create a mask). Everything needed for the production is there in the performance space throughout, objects are transformed simply by the actors' use of them. Text is used but it is reformed, deconstructed and reconstructed text; displaced and given new meaning by the way it is employed by the performers. The performance space envelops and includes the audience – so that they and the actors share the same space and time, the same event.[5] In the end, for Grotowski all performance is an encounter between the actor and the spectator - and between the actor and himself. Throughout the early work there develops the idea of the actor making a total gift of himself – the 'total act'.

Grotowski's *theatre* practice - as distinct from the *paratheatrical* work which we shall discuss shortly – can be seen to be implicitly based on a theatre of signs: it is a semiotic theatre, in which texts, objects, actors are infinitely redeployable. Words are relexicalised; texts are intercut and their intertextuality made evident - often blasphemously: the actor searches for the archetypal physical sign of the character's condition. But, beyond the semiotic, even in the early days we can see the quest of the actor to escape from role: to be himself. The theatre exercises (described first in *Towards a Poor Theatre*) and the daily training routines may give a slightly misleading impression of Grotowski's aims. The exercises were not a 'training' for the act of performance. They used improvisation in training, certainly, and they developed remarkable physical and vocal skills, but the aim was not purely to develop bodily and imaginative *skill*. Rather the aim was to bring about the spiritual condition in which:

the body would not resist the actor. . . . For as long as the actor has the feel of his body, he cannot attain the act of divestment. The body must totally stop resisting; in effect, it must cease to exist.[6]

Part of Grotowski's aim, then, was to *subdue* the flesh. The body is seen as an obstacle to be overcome, and the harsh yogic exercises are as much a means of fighting the body as training it. The same stricture applies to the mind of the performer (at least as it is evident in the teaching work of Rena Mirecka): the mind's desire to shape, to form, to 'script' the event, the intellectual ambition to create 'meaning' (by making intertextual references), hampers the ability genuinely to experience the event. The famous *via negativa* approach of Grotowski's rehearsals is an attempt to prevent physical or mental habits from interfering with the process of *giving* oneself utterly to the event. Acting in 'Poor Theatre' is not dressing-up and pretending: it is divesting – sometimes physically, always spiritually – and being. One is aware of the actor *as* an actor, not in the Brechtian manner of calling our intellectual attention to the fact, but in the sense that, beyond the matter of the play, the event is an encounter with the actor as a human being. He is not so much a *character* of the play, as the *subject* of the play. His skill may amaze us, but what moves us is the actor's gift of himself.

Grotowski believes we use art 'to cross our frontiers, to fill our emptiness'.[7] For him this is a slow process in which we 'peel off the life-mask', and the theatre thus becomes (as, in somewhat different ways, for Artaud and Brecht) 'a place of provocation'. Workshops and performances are a confrontation with the vulnerability of feeling and experiencing which lies behind public and private roles. We often avoid this exposure: we screen ourselves by adapting our feelings to the image we have of ourselves, or that we would like others to have of us. It's as though we pre-empt feeling by saying 'How should I feel?' A Sartrian game, certainly, and a continual imposture, which actors, even or especially in (dangerous) impro situations, are equally prone to: it's much easier to adopt a stereotyped role. But this easy route out is so tempting precisely because the alternative is frightening: it's facing up to the fact that I don't know who or what 'I' is or how it might respond if it abandons all *a priori* models. Before filling our emptiness we have to experience it, and that is uncomfortable. But until we do this we can only go on 'acting' what we think we ought to feel, which is a loss to everyone.

> We arm ourselves in order to conceal ourselves; sincerity begins where we are defenceless . . . if a method has any sense at all it is as a way to disarmament.[8]

So Grotowski uses 'obstruction exercises' aimed at locating and neutralising individual blocks or tendencies to hang on to comfortable habits; the participants must renounce any temptation to avoid such obstructions, and the elimination of resistances is what achieves 'liberation'[9] for the actor.

One technique used by Rena Mirecka in workshops is related to this coping with avoidance of confrontation. When the situation is pointed out, it can be recognised: the instruction then is to act on that recognition. As soon as the participants become aware that they are no longer fully 'with' whatever they are doing (that is, starting to decide what they ought to feel or do instead of doing it), they must immediately do a backward roll (without looking behind) and come up facing in a different direction. This physical breaking of the situation allows a fresh start. (To what, you may ask? This is difficult to answer, because such workshops usually follow an internally generated structure that could be different for each participant. The new activity may not be to 'do' anything but to be aware of what is happening, begin to explore what it feels like, see what physical positions or imaginative activity it might set in motion.)

In Grotowski's process, we find many of the basic assumptions of improvisatory work in theatre and outside: work on actors and audience, in the awareness that their relationship creates theatre, and centred on the establishment of a state which may be called neutrality, being wiped clean, deconditioning. This last aspect is comparable with Copeau's neutral mask-work mentioned earlier, and involves an element of fear and crisis. It is only moving through this that allows us to experience without masks, without the familiar filters of habit. (When you put on a theatrical mask, especially a neutral mask, the body suddenly 'sticks out', all its awkwardnesses revealed; you can't 'hide' it behind the attention-catching expressions of the face.)

Curiously, if we *do* move through, if we abandon ourselves to what may seem like chaos, to the totally unknown, we may find that there is an unsuspected order to feeling. In the backward roll exercise, people rarely bump into each other: the body orientates itself in space without conscious thought (just as blindfold trust exercises, or the 'eunuch/pauper' game described in Part II may produce an extension of spatial awareness and other subtle operation of the senses). We may begin to 'know' and to 'behave' in different ways, which change our patterns of relationship to others and to the environment.

Grotowski's work – with performers and audience – thus implicitly moves beyond the boundaries of what we conventionally designate as 'theatre', and seeks to set in play fundamental physical and psychological capacities. But it arises in the first instance from a concern to establish a more acute experience *in* the theatre, and from an understanding of what that involves. In his later Theatre Laboratory performances, the audience (strictly limited in numbers) is assigned a role (accomplices, judges and so on) which inhibits the passive or detached gaze. Provocation is physical and psychological, and thus personal and political. It affects the audience as a whole, making them uneasily aware of collective responsibility, and, as individuals, making them confront the limits of their capacity to understand and respond. What is created first is the sense of panic at being cut off from familiar behaviour, which is exactly paralleled by the demands on the actors: 'Grotowski stresses the moment of surrender . . . the extinguishing of individuality, and then the elation and regeneration involved in the recognising of 'another' reality unobtainable in everyday life.'[10]

Grotowski's work with the Theatre Laboratory, in its various phases, always focused on small groups (of actors and audience members) exploring or being subjected to very intense experiences and sometimes reaping rewards in the form of profound personal 'breakthroughs', revelations of suddenly liberated or unblocked capacities for doing and understanding. There is, in addition to the emphasis on psychological process, something slightly esoteric, hermetic and élitist about this kind of activity, necessarily largely self-selecting in terms of participants. Of course, all intense work with actors requires relatively small groups, and improvisatory work is certainly no exception: but there are many instances in which that work aims to open itself up to a wide public and to formulate its presentation in a 'language' of directly accessible physical or symbolic signs. Grotowski's approach is even more 'difficult' than, for example, *commedia* or Lecoq's work. But it's clear that Grotowski himself is aware of this, and that this awareness contributes to the move towards 'paratheatre'. In the course of this move, the boundaries between performers and spectators are broken down, and thus although the total number of participants at any one event is not necessarily very different, their function and relationship to each other changes significantly. *Performance* as psycho-physiological process opens itself to a wider clientele, but in doing so performance as theatre is left behind.

After *The Constant Prince* in 1969, the search for technical mastery becomes less important: the exploration of personal authenticity through group activity becomes central. Richard Fowler describes it as a move from a Theatre of Performance to a Theatre of Participation.[11] *Apocalypsis cum Figuris* forms the transition, and was itself used to bring interested spectators into the group work. Throughout the 1970s the Laboratory mounted a series of Special Projects of various kinds. In some renovated farm buildings at Brzezinka (25 miles from Wroclaw) the Laboratory set up the first paratheatrical Special Project (originally called Holiday) in 1973. The research continued into the Mountain Project and the Earth Project (from 1975 to 1978). The actors of the Laboratory became the leaders (and co-participants) in a series of 'meetings':

> One day we found it necessary to eliminate the notion of theatre (an actor in front of a spectator) and what remained was a notion of meeting – not a daily meeting, and not a meeting that took place by chance.[12]

Such meetings needed specially prepared spaces (often made ready by the actors' labour in advance of the other participants' arrival), and a far longer span of time than that occupied by the performance of a play. Most of the Special Projects lasted several days, with the participants living together in seclusion. Money would be pooled to buy food. Wristwatches would be put away until after the event's conclusion – this was a special time, out of time. Though each phase of each project was different, they occurred typically in natural surroundings (woods and fields, hills and mountains), with long hours of various physical activities (running, climbing, singing, chanting, dancing, music making . . .), using natural elements (water, fire), and taking place both by daylight and throughout the night.[13]

Work of this kind is necessarily 'improvised' in the sense that there can be no reliance on a 'script'. Even the pattern of events, though it may contain common elements, is subject to reorganisation according to participants and circumstances; and any subsequent recording of events cannot hope to 'fix' them for future use, since each occasion will necessarily be different. All of this does not imply a lack of structure or precision, or of clarity about the intended outcome. But the structure is (as Roland Barthes puts it in *S/Z*) more a 'structuring' – an evolving sequence not a rigid framework; the precision has to do with a sure sense of how to respond to actual needs and keep the activity focused, rather than with maintaining any abstract ideal design.

The major focus is on the discovery or disclosure of the full self (or Self, to give it its Jungian emphasis) through group activity. In its various phases and locations (for example, USA, Australia, France), the work is seen as 'research' (the 'University of Research' operated in Warsaw in 1975), sometimes with a small select group, sometimes with participants from a slightly wider public, though these too were carefully screened and selected. The aim is to achieve a condition of personal and interpersonal behaviour where: 'a man does not impose himself. . . . He comes forward and is not afraid of somebody's eyes, whole. It is as if one spoke with one's self: you are, so I am.'[14]

'Meeting' is used as an organisational and psychological strategy: people do things together, and that, rather than any extrinsic aim, is the point. The sessions are thus a kind of continuous encounter, with space for personal reflection. They often take place in isolated rural settings, and links can be seen here with Copeau's 'retreats' to Marne and Burgundy, and with some of Peter Brook's work (Brook, along with Jean-Louis Barrault, was present at the University of Research proceedings.)

Activities include work on aspects related to acting (release of vocal and physical blockages); the use of language to penetrate to, rather than conventionally mask, the personal; exploration of the 'oscillation between game and play'; workshops leading to interpersonal contacts. Clearly the context is that of the 'quest' previously instigated by Grotowski during his earlier period, for an 'authentic and revelatory encounter between individuals',[15] which cannot proceed except through rigorous work on the self. Grotowski speaks of a 'second birth'.[16]

The experience of paratheatricals directly fed the later work of the Laboratorium, whose members have continued to teach around the world and to find their way back towards the theatre – a transformed and far more inclusive style of theatre. In 1981, three years before the dissolution of the Laboratory, Ryszard Cieślak directed *Polish Thanatos*, in which the audience was informed: 'It is possible for those present – without constraint – to enter the action. Your participation in the particular life of this group may be active, vocal, or simply by being with us.'[17]

From 1976 onwards, Grotowski's attention has turned towards a new research focus, which he has called the 'Theatre of Sources' and, since 1983 (when he became a professor at the School of Fine Arts, University of California, Irvine) 'Objective Drama'. In essence, this has meant a multicultural exploration of the ritual, communal roots of the theatrical experience, and an attempt to study their foundation techniques, or sources. In many ways, his study of non-Western ceremonies, liturgies and ritual forms seeks a return to the original, shamanistic experience of inner transformation – of making over one's body and one's self. And still beyond the development of such re-sources lies the necessity of meeting:

> I am water, pure, which flows, living water: and then the source is *he*, *she*, *not I*: he whom I am going forward to meet, before whom I do not defend myself. Only if *he* is the source, I can be the living water.[18]

Although there are some parallels, the use to which Grotowski puts improvisation is, in the long run, clearly different from that of Copeau and Lecoq, and even, though to a lesser extent, from the direction taken by Johnstone and Maude-Roxby. For all of these people, theatrical performance is still the issue, whereas for Grotowski it has been superseded by other concerns, however much these arise originally in the context of performance. But what Grotowski represents is also a way of thinking and working which has had very important effects on developments in theatre, and indeed perhaps most of all on the theorisation of theatre – thinking *about* it, developing an aesthetic and a range of theoretical approaches which account for its influence in various spheres.[19] Curiously, perhaps, the most extreme form of improvisation in the end leads to important theoretical and intellectual reformulations of the nature of the act of performance and the relationships which it predicates; and that theorising has itself fed back into the work of directors and dramaturgs working in more traditional fields.

Improvisation is now used widely in other contexts, ranging from 'psychodrama' as a recognised form of therapy, to various educational and developmental applications (role-playing in language learning, in project-centred work in schools, in the acquisition of interpersonal skills in counselling, in training for management or negotiation situations in business). The bibliography lists publications which deal with some of these areas. Part II sets out some of the techniques and exercises available, and we will discuss the implications of the use of improvisation in a wide variety of contexts in Part III.

Part II

What? The Practice of Improvisation: Improvisation Exercises

Introduction

This section describes in greater detail the kinds of practice outlined in Part I, and is intended as a summary and source of reference for both students and theatre practitioners.

There are a number of techniques commonly used by teachers and directors of improvised drama. Individuals place different emphasis on different exercises. Some are only important for specific types of work (for example, for creating a very structured piece); others are fundamental to all acting. One thing is certain: techniques cannot be adequately learned from books. Improvisation is learned experientially, in the rehearsal room and on the stage. The improviser learns from his mistakes (and, if he's clever, from other people's mistakes).

What follows, then, is not a DIY manual on 'How to Improvise', but a discussion of a number of the most important techniques and approaches. It looks at most of those techniques we consider to be part of the improviser's repertoire and, in addition, considers a number of specific techniques central to the work of some of the most distinctive teachers of drama and practitioners of improvisation. The techniques we discuss fall into a number of groups, although they ultimately run into one another, so that distinctions of grouping soon dissolve. Equally, many of the techniques discussed are by no means specific to improvisation work, but are common to all types of drama and actor training. We discuss them here, none the less, either because they have a particular usefulness in training improvisers, or because the picture would be incomplete without them. The list is by no means exhaustive, and we have probably missed out as many techniques as we have found room to include.

The first group is about *preparation* for work:

Relaxation
Games
Balance and 'body/think'

Space and movement
Concentration and attention
Impulses and directions

The second group is about *working together*:

Trust and respect
Making a machine
Showing and telling
Entrances and exits
Meetings and greetings
'Blocking'

The third group is concerned with more difficult exercises, *moving towards performance*:

Senses
Tenses
Status
Masks
Another view of masks

The last group is about *applied* improvisation work:

Who/where/what?
Objectives and resistances
Point of concentration (focus)
Memory
'Set'
Character
Narrative

The exercises lead towards particular *objectives*, which develop psychomotor, cognitive and affective skills in individuals and group relationships. These objectives imply an underlying network of processes and significations inherent in improvisation work. These *active meanings* are generated through impro activities, indicating that improvisation keys into fundamental ways of creating the structure of human existence. In the following chapters we outline the practice; in Part III we will follow up the implications.

Chapter 4

Preparation

Relaxation

The actor's primary resource is the body. It has to be fit, flexible and capable of a great range of expressive movement. Everything that the actor communicates is expressed through the body, through the conscious and unconscious tensing and relaxing of the musculature, which controls posture, gesture, movement and vocal expression. It follows that, if the body is inappropriately tense, the channels of communication will be interfered with, or blocked altogether.

Relaxation does not mean 'to go limp'. Going limp means that the actor falls over and lies like last week's blancmange on the floor, without the energy or the inclination to get up and do anything. Tension is necessary for balance; *unwanted* tension is unnecessary, and can be relieved by a 'draining exercise', where physical tension is imagined as a liquid pooling in the body's extremities and is made to 'flow' towards the centre, from where it is 'drained away'. Laban – or Alexander – based techniques for understanding and correcting posture are extremely valuable, as are yoga or Tai Chi Chuan exercises. They leave the actor physically composed and mentally refreshed – in the perfect condition to begin work.

Games

Clive Barker, in *Theatre Games*,[1] speaks of 'taking the pressure off the actor'. The ideal way to do this is through game playing. One of the primary functions of childhood play is the acquisition and development of motor skills. Games are a heritage we all share, a language we can remember with the minimum of prompting. Most of all, games are *fun*. 'Opening the pelvis', freeing the pelvic joints to facilitate movement, is very difficult to learn, and painful to practice. But sit the actors in a ring, legs outstretched and wide apart, feet touching those of the people on either side, and let them roll a ball at each other's feet, scoring and losing points if the ball makes contact, and the exercise is accomplished automatically. Actors and students will stretch their arms, backs, hamstrings to prevent the ball touching them, or to sweep it away to score off someone else, without complaint. The ball also provides an external focus. Such a focus, which provides a purpose to the movement beyond trying to lengthen muscles and develop suppleness, is invaluable, both to actors and to students of physical education.

The game takes away the pressure of formal training, and replaces it with a focus which is external and purposive. It *socialises* the training. The body becomes more supple; but so does the awareness. The actor's energy is directed outwards, towards the world and towards other actors. The work is in harmony with the body, and the body responds by flowing naturally. The spine stays erect, the head lifts, the posture straightens, the actor laughs rather than grimaces.

Games can be played over and over again. The more proficient the players become, the more they become free to experiment and to develop. Games have myriad uses in actor training. Barker's book (subtitled *A New Approach to Drama Training*) offers a wealth of examples of ways to tackle difficult scenes, to encourage social interaction or to release the imagination.

Balance and 'body/think'

Two very simple games can be used to develop balance, and that awareness of the self in space that Clive Barker calls 'body/think', or the *kinaesthetic sense*.[2] Balance is essential to the improviser who cannot prepare to change direction in advance, but must instinctively respond to each new impulse fully and openly. Japanese swordsmen long ago realised that there is no ideal, preset position in which to stand before a fight. To adopt any one stance reduces the possibilities of all the other stances, and therefore creates a potentially fatal weakness. The ideal position is 'no position' – that is a condition of alert or 'armed' neutrality – containing all potential within it. If the attack comes from the left the sword *sensei* can move right and counter-attack instantly, and vice versa. For the improviser, too, balance is that 'armed neutrality', expressed physically as well as imaginatively. The best game for developing it is itself based on the idea of swordsmanship (though Chinese rather than Japanese): the Fight in the Dark.

The games comes originally from a favourite scene of the Peking Opera. Two men armed with lethally sharp swords hunt one another in a room which is supposed to be pitch dark. The actor has to convey to the spectator the idea of darkness, though his eyes remain open throughout. The swords slash the air centimetres away from the opponent's body and face as the actors manoeuvre in a terrifying and wholly credible dance of danger.

The game version of the fight in the dark (played under the title the Pauper and the Eunuch) is a little safer. A square or ring of chairs facing outwards forms the outline of the room, perhaps 15 ft. x 15 ft., with a single chair missing somewhere around the circumference to provide the only entrance and exit. On the chairs sit all the members of the group except for the two players. In the space lies, somewhere, a bunch of keys – which the players are told represents 'a jewel of great price'. The room is 'totally dark', and in the room, guarding the treasure, which he is unable to see, waits a Eunuch armed with a scimitar (the lights are on, and the 'scimitar' is a rolled up newspaper). Into the room comes a Pauper – sometimes armed, sometimes not. The Pauper is starving and desperate enough to try to steal the jewel. He knows the Eunuch is there, and he has to find the jewel, and then find his way out again without being 'killed' (that is, dealt a hefty whack with the rolled tabloid). Those are the rules.

The game is played in three stages, with the other group members watching in total silence (as far as possible), and commenting later on what they have seen. First, the Pauper and the Eunuch try to imagine themselves in the dark room, with their eyes open. They *act* the darkness. Then they play the game again, after hearing the comments of their peers (or they can watch two others play) – but this time the combatants are blindfolded. They *experience* the darkness. The third stage repeats the first, assimilating what has been learned, and when the players are blindfolded, there are a number of marked changes.

The actor's personal space extends to include the other player.

The head is raised, the posture of the spine naturally corrects itself, balance improves, the actor tunes in to the slightest vibration in the air around him. The distance between the two players becomes very clearly defined as dangerously close, and the watchers thrill as the 'swords' come ever closer to the players' bodies. The tension generated is often cathartically discharged as laughter in the culminating collision. In the open-eyed version the actor is concentrating on a *result*, on playing the darkness. Blindfolded, he is forced to enter the *process*. His body relearns how to 'think'; how to balance; how to wait, poised and still for the slightest betraying rustle. The audience cannot help but be drawn into the same process, holding its breath with the actors. The final version tries to use what has been learned, with the eyes open once again.

Play is innate. It links directly to the actor's experience, and has pleasurable associations, lessening the actor's resistance to the exploration process. Sometimes, though, it is essential to contextualise the use of play and games. This should always be done *after* the practical session rather than during it, unless absolutely essential. To explain what a game is useful for actually changes the objective of the game: the players begin to strain after what they now see as the desired results, instead of just playing the game and letting the process provide that result naturally and organically. Sometimes students and actors do need to know why what they see as precious rehearsal time is being 'squandered' on games, however pleasurable. Once they understand the intrinsic value, and are aware that there is a justification for each and every game, this resistance vanishes.

Space and movement

The individual actor's space intersects with that of his fellow performers, and with that of the audience, however large that may be. The actor's skill is to *fill* his space, to inhabit it fully: to be *there*, totally, in the moment of performance. This is what relaxation and 'body/think' enable to happen, and allow to be seen happening.

'Presence' means the performer is fully *there*, 'present', in the present tense, inside the moment. His attention is wholly on the task and yet, most important, his awareness extends beyond the immediate space around him to include the audience's space. This does not mean that the actor is 'playing to the audience' all the time, or that they are even consciously acknowledged. Simply, the actor is aware of all the potential space around him, and wants to fill it. His energy level is geared to this; he cannot be too small, or too quiet. His body naturally conforms to the demands of the given space.

Improvising pure movement in space is difficult. The body quickly loses orientation, and movement becomes aimless, unless some way of imaginatively coping with the surrounding void is internalised. Up and down present few problems; movement works with or against gravity, and the floor is the primary reference point. Now imagine a large, invisible cube, centred on, and moving with, the performer's body. A movement can be seen to grow from the actor or dancer's centre and flow outwards towards a given point (say, the top right-hand corner of the cube). The idea of the cube encourages both spatial precision and the fullest possible gestural extension. Movement flows from the performer's centre to the periphery; a physical and emotional impulse begins in the sensoric centre of the body, the abdomen, and is extended outwards into the world around the performer through the expressive limbs – and the world flows back *into* the performer, too. Every movement, every foray out into the void, is accompanied by a *recovery*, a return to inward poise and stillness preparatory to the next exploration or offering.

This Laban-derived work is totally compatible with Lecoq's teaching, which also centres on the actor's body in space:

> You can't talk about movement unless you have equilibrium. You must know about the horizontal to undertake being vertical. What we give the public comes from within. There's a link, a reverberation between inner and outer space. If I make a physical action – pulling or pushing – it's analogous to internal emotion, love or hate. . . . I indicate passions in space.[3]

Both methodologies get students to observe things with and in their own bodies, and thus to develop an active vocabulary of appropriate signs in movement.

Concentration and attention

The central principle of 'presence' is mental and imaginative. It is a matter of concentrating without straining, attending and behaving in accord with the situation. Copeau's and Lecoq's work with neutral masks, or relaxation exercises, are ways of tuning up in preparation for this.

Stanislavsky, in *An Actor Prepares* (a better translation of the title is, perhaps, *An Actor's Work on Himself*) underlines the importance of the principle of 'concentration of attention':

> The eye of an actor which looks at and sees an object attracts the attention of the spectator, and by the same token points out to him what he should look at. Conversely, a blank eye lets the attention of the spectator wander away from the stage.[4]

Everything on the stage has significance; so does everything surrounding the stage. But the actor can encourage the spectator to give his attention to what the play requires be most significant. If he himself is unfocused, he ceases to be significant to the audience, he ceases to be 'present', he is, unconsciously, signing to the audience 'I am not here, ignore me'.

Stanislavsky's Circles of Attention exercise is very useful for overcoming this. Using first a spotlight in a darkened room, he placed objects within the circle of light, allowing the actor to examine them. The surrounding darkness contrasted with the brilliant illumination of the objects makes it easy for the actor to ignore everything but the objects of concentration. Using a larger circle, including other objects within the larger space, the actor finds it at first more difficult to concentrate, to attend only to the illuminated area. The largest 'circle' is the whole space, fully illuminated. Now everything competes for the actor's attention, and focus is dissipated, unless the actor learns how to regain the original sensation of 'public solitude', imaginatively selecting the smaller circle out of the large one, and concentrating wholly upon it. The actor's *attention* replaces the spotlight. As soon as concentration wavers it can be regained by this act of imaginative focusing.

A related but slightly different exercise can be done with sound. The actors lie still on the floor and listen. First they listen to the sounds emanating from their own bodies, their breathing per-haps, or the noises of digestion. Imaginatively, they are listening to the sound of their own heartbeat. The actor is still, and silent, but concentrated and aware. Next, without losing the first set of sounds, if possible, they expand their awareness to include other sounds from within the room. The sound of others breathing, most especially, as well as the incidental background noises of the plumbing, and from time to time the quiet, reassuring voice of the teacher or director. Then, the actor listens to *all* the sounds from within the audible range. He admits into consciousness the noise of traffic from outside the room, birdsong, people talking along the corridor, whilst trying not to lose the original sets of sounds. This magnified consciousness is too diverse at first, and so the actors are asked to come back to the middle stage, of listening to all the sounds within the surrounding room, and stay at that level for some time, making occasional forays into the smaller and larger regions. Actually, it is the middle level that the actor must learn to operate in. He has to be aware, albeit subliminally, of the whole space within which he operates, and of all those who share it with him. Whenever concentration is destroyed, or misaligned, it can always be pulled back by regaining the sensation of alert stillness, or 'armed neutrality'.

Impulses and directions

Direction in movement and speech once begun can be worked on. But what starts the movement? Every movement starts with an impulse to move. Whether voluntary or involuntary, all physical movement originates with nerve impulses that activate the muscles.

There are exercises which develop the motoric and impulsive functions, like 'The Starfish'. The actor lies on a mat, curled up, closed and protected. On some agreed signal – say, a sharp noise – he instantly (and without thinking about it first) flings himself into a starfish shape, arms and legs fully outstretched. It doesn't matter whether he is face down or face up. At the next signal, the exercise is reversed. A soft fall-mat is essential if the actor is to feel confident about this.

In this exercise, the impulse to move is being both controlled and liberated. The actor knows what movement is to be made, but the random timing of the signal means that the impulse has to be generated and obeyed instantly, without the intervention of 'insurance policy' thoughts of personal safety (which is taken care of for him by the mat, and by having properly warmed up first!). He learns to obey the impulse.

The 'backward roll' exercise used by Grotowski's actress Rena

Mirecka (described in Part I) is an example of this, involving a sudden shift of relationship. As soon as the performer realises that he or she is trying to force something to take shape, rather than letting shape evolve organically, the necessity is to leave it and to begin something new. The kinaesthetic awareness of one's body in space is also developed, together with the confidence to impel oneself into that space in any direction.

The activities we have here classified as 'preparation', then, open out physical and mental skills, get the system balanced and alert, begin to work on focus and leave the actor in a state of readiness to work for himself and with others.

Chapter 5

Working Together

Trust and respect

When an improvising actor gets into difficulties, he or she has to *know* that somebody will come to their rescue, and that somebody will take what they are offering and develop it. Every member of the group is responsible for every other.

One way of developing this is the use of the many 'trust games' which actors employ. For example, the 'Trust Circle'. The group stands in a circle, facing in, shoulders touching. Each member in turn (and all of these exercises include the director or teacher) enters the circle, closes their eyes, relaxes and leans in any direction. The surrounding circle takes the person's weight and passes him or her upright across the circle. The one in the middle has to do precisely nothing; the group takes the weight. The others take responsibility for not letting him or her fall. The actor in the middle gives up responsibility to the others. This process of surrender is highly enjoyable. Should anyone be allowed to fall (which is unlikely) then the exercise should be repeated, with plenty of encouragement. This should be part of the daily warm-up.

The necessary corollary of trust is respect. So much of this work is personal and difficult to learn. The group - and it is almost always *group work* that we are talking about – has not only to trust its members equally, but to have respect for them, for the work and the ultimate goals of that work.

When an exercise is in process, for example, some people will finish before others. They should go quietly to the side of the room and sit down, watching their fellows until they, too, have completed the sequence. If that is not possible, they should just remain silently where they are and wait. They cannot just get up, walk out, start smoking and chattering to one another. They have to respect the needs of those who are still involved in the process.

Making a machine

One of the simplest ways of getting a group to start working together is the 'Making a Machine' improvisation. One member of the group is asked to get up and make a mechanical and repetitive movement; others join in, fitting in with the original movement one by one, adding their own until the whole group is physically involved.

As well as being about personal responsibility, and following impulses, the 'Machine' exercise has other benefits. It encourages listening and observing, and practises rhythm. The combined noises are often very musical. If the exercise is repeated, and the students or actors are encouraged to relate physically to one another, by contact as well as by isolated movements, then the exercise helps to break down tactile inhibitions. If the first person to begin, once the entire 'machine' has been assembled, is told to move or adapt within it (followed by all the others in sequence) then the 'sterile' machine can suddenly become an organically living 'monster', sinuously writhing and moving as one. And this can lead to a whole series of related tactile explorations involving the whole group.

An excellent example of this is the 'Laughing Snake'. Everyone lies on their back on the floor with their head on someone else's stomach. If they haven't done it before, don't tell them what it's about. It takes some time to get everyone arranged properly (either in a serpentine diagonal line or, if possible, in a circle, or two lines or circles if it's a big group) so ask them to do nothing, just lie still and compose themselves. After a while someone will giggle. When people lying on their backs giggle, their abdominal muscles vibrate. The head resting on their stomach begins to bounce up and down. The owner of the head usually begins to giggle, too, infecting the next person in the chain. The sound of giggling is enough to set off some of the others and, in no time, there is a room full of people cackling away dementedly, heads bobbing up and down on each other's stomachs. It goes quiet, and then somebody's stomach rumbles, right beneath someone else's ear – and the laughter bubbles up again. It's an excellent exercise for de-inhibiting a group (and, when necessary, for stopping a workshop becoming too serious).

Work with *sound* can extend the feeling of interconnectedness. A group can build up a rhythmic weave from different individual noises (percussive, vocalised, clapped and so on); or can explore relationships between the close proximity of sound and physical distance (start far apart, with a range of different pitches and notes; move closer together, shifting through harmony towards unison). The effects of chanting and choric work can be very powerful, and specifically in terms of improvisation they create a strong physical sense of unity, as well as freeing the voice – a significant method of de-inhibiting and relocating the sense of self and its potential.

Showing and telling

One of the hardest things to grasp is often the difference between 'showing' and 'telling'. The most common and useful direction here is 'Don't tell us, *show* us!' 'Telling' avoids the full physical involvement of the body. It substitutes codified signs (words, pantomimic gestures) for full body response. An actor can 'tell' the audience he is 'walking through a doorway' by miming reaching out and turning a door handle and stepping forward (or by saying 'Oh look, here's a door. I wonder what's through here . . . '). The audience will understand what is happening but they won't believe it. The actor 'shows' us the doorway by first imagining the door (creating its reality in his mind) and then changing his whole posture as he steps from one visualised space into another. When a person steps from a small room into the open air, the spine lifts, the head rises, the eyes change focus. This happens naturally in life. As long as the actor imaginatively re-creates the circumstances and obeys them (that is, creates the 'set' (see below) and conforms to it imaginatively), he will 'show' the audience where he is. If, through haste, he just wishes to signify the change, he will 'tell' the audience. The result is significantly different, and showing is nearly always more telling than telling.

Exercises to develop this habit of mind and body are primarily non-verbal. Roddy Maude-Roxby and others use variations of the 'Mime-stick' exercise. In this exercise, derived (as its name suggests) from mime teaching, the student is given a simple stick (or equally basic object, such as a jumper) and has to assign it a reality other than its own. The stick may become a telescope; the jumper may become a baby. But, whatever the transformation, the new reality of the object has to be conveyed physically, and truthfully, within the improvisation. In the early stages, the transformations tend to be signalled rather cheaply (we read the stick held to the eye as a telescope almost without the actor needing to do anything else). Notions of 'showing' and 'telling' can then be brought in, and the actors encouraged to use the object as an imaginative trigger for a scene. When the actor's whole body begins to conform naturally to the imagined reality, 'showing' replaces 'telling'. At that point, too, the prop itself will be subsumed into the scene which has been created from it. The audience's attention, like the actor's, will no longer be on the sign but on the signified. We will forget the telescope and, with it, see the ships in the distance.

Entrances and exits

In the theatre, the entry of a new character signals an intensification of energy. This is partly attributable to learned expectations. The audience knows that the playwright has sent him or her on to *do* something – that is, a new action is about to develop. (That is the reason for the Neo-classical system of scene division in play texts. A new scene means a new action within the main 'Act' of the play, and that usually coincides with a character's entrance.) So entrances are vitally important.

In improvisation this is equally true. In rehearsal, the group watches a scene developing and is encouraged to join in as soon as possible with it. As each actor joins in – that is, enters – the energy of the scene lifts. As soon as it begins to flag, someone else *must* come in to help out. The actors mustn't be left stranded. That is the First Cardinal Sin in improvisation. The new action doesn't have to be highly significant, as long as it's sensitive to either the demands of the developing scene or the energy level of the situation. If this is learned as a principle, then there is very little difficulty in sustaining the spontaneity of improvisation. Actors learn to look after one another, to take the pressure off each other rather than increase it. It encourages structure, altruism and genuine spontaneity, because the people on the stage now have to respond to whatever the new entrant brings on.

It may seem obvious, but it's worth pointing out that exits, too, are important. They finish the scene: ending the action for the person departing (though not necessarily for those who remain). It's a good idea to encourage people not to hang around once their contribution has run out, but to think up a good reason for leaving and to play it. This can develop a sense of shape in the actor's mind; making the actor work through every moment of a scene. Sometimes, of course, this will be used as an excuse to get off as fast as possible, but just as often it will open up a whole new reason for staying on.

Meetings and greetings

All theatre is an act of encounter. Characters meet each other and we understand from their meeting how they relate to one another: this is a husband greeting his wife upon awakening; that is an underling receiving his boss into his home; these are two lovers who have been apart. But there is also a deeper level of encounter implicit in the act of theatre. Clive Barker writes:

> The theatre is the art of human relationships in action. This definition will apply to modern unstructured forms of improvised drama and rituals as well as to older established forms. In the theatre people meet, and plot is the result of their interaction. At the end the situation is not what it was at the beginning, because human beings have experienced a process of change. Change takes place in the audience individually through their meeting with the actors/characters/dramatist.[1]

There are a number of implications here. On stage, *people* should meet, not machines repeating the fixed formulae of lines learned in rehearsal. In one type of theatre (say, the Chekhovian) the implication is that *characters* encounter one another. In another (say, in *commedia*) the *actors* meet – and so do the *masks*.

Exercises about meetings and greetings abound. They include sitting in a circle and introducing the person next to you to the rest of the group; walking round the room and stopping first to acknowledge silently, then to greet, finally to introduce oneself to, each other person; throwing a name (maybe accompanied by a ball) across the circle, focusing total attention on a chosen person for an instant. Here the idea of meeting is enhanced by a directing of energy and purpose.

But the audience, too, encounters the actors, and through them the characters, and beyond them the dramatist, or the idea of the play. This is the deepest level of encounter; an audience comes to meet itself; touching physically (at the elbows if nowhere else) and touching spiritually via the play's depiction to the audience of their own concerns. And the individual audience member encounters himself, recognises some truth about himself in what he sees.

Blocking

'Blocking' – the Second Cardinal Sin of improvisation – is a denial of the possibility of encounter. Blocking occurs when an actor tacitly refuses to accept what another actor is offering (or, indeed, when he refuses to accept the impulses and ideas of his own psyche). Keith Johnstone calls it 'a form of aggression'. He sometimes uses video to record improvisation sessions. It's difficult at first to show people (even those who are watching) how the blocking is inhibiting the development of a scene. On video it becomes obvious what has been offered and either missed or denied:

> Each actor tends to resist the invention of the other actor, playing for time, until he can think up a 'good idea', and then he'll try to make his partner follow it. The motto of scared improvisers is 'when in doubt, say "NO".' We use this in life as a way of blocking action. Then we go to the theatre, and at all points where we would say 'No' in life, we want to see the actors yield, and say 'Yes'.[2]

There's a good reason for this wanting to hear the actors (the interchange going on in the play) saying 'yes': it offers us a chance to experience those aspects of our 'character' and those possibilities of action which we do not feel confident about trying for ourselves in normal situations. The freedom of the stage action allows us to live a little more fully, and that is also what can happen through improvisation.

As Johnstone says, good improvisers develop action, even when they aren't sure where it's leading; bad improvisers block it. And in blocking action, they deny the possibility of any kind of encounter happening between the actors, and between the actors and the audience.

Some useful exercises which promote unblocking (though almost everything done in impro works towards this) focus on response situations: making machines and body-sculptures, telling stories one word or sentence at a time, adding noises or gestures to a partner's story. In 'Yes/Yes, but' scenes, one actor is allowed to say no more than 'Yes' (twice in succession) and then 'Yes, but' every third response. There is a version of this which figures in Indian folk-theatre such as *Yakshagana*, where the narrator-cum-director (or another character) intersperses 'comments' into an actor's speech, for example, 'Um', 'Ah', 'Eh', 'Oh' and so on. With very little or no vocabulary, the interlocutor can incite all kinds of interesting possibilities depending on tone of voice, timing or inflection.

Blocking is both a physical and a mental problem (discussed in Part III as censorship and psychodrama), and everything from gentle warm-ups to the most intimidating Grotowskian encounter-strategies can be appropriate to tackle it, depending on the context. The things we have referred to here relate mainly to working in pairs or groups; that is, to the importance of unblocking in developing the ability to work together, which is basic to all acting.

Chapter 6

Moving Towards Performance

Senses

The actor's senses are of paramount importance if he is to be fully responsive to his fellow performers and to the audience. They are the actor's only means of experiencing and contacting the world around him. Sight and hearing are crucial, of course, but smell and taste and, particularly, *touch*, are equally important. Sight is the actor's primary means of spatial location – remove sight (with a blindfold) and the actor has to reorient himself physically, and reach out through space. If the actor can learn to extend himself spatially with his eyes open he will automatically become more physically expressive – less 'bound' or 'closed' (as the 'Fight in the Dark' game demonstrates).

But the senses also have an imaginative dimension. We have sensation memory, which Stanislavsky used as the key to 'emotional recall' – allowing the actor to get in touch with memories of childhood, say, by recalling the smell of soap, or the roughness of school clothes. It is impossible to say whether 'emotional recall' is actual recall – or if it is an imaginative creation of the present. Proust calls it 'involuntary memory', and believes that it gives us access to the *moi permanent* (a sense of self as more than transitory, extending across time; as a *capacity for* cognitive and affective experience), and makes it the core of his life's work about the processes of memory, imagination and artistic construction. But the use of recalled sensory information is certainly central to the process, personalising and concretising the imaginary reconstruction. The group can be taken on a mime 'journey', for example, through an imaginary sensory landscape.

Lecoq makes the journey involve a passage through each of the elements – earth, air, fire, water – and an exploration of how the body functions in relation to weight, speed, balance and so on.

Tenses

Acting occurs in the present tense. It is experienced in the moment of its creation, the actual present – the 'now' of the performance. That is another reason why we speak of the good actor as having 'presence' – his concentrated attention fills the space, and fills the time. It doesn't matter whether the play is set in the remotest past or the farthest reaches of some imagined future: in order for it to be experienced it has to be performed in the present.

But Clive Barker (following Brecht) has importantly qualified the process of acting 'in the present' in a way which throws light upon one of the basic principles of improvisation: the actor's use of the imagination. The performer can vary the tense – and the person – to produce a clearer mental and physical narrative of the action being portrayed. The actor moves from the understood 'I, the character, am doing this', via 'He, the character, is doing this' to, ultimately, 'The character did this' – which the actor then *re-enacts*. He explains it thus:

> The activity of the actor is not the illusory *reliving* of an imaginary event, but the *re-enactment* in the present of an event which we accept as gone for ever, in which we personally had no part, and which is no longer a direct issue. Whatever terms we work in, the actual event is the performance of a play by actors.[1]

Actors can discover for themselves the 'tenses of acting' and have little trouble with changing person from first to third, or tense from present to past. But how do you act in the future? Through dreams, prophecies, visions which take you forward into the future, just as memory takes you back into the past.

While Clive Barker's theory is demonstrably true, both as a

description of what the actor does and as a method of approach, it is rather problematic for improvisers to work in this way. In pure 'impro' there is no past, only the immediacy of the present. There is only action, not re-enactment. Barker's work does have relevance to improvisation, but of a specific kind. His criticisms of improvisation (which he is at pains to point out he regards as both productive and creative) reveal a fundamental separation between two understandings of improvised acting – that which is 'pure' and that which is 'applied' – and a necessary corrective to the effusive assumption made by some practitioners that improvisation is a universal panacea.

Barker doesn't acknowledge pure improvisation at all. He regards it only as a valuable rehearsal device (if properly used) in the service of the traditional play. He sees it as a process of *programming* the body/think to respond and adapt instinctively:

> If it has not been programmed with a mass of material about the play, the situations, the characters and their interrelationships, it will only produce the material it has, which will naturally relate directly to the here and now, the situation in which the actor is actually present, along with a mass of cliché responses he has learned from other situations. This is not improvisation. It is 'mugging', 'fooling about', a totally self-indulgent activity.[2]

Barker is right; the production of cliché responses is not improvisation, and improvisation does demand enormous technical prowess. Where we disagree is with the dismissal of the 'here and now', the real situation of the actor. 'Impro' makes that situation its subject. Every actor is the sum of his experiences (real and imagined) learned from other situations in life and on the stage. To draw upon them (often unconsciously) is not to submit to cliché: every actor does it. If the actor is responding genuinely, truthfully, to the here and now of his situation, then improvisation can be divorced from the preparation process and become the performance itself.

Status

The two chief sections of Keith Johnstone's *Impro* are devoted to *status* interactions and to *masks*. Both are extremely complex subjects and the reader is advised to consult Johnstone's book directly, since space here will permit only the briefest discussion of these crucial topics.

Status, for Johnstone, implies far more than just given power relationships, or questions of submission and dominance. The word 'status' is best understood as both noun and verb. It does not simply define a state or condition, the social status, it is something one *does*, or plays.

> TRAMP. 'Ere! Where are you going?
> DUCHESS. I'm sorry, I didn't quite catch . . .
> TRAMP. Are you deaf as well as blind?

> Audiences enjoy a contrast between the status played and the social status. . . . Chaplin liked to play the person at the bottom of the hierarchy and then lower everyone.[4]

Status is a dynamic interactive process of continual adjustment. One can work to raise or lower oneself and those around one – what Johnstone calls 'the see-saw principle'. In Johnstone's view, people train themselves in life to become 'status specialists', manoeuvring themselves in any social situation into their preferred position and feeling uncomfortable when asked to play the alternative position. So a lot of his work consists in training his students to recognise and to adapt their preferred social positions. His exercises often centre around scenes in which pairs work together on status transactions. First both will lower status; then both will raise it; then one will raise while the other lowers; finally status will be reversed during the scene. He emphasises that the chosen position should be just a *little* bit higher or lower than the partner's; this means careful observation and delicate modulation. The actors have to learn the subtle dynamics of transition.

Status can be played to the space, and to objects as well as to people. One can, for example, play high status to an empty room – rubbing a finger over surfaces and finding dust will raise one's status and lower the room's. Or one can play low status to a chair – avoiding it because it looks too posh lowers oneself and raises the chair's.

One very important point about status information is that it may be all an actor needs to begin improvising. Talking of the 'Method' actor's wish to know all the 'given circumstances' in detail before attempting improvisation, Johnstone says:

In order to enter a room all you need to know is what status you are playing. The actor who understands this is free to improvise in front of an audience with no given circumstances at all![5]

The basic status game is 'Master–Servant'[6] in which each plays the status of his respective role to the limit, so that the interaction becomes a battle (by grovelling to the utmost, the servant implicitly attacks the master, who has constantly to reassert himself). This game and its variants allow actors to recognise and begin to use status as a part of their repertoire. Like other improvisation games dependent on a rapid response, it liberates the player from any one habitual mode and moves him towards becoming a kaleidoscope of available choices. Important for actors, of course, but equally so for actors as people, because it produces an extension of the range of existential choice, which is the most serious and far-reaching effect of the play element in culture.

Masks

Masks are used in various ways in improvisation and related forms of teaching. Copeau, Lecoq and Maude-Roxby all made or make extensive use of them. We have described some of this in Part I, particularly from the point of view of the aims of mask-work. In what follows, aims are naturally also relevant, although here we are more concerned with different techniques or ways of working. It may therefore be helpful to have a short overview of the principal kinds of mask-work associated with improvisation. Of all the teachers we have mentioned, Lecoq is most systematic in this, since he incorporates work with five different kinds of mask into his training. They provide a handy check-list.

Neutral Mask

Lecoq starts with this:[7] it is the Mask most fundamental to improvisatory work because learning to wear it is learning to achieve the state from which new creative structure can arise. It works as a kind of 'unlearning', liberating the performer from preconceived notions, from any 'recipe'. It requires – almost like a Grotowskian *via negativa* – a complete letting-go in order to reach a condition of unprejudiced being; whilst at the same time one must remain acutely focused and alert, ready to respond with the whole organism.

Lecoq uses this Mask to erase the past, as part of the process of 'forgetting': 'Neutral . . . means without a past, open, ready.'[8] He aims for 'a liberation that permits the mime to rediscover the world in a newly attained state of nonknowing'.[9] In this condition 'the individual becomes a blank page. . . . Everything is erased so he can start from scratch, seeing things for the first time.'[10]

The 'waking-up' exercise asks actors to explore movement and expression from a situation of no prior knowledge, evading preconceptions; the features of the Mask itself are of a male or female in repose, without particular characteristics. It is actually almost impossible to 'behave neutrally' and this is the first discovery one makes. Out of that, with patience, the ability to recognise and discard habitual postures and gestures begins to emerge.

This is the all-important process of getting back prior to habitual reactions and fixed notations, including language. Lecoq goes on to use exercises derived from Copeau and Bing:

> We play people, elements, plants, trees, colours, lights, matter, sounds – going beyond their images, gaining knowledge of their space, their rhythm, their breath through improvisation.[11]

All Lecoq's work on rhythm, matter, plasticity and relationships in space is rooted in what he does with the Neutral Mask. It is interesting that he also uses this Mask for work on the Greek chorus, both in terms of the way it responds as a single organism rhythmically and spatially balancing the protagonist, and because he regards it as incorporating a neutrality that is 'all-knowing'. What Lecoq sees in the Neutral Mask is precisely this leading into a kind of total and potent organic knowledge.

Expressive Mask

This Mask represents a fixed psychological type – rather like Pirandello's *Six Characters*. Wearing it forces the body to find gestures and emotions in direct response to the stimulus it offers. (Some *commedia* masks may be of this type: the difference lies in the degree of intensity with which they are invested.) Lecoq also uses this Mask for *contre-masque* work where the actor has to be a character *opposite* to that represented by the Mask he is wearing. Impro work with this Mask thus leads to the experience of what if feels like to be a 'split' character with an internal conflict; one whose inner sense of himself is always at odds with his appearance, for instance. The multiple possibilities of self-regard and self-deception begin to emerge as physical experiences.

Larval Mask

Larval Masks are abstract forms. Non-human yet evoking psychic and emotional states, they lead, like the Neutral Mask, to a kind of precognitive situation where physical gesture precedes emotion and both precede conceptualisation. Wearing them, actors experiment with the position of different parts of the body and discover that emotional changes may result. Lecoq's hierarchy, similar to Copeau's, runs from gesture through emotion and then to thought and finally language. The *mime de fond*, which Lecoq also calls *mime du début*, arises at the gesture level. The Lecoq-trained Swiss company Mummenschanz use Larval Masks which are none the less powerfully evocative, working at a kind of pre-verbal level. The English troupe Moving Picture Mime Show also centred their work on the Larval Mask.

Commedia

In Lecoq's teaching, the essence of *commedia* lies in the fact that it takes stereotypes to the extreme, and is always played at the highest level of intensity. Here too 'fixed external movements and the mask create the internal character'[12] so it's a matter of working off the Mask through the body, not of thinking up suitably typical actions (or words, since *commedia* uses language) in advance. Lecoq progresses towards use of *commedia* Masks both through work on breathing and through exercises which raise the level of intensity of expressing emotion: each feeling, for instance, can be progressively 'scaled up' by every new character entering a scene.

Clown (red nose)

For Lecoq, this smallest Mask is the ultimate in self-revelation: 'self-humour is the only true alienation effect.'[13] Here one confronts and confesses by sharing what one normally represses: brings out one's 'shadow', as it were, and lets it dance in the

1 I Gelati in Commedia masks (photograph © I Gelati).

2 Copeau's *Comédie Nouvelle*: Saint-Denis as Knie, Suzanne Bing as La Célestine, Dasté as Cesar (photograph © Et. Bordas, from J. Lecoq (ed.), *Le Théâtre du Geste*, 1988).

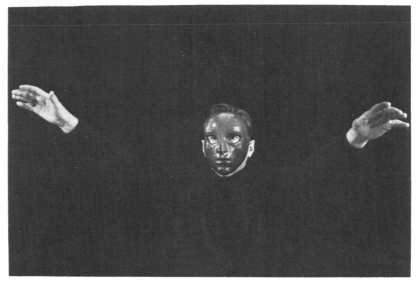

3   Jacques Lecoq in a neutral mask (photograph © Patrick Lecoq).

4   Jacques Lecoq teaching at his Paris school (photograph © Et. Bordas, from J. Lecoq (ed.), *Le Théâtre du Geste*, 1988).

5 'The Fight in the Dark', from *The 1984 Game*, University of East Anglia, 1983 (photograph © Anthony Frost).

6 Free improvisation with Roddy Maude-Roxby and Theatre Machine (photograph © Jo Rice).

7   Théâtre de Complicité in *Please Please Please* (photograph © Théâtre de Complicité).

8   'Croquet': Ric Morgan and Roddy Maude-Roxby of Theatre Machine, 1981 (photograph © Bernard Phillips).

light. As with all Mask work, the 'technique' has to do with *not* acting, with letting the Mask speak. Here, it speaks for the self, and the actor is most naked, most offered to the audience.

The first problem is one of language. Johnstone in particular uses a kind of 'magical language' when speaking of the power of Masks (this is implicit in his capitalisation of the initial 'M'[14]). It is perfectly possible to put on a mask (small 'm') and pretend to be someone else. But Johnstone is concerned with the induction of trance states in the performer via Mask work. For him, it is almost impossible to define the changes wrought in the performer by the assumption of a Mask without resorting to terms like 'possession'.

It can be difficult to persuade actors to see masks in this way. The language itself can be a barrier. It suggests either something very dangerous, or something too reverent by half; and it can set up a resistance in actors who haven't experienced directly the transformative power of the mask. So it is essential to create the right atmosphere from the outset. Keith Johnstone and his colleague Roddy Maude-Roxby are experts at creating the right sort of anticipation in their students. The rules they set up are crucial for overcoming the actors' initial resistances. The primary aim is to let the masks do the talking, as it were. The actors can be asked to encounter the masks as characters, encouraged to find out about them – what they like to do, whom they like to be with and so on – treating them rather like intelligent children, perhaps (which is appropriate, because masks *are* childlike by nature – always eager to meet, and learn and do new things). So the actors should be childlike (never childish) too, and begin simply by putting them on and seeing what the mask suggests to them. Mirrors should be provided to stimulate and later 'recharge' the masked actor. But mirrors should not be overused. Far more essential is for the actor to work off the *feeling* that he is experiencing in the mask and the *feedback* he is receiving from the audience. Too much gazing in the mirror tends to trap the wearer into unproductive narcissism.

Too little respect, and the masks will remain lifeless cardboard props; but too *much* respect – treating the masks as if they were truly the repositories of ancient demons – can stifle creativity altogether. The latter course places entirely the wrong sort of

demands upon the improviser. It suggests that there is only way
of behaving that will animate each mask, some kind of arcane
ritual. The performer will spend all his time gazing reverently at his
reflection and wondering why nothing is happening. Masks begin
work by ambushing their wearers. If the atmosphere is good, the
work respectful, open, honest and good-humoured to begin with,
the mask will animate the actor rather than the reverse. (This
statement can be applied to *all* kinds of impro work, though
mask work is its best example.)

The second problem is one of technique. There are rules
for working with Masks (and with masks, too). Some masks
can speak, others are inappropriate for speech work. There are
rules governing the actor's presentation of the mask: profile may
destroy the image; the mask is a frontal thing and it may lose power
when it presents a side view (consisting of its edge bisecting the
side of the actor's face, with the actor's ear and hair visible – a
Larval mask or a whole-head mask is preferable for this degree
of movement). These rules need to be learned, but learned in a
way which does not conflict with the free expressiveness of the
mask itself.

The rewards can be extraordinary, as anyone who has seen a
good Mask company (like Trickster, or Trestle Theatre Company)
will testify. Johnstone quotes some of his students on what the
Mask state feels like. One student wrote: 'As an improviser I
am nervous about appearing "right", but once in a Mask,
there's no such feeling and the Mask can improvise indefinitely
(if happy).'[15]

Masks take the actor back to the original state of transformation
– the shamanic act of self-annihilation (note the way in which the
student here makes the distinction between his own feelings when
improvising and those of the Mask: the Mask is improvising; the
Mask is happy). They allow the transformation to happen safely,
providing a format within which a new, creative self (called 'the
Mask') can appear. Thus they are crucial in improvisation work.
But it is essential that the work be undertaken with care, so
as not to stifle the emergence of that new self. A good way
is to encourage the actors to make and to decorate their own
masks – and from as many materials as possible (paper, papier
mâché, leather, wood, plaster bandage, photographs stuck on
cardboard). What is important here is the emphasis on working
with the mask, developing a relationship with it from which the

new self can emerge, as a seamless 'fit' between mask and actor's body.

Masks – another view

As an alternative approach to the 'entranced' Mask work described by Johnstone, there is another way of working that is equally valid and essentially improvisatory, and leads equally to trancing, as the writers can testify. Fifteen minutes under the Mask of Arlecchino can seem like hours of relentless pressure. When the mask is removed it has taken, literally, an hour or two to 'come down' from the high induced by intense physical and mental concentration, and perhaps also by changes in breathing due to the mask's demands. This type of work is, in the end, a validation of Johnstone's claims for Mask states of consciousness rather than a negation of them. But the process involved is very different, for where Keith Johnstone and Roddy Maude-Roxby's work is relaxed and exploratory, this style of mask improvisation is intense, physical and highly technical.[16]

The first half of a three-hour session consists of a devastatingly thorough physical warm-up, designed to inculcate professional discipline, and to work on all parts of the body, especially the legs and the torso. The exercises stress co-ordination, flexibility and rhythm. The aim is simple. Under a mask, it is the rest of the body which must be expressive. The thorough bodily warm-up aims to awaken each part of the body, leaving it ready to become expressive, preparing it to help to *carry* the mask in an appropriate way.

Having selected a mask, the actors are asked to walk around the acting space. At first it is evident that the masks do not 'belong' to these bodies. There seems to be a discrepancy between the mask and the body that is failing to 'carry' it appropriately. So the work proceeds by requiring instantaneous organic response. Snap changes of bodily position, direction of gaze, gesture and so on have to be found in response to the beat of a drum or tambourine. Then the actors are asked instantly to assume a posture which (a) involves the whole body and (b) seems to suit the mask. As the actors adopt specific, grotesque positions and freeze them, the masks do seem to flicker into life.

The first two or three postures are superseded quickly by banging the drum again. On a final drumbeat the actors adopt their new postures and are still, waiting, instantly forming a remarkable tableau.

With the masks 'alive', and all the group working together, the session proper begins. The method is simple enough. Verbal instruction, coaching, comes continually from the sidelines, punctuated by cues from the drum.

The group is told that it is at a zoo, looking at the exhibits. But rather than being allowed just to wander through a loose improvisation, the group is continually told what it is seeing. At one side of the space (the group instinctively crowds towards it) is a magnificent bird of paradise on a high perch. At first the actors imagine the bird and 'pretend' to see it. But then the description from the sidelines becomes more precise.

The imagined bird has a sharp crest with three upright feathers. The actors' heads begin to lift three times in unison as the eyes of the masks – and the *always open eyes* of the actors (for to close the eyes for longer than a blink is to close out the watchers, to introvert the mask) – begin to trace the imaginary plumage.

The beak is long and angled down to the left, ending in a sharp point. The heads and bodies turn, following the line; noises begin to come freely from the masks, expressing the shape vocally and ending up in a sharp point of sound. The actors are beginning to show us, physically, what it is that they are imagining and responding to.

The bird has a magnificent swirling tail that reaches the floor. The actors' heads swirl downwards, and then bob back up again so as not to lose the whole image, and so as not to lose contact with the watchers.

The bird of paradise is just one example of this way of teaching mask technique. (A similar exercise involves looking at an imaginary exhibition of abstract painting; the masks respond to the described shapes and colours with the same broad, whole-body movements and with naturally descriptive sounds.) It illustrates a number of key ideas.

The mask is, of course, a *frontal* medium. It is often difficult to see properly when wearing a mask, and improvising in one is made more difficult by the fear of losing contact with the audience – letting the mask 'go dead' – while trying to keep contact with one's partners on the stage. The answer to this problem lies in what one may call a 'whole-body awareness' of the other performers, rather than in the 'eye contact awareness' appropriate to other forms of improvisation and, indeed, naturalistic acting.

The whole body listens: it isn't necessary to look at one's interlocutor in order to convince an audience that one is paying attention, nor to establish and hold eye-contact in order to communicate with a fellow actor. It *is* necessary to give one's attention totally and to communicate; but in the frontal style, that communication is always mediated via the audience.[17]

The mask has to *show* (not 'tell') the audience what it is seeing, and it has to do so with the whole body. It is carried by the physical being of the actor – which starts from a physical posture in some way appropriate to that mask (as Il Magnifico's beaked nose is naturally avian and everything else is consonant with that; or as Arlecchino's mischievous agility is naturally consonant with the feline smile on his black face. Actors working with leather masks re-created by Amleto Sartori found this catlike quality in Arlecchino, no matter what the Mask outwardly suggested).

Dario Fo, in his famous master-classes in Umbria and elsewhere, demonstrates just how the Masks of the *commedia* tradition require the involvement of the actor's whole being to bring them to life. He dons the Mask of Il Magnifico – an aristocrat stranded in a bourgeois era. The key to animating this Mask is that sense of contradiction. The actor's arms begin to make contradictory movements; they move apart or cross one another, or contra-rotate across the turning body. The feet lift high, stepping over-cautiously; the head turns from side to side, as if the eyes were placed far back on the sides of the head. The movement is birdlike and, indeed, when the voice is heard it is a high-pitched, raucous squawk. Il Magnifico (Pantalone) is rendered as a fantastical kind of chicken, an ageing rooster whose power has gone forever.[18] Thus the Mask comes instantly alive for the spectator but, as Fo (and Bertolt Brecht) would remind us, there is also a powerful political *gestus* inherent in that incarnation. It is part of the conception of the role, not a gloss upon it. Together with the physical there is also a mental set, and a specific attitude to the character. The Mask remains dead without it.

Physical considerations matter a great deal. The half-mask, for example, may depress the actor's upper lip, or the large cavity behind a grotesquely extended nose may create an extra resonator, both of which will naturally transform the sound of the voice, adding and subtracting tonal qualities, and these changes have to be accepted, used and developed. To do anything else is to attempt to deny what the mask is demanding of the actor. Finding this physiological quality is a measure of integration of actor and mask.

Once the technical skills have been inculcated, the teachers home in on each mask in turn. They *provoke* the mask: somehow the actor always knows (although the watchers may be unsure) that it is the mask that is being provoked, not its wearer. They provide the performer with a constant source of external stimulation. They instruct ('Keep that voice'; 'Eyes open!'; 'Look at *us*!'). They ask questions ('What's that you're holding? Show it to us. Do you like it? Well, show us. Show everybody, not just us. Aren't you proud of it? Well, you're even *more* proud of it'). Sometimes they cajole and flatter; at other times they seem to want to belittle or humiliate the mask ('You're boring!'), until the mask responds with something new, or something true.

They pick up on every little thing the mask is doing, or failing to do, and instantly suggest a way of extending or developing what is happening. For instance, one way of getting the performer to understand the crucial mime notion of *le point fixe* is to suggest that the mask is in a television studio, on camera. They ask for a retake because 'Camera Two has packed up and we didn't quite get that, love. Could you do it again for Camera Three over there?' The mask loves being the centre of such attention and happily repeats and enlarges the activity. Or they suggest that the mask freezes certain moments for the benefit of an imaginary stills photographer ('A few shots for the publicity people'). The mask, happy to oblige, naturally begins to find those fixed points, those moments of stillness which allow the action to be clearly read.

Sometimes the sideline coaching is more belligerent; the watchers will refuse to accept an explanation, say, or demand that it be sung first, or spoken like Shakespeare, or danced (while keeping the basic posture). This serves to renew energy and continually to pull the focus outwards, away from any relapse into introversion.

This form of mask work is difficult and initially scaring, in that it involves overcoming resistance (arising from a lack of trust in oneself, but liable to be transferred to the teachers and the work) and operating at intense pressure under constant 'nagging'. It also requires discipline: once the mask is on, the actor has to stay within that mental set.

But if these conditions are accepted – and in the end they represent that willingness all improvisation work aims to initiate, to prise open the protective shell of the narrowly conceived self – the results can be exhilarating. Some students reach and sustain a high level of creativity very quickly. One Mask, on trial for the theft of a can of soup (from a soup-ermarket), spontaneously made up and performed a rhyming aria on the merits of various brands of broth, while another operatically demanded the soup-reme penalty for the malefactor. Students who find it difficult to give their whole body to a performance (scripted and rehearsed as well as improvised) can be coached through a revelatory learning experience while wearing a mask.

Masks do have to be treated with respect, as do the people carrying them. Masks have strange and powerful hypnotic qualities which affect those who wear them. They *constrain* the performer and reduce some of his or her expressiveness (facial expressiveness most obviously, but also they remove a lot of habitual acting techniques by altering the voice and making strenuous demands on the physical carriage and movement of the actor). But, by this very process, a mask *liberates* the actor. The mask suppresses so many facets of the actor's habitual stage-self in order to liberate other, deeper, creative resources. It suspends the judgemental self: the technical demands are too great to allow split concentration. It frees the actor from the heavy burden of creative responsibility (as, indeed, all impro work can). The *mask* is creative; it knows what to do. Locked into its shape – into the way it makes the body feel – are all the answers the actor needs. The actor only needs to trust that feeling and the result will be magical. In reality, the effect is of having taken *off* a false mask in order to put on a true one.

Ultimately, the 'trance' or power to change is not in the *mask*: it derives from the conjunction of mask, actor and audience. The wearer responds to stimuli both from the mask and from teachers and/or audience: what is involved is a dynamic process of co-creation.

In this chapter we have looked at a variety of ways of developing whole-body awareness, opening up the actor's resources and developing his performance vocabulary. In the process the imagination is liberated and rechanelled to offer the possibility of new physical and intellectual invention and expression.

Chapter 7

Applied Improvisation Work

Who/where/what

The 'who/where/what' exercises stem primarily from the work of the American teacher of improvisation Viola Spolin.[1] Keith Johnstone finds this technique unhelpful,[2] but this is because his aims are different. We have found this approach most useful in the creation of a consistent piece. It concentrates the attention, and removes distractions, without limiting creativity. It gives the actor something to start with, and to build upon. Given either a 'who', a 'where' or a 'what', the actor can create the other two. Given nothing, the actor can still choose one of these and generate a consistent and coherent piece of improvisation. For example, the 'who' might be a 'a farmer'; this suggests the 'where' (for example, in a field) and the 'what' follows quite naturally (for example, planting potatoes). But the 'who' might just as easily be 'yourself', in the same field doing the same thing – or some other 'where' doing something else. Or the 'who' might be the character that one is developing in a formal, scripted play – which can then be examined carefully in another context. The exercise asks that the imagination remain constant to the 'set' chosen or specified. If the 'who' is a king, the actor has a constant imaginative focus to return to; he must behave consistently like a king (and that, of course, implicitly involves status work too) or he must consciously choose to alter the imaginative set.

One problem that the 'who/where/what' exercise can overcome is the automatic tendency of any group of inexperienced
improvisers to 'play for laughs' at inappropriate moments – to
make the scene as absurd and laughable as possible.

The reasons for doing this are fourfold. First of all, the
actor hasn't entered fully into the piece, either through not
concentrating or not listening to what the other actors have
created. Second, it's a subtle but very aggressive form of
'blocking', which rejects the creativity of the other performers
(effectively saying 'NO' by ironising their work). Third, it's an
easy way out, avoiding the responsibility of having to remain
consistent and 'true' to the situation. Fourth, it evinces a deep
insecurity about this type of work felt by the actor.

This fourth type of response is very common. In a scripted play,
the actor has a set of reassurances to rely on: the rehearsal process,
the learned moves and gestures, the other actors doing pre-
ordained things. Above all, the actor *knows where he's going*; he
knows what the outcome should be like, and works towards that.

In improvisation the actor doesn't know where he's going, and
isn't always comfortable going there. He isn't at all sure that he
doesn't look very foolish. His defence against this can be to make
the scene funny. It disarms criticism and, at the same time, gives
the actor the reassurance that those watching accept that what he's
doing works (they laugh). He is reassured by a response, even the
wrong response, from the audience or from his peers.

The 'who/where/what' discipline helps to remove these anxieties
and these blocks. It gives the performer a reassuring and familiar
structure within which to operate, and it also insists that the
creativity keep within the logical bounds of the initial idea.
It's another way of taking pressure off, without losing genuine
spontaneity.

It probably doesn't suit Keith Johnstone's freer 'impro' work;
and its use is therefore limited to specific exercises on plays, or
to the creation of sustained and 'true-to-life' scenes.

Objectives and resistances

Improvisation workshops and rehearsal situations are a great
means of teaching the fundamental principles of acting *and*
dramatic theory. A group of students will almost always organically 'discover' many of the major theories of acting for

themselves, among them the Stanislavskian idea of the 'want' or 'intention' and how to play it against the conflicting wants of other characters. This playing of 'objectives and resistances' can work in some very strange ways, and not only ways connected with Stanislavskian theatre.

For example, an actor wants to pass through a doorway. What might happen if the doorway (played by another actor) chose to resist him – or if he imagined that it did? He would have to talk or fight his way through, or invent a way round or over the obstacle. Whenever a scene is flagging, or lacking in impact, it helps to devise or strengthen a resistance, and make the actors overcome it. This invariably produces new improvisations. The Stanislavskian terminology is very useful, keeping the 'want' active by shaping the idea (always using the most active verb possible) and getting the actor to concentrate on physical objectives.

Point of concentration (focus)

Viola Spolin uses the term 'points of concentration' (abbreviated to POC) as the focal point of her system. She regards it as the 'ball' with which the game is played. It is related to the idea of concentration of attention which we have already discussed, but disciplines the work and enables each exercise – and each moment of performance – to be worked on in isolation with the actor totally given to the moment and to the action being played. Most of her exercises have a specific POC to which the actor can attach himself, enabling the aspects of acting to be separated out and put together afresh (she also provides for evaluation of each exercise and gives the session leader a 'point of observation'. For example, describing an 'orientation session' in which a single actor becomes involved with a large, entangling object, she writes:

POINT OF CONCENTRATION: on the selected object.

EXAMPLES: spider web, boa constrictor, tree branches in forest or jungle, octopus, parachute, man-eating plant.

POINT OF OBSERVATION
Watch the wording when stating the POC to be certain that the player's concentration is on the object and not on disentangling himself from the object. This is an important

difference and one which comes up continuously throughout the work.[3]

Spolin's work is highly systematised and at first may hardly seem to relate to Johnstone's pure spontaneity of response. But she is concerned with focusing the individual performer very tightly onto the work at all moments during the training in order not only to liberate, but also to *channel* that spontaneity.

Memory

Andrea Perrucci wrote in 1699 about the internal consistency of improvised comedy:

> The actors must, above all, be careful not to make a mistake with regard to the country where the action is going to take place; they should realise whence they come, and for what purpose; the proper names must be kept well in mind. . . . Moreover, the actors must pay attention to the distribution of the houses, so that each player may know his own house, for it would be too ridiculous for anyone to knock at or enter into somebody else's house instead of his own: one would regard such a person as a booby or a drunkard.[4]

In any kind of consistent piece, memory plays a large part. It stores the 'rules of the game' and allows the player to improvise within them. Memory games are, therefore, very useful as 'mental warm-ups'. Simple games of mental concatenation can be great fun. Player 1 announces that he's going to a party and taking 'some yellow jelly'. Player 2 announces that he, too, is off to a party and is taking 'some yellow jelly and a trilby hat'. Player 3 (by a great coincidence) also has an invitation to a party and plans to take 'some yellow jelly, a trilby hat, and a dustbin full of red knickers'. The game passes to Player 4 and so on around the circle until it arrives back at Player 1 who has to reel off the whole string of unlikely objects. It's good, too, if the players can relax into this, and have an attitude to what they are taking (maybe 'yellow jelly' is yummy!) If anyone breaks down, or goes wrong, the game starts all over again from the beginning with new objects. After a few breakdowns, the relationship between concentration, memory and the body is quickly learned. The mnemonic tricks for learning which we all possess are sharpened in an enjoyable way.[5]

'Set'

A paper by the Georgian psychologist R. Natadze poses the following question:

> When, with a spontaneity convincing to the spectators, the actors acts in conformity not with a real, but with an *imagined* situation imposed upon him by the play, embodying this in his stage performance experiences and conduct not his own – what is the psychological mechanism of such behaviour?[6]

Natadze implicitly recalls Diderot's *Paradoxe sur l'Acteur*, and the controversy between the ideas of 'real feeling' versus 'cold virtuosity'. The hypothesis advanced in the paper is that it is:

> *fixated set* evolved on the basis of picturing to oneself the particular imaginary situation imposed by the play that constitutes the foundation on which stage impersonation rests.[7]

His experiments with gifted actors and promising students of the Tbilisi Theatrical Institute, as well as with non-actors and a comic performer, strongly suggested 'a high correlation between the ability to evolve a set on the basis of imagination and the capacity for stage impersonation'.[8]

By 'set' is meant a mental construct; a set of rules which apply to the world of the play, which then becomes 'fixated' through rehearsal. The actor has the ability to behave in conformity to that 'set', even though it isn't real. The non-actor finds it difficult (and the comedian finds it downright impossible!).

Natadze's work implies that actors have a combination of a powerful imagination allied to strong concentration (which enables them to hold onto the construct and to shut out perceived contradictions). His work rewrites Stanislavsky in psychological terms. But that is in itself important.

The improviser makes use of Stanislavsky's 'magic If' all the time. And he does so without the benefit of rehearsal to fixate the evolved set. He plays the set *as it evolves*. So the training of the improviser must be in the evolution of set, of imaginary and self-consistent worlds. His training must encourage him to accept and act upon them – to go with the products of his imagination as if they were real, to accept their rules and statements as if they were not fantasies.

Character

Character work is not central to most improvised drama. In a loose sense, it may be the sum of all the other types of work going on. But in *pure* improvisation, 'impro', it is not something that the actor strives for. In *applied* improvisation, however, the rehearsal 'improvs', character is the dominant concern.

Most Western actors and drama students *use* improvisation (when they do use it) rather than just simply experiencing it. It is a rehearsal technique, a means towards the scripted end, through the exploration of character. Actors undertake improvised explorations about 'previous circumstances'; for example, meetings between characters that have happened before the action of the play begins.

This exercise puts the *actor* in a situation where he has to respond 'as if' he were the person he portrays. It can, at the very least, offer the actor an experiential measurement of the difference between himself and the character. (On reflection afterwards he can decide that Hamlet would have chosen the game pie rather than the Scotch egg because he's a prince.) But, more importantly, it allows the actor to develop what Natadze has called 'set', and practice being within it, with other actors, exploring its rules and its boundaries. And, finally, as Stanislavsky (in the person of 'Tortsov' guiding the student 'Kostya') wrote:

Now I hope you realise the difference between approaching and judging a role in your own person and in that of another, between looking at a role with your own eyes instead of those of the author, or director, or drama critic.

In your own person you live your role, in the person of someone else you simply toy with it, play-act it. In your own person you grasp the role with your mind, your feelings, your desires, and all the elements of your inner being, while in the person of another, in most cases, you do it only with your mind.

Purely reasoned analysis and understanding in a part is not what
we need.

We must take hold of the imagined character with all our
being, spiritual and physical. That is the only approach I am
willing to accept.[9]

The improvisation is not about the *character's* inner life, but
about the *actor's*. It awakens responses in the performer which
are primal, and personal. Afterwards, they can be analysed and
adapted and assimilated into the actor's conception of the role.
As they are happening, though, they force the actor to respond
directly and imaginatively to the situation. They encourage him
to see his fellow actors as the characters they are portraying (he
needs this imaginative leap to help sustain his own imppovisation
and to prevent 'corpsing') and to respond to them within the
agreed rules of the 'set' they are jointly constructing. They
tighten his concentration on the role, since distractions will
destroy the edifice the actors are building – and the greatest
distractions arise from his own intrusive thoughts. The actor
is given no time to think, to stand back and judge, to split
himself into simultaneous performer and critic. And it makes
the acting company into a genuinely creative ensemble, involved
in the 'writing' of their own play, bonding them and tuning them
into their own group wavelength.

Clive Barker, however, offers a salutary warning about the
misuse of improvisation in rehearsal which ought to be borne
in mind by any director tempted to rush in and apply it.

I rarely use free improvisation, preferring to use some
games activity as a structure within which the actors can
improvise.

The principal use of improvisation, as far as I am concerned,
is to overcome the actors' failure to penetrate the text to the
actions which underlie it. The words make sense, but have no
real meaning.[10]

Improvisation work before textual rehearsal begins may be
immensely useful. It may bond the group together and establish
a common language and way of working. But it isn't of much
use as a method of working on the *play* at an early stage. That

will come later, when the actors have a more thoroughly worked
out idea of what the play demands. And there is a further danger
that these improvisations will become only verbalisations, with
actors standing, talking and *explaining* at each other – rather
than discovering action.

This is where the 'impro' or pure improvisation training comes
in; the director (at least) must be able to intervene, cut away the
'telling' and demand the 'showing'. The actors have to communicate – perhaps non-verbally at first, through touch and movement,
or through sounds other than words – rather than simply translate
their ideas into words which will only block interaction. If this
can be achieved, then the two primary goals of applied improvisation will succeed: the inner actions will be explored, and the
inner life will be felt.

The character to concentrate on is not always one's own. In
a solo improvisation piece the actor feels the burden of having
to create everything on his own. This can be overcome by sharing
the responsibility for initiation (just as in a group piece) with one's
own partners – except that, in this case, the 'partners' are the
imaginary characters in the scene. Create the other characters in
the scene and take the *time* to stand back and 'hear' what they
have to say. To take a specific example: the chosen 'who' might
be 'an auctioneer', the 'what' and 'where' conducting an auction
in a posh sale-room. Having accepted the 'set', and decided the
rhythm and physical shape of the central figure of the auctioneer
(who is the only character the audience will actually see portrayed)
the actor needs also to create selectively the other participants in
the scene. If the actor imaginatively characterises them, visual-
ising them in the acting space, they can be made to do most of the
work for him.

The little old lady in the grey pullover wonders if she can
afford a few pounds more, and the auctioneer has to cajole
a bid from her. The red-faced farmer in the pork-pie hat can
easily afford it; the auctioneer need only appeal to his greed.
Is the housewife continually gesticulating to her friend in the
red coat making a bid or not? The foci of the scene have
become the invisible other characters, each of them a series of
prompts for the solo actor's imagination. Without these external
foci, the scene will quickly lose shape and rhythm; and the actor
will probably lose his grip on his own character, and descend

rapidly into cliché. With them, even a solo performer can develop the simple action (Spolin's 'what') into a consistent and coherent narrative.

Narrative

At all points in the process of improvising drama, the actor is involved in creating narrative. This does not mean simply 'telling a story'. That might be the result; but the process is concerned with other activities. All good improvised scenes have content and meaning: the improviser need not strain to impose them on the work, however. Handled properly, they arise organically, often created as much by the audience as by the actors.

Keith Johnstone stresses two narrative skills, *free association* and *reincorporation*. In fact, these two processes sum up many of the techniques we have already discussed, and turn them to account in the creation of a piece to be shared with an audience.

Free association means spontaneous response, 'going with' whatever has been offered, by oneself or by one's collaborators. It means letting one idea generate the next without trying to force it into shape: without trying to *make* it mean something (it undoubtedly *will* mean something). It means accepting, too, that part of the meaning (the true 'content' of the story) will be the performer's revelation of him/herself. Free association exercises (like Johnstone's 'Automatic Writing', 'Lists', 'Dreams') if used properly can encourage the actor to bypass the 'censor' in himself. It takes a lot of trust. That is why it shouldn't be concerned with interpretation; if the actor realises too soon that the underlying content of the story is sexual, for example, he may not wish to continue it, or may try to force the story to change direction.

Johnstone abandons the notion of content, and concentrates instead on structure – the key to which is reincorporation. When telling a tale, either singly or with others, reincorporation means making use of what has already been introduced. It means coming back to ideas previously established, and then using them in ways that both bind the story together and take it forwards. Free association takes care of invention and development; reincorporation takes care of structure.

The improviser has to be like a man walking backwards. He sees where he has been, but he pays no attention to the future. His story can take him anywhere, but he must still 'balance' it, and give it shape, by remembering incidents that have been shelved and reincorporating them. Very often an audience will applaud when earlier material is brought back into the story. They couldn't tell you why they applaud, but the reincorporation does give them pleasure.[11]

The audience, in fact, is enjoying structuring the story in its mind. They are looking for meaning, and making meaning out of what is being offered. Apparent randomness is given sudden illumination by reincorporation. So the applause, laughter or cheering that sometimes greets this reincorporated material is often the audience congratulating *itself* as much as the actor. They are saying 'Got it! Now it makes sense!' – and it's also an affirmation, a way of saying 'Go on! What will happen now?'

Taking the process further, however, into working on presentation of a given story requires other skills. The actor must be able to meet the audience face to face, must want to tell them the story directly, must be able to make eye-contact with as many people as possible.

Mike Alfreds, the founder of Shared Experience, reminds us that

the audience are usually very much with the actors *as* actors and seem willing to allow them the right to fail as long as the attempt is honest. The actor's process is almost as interesting for them as the piece he is creating.[12]

Alfreds works on 'trampoline' words within the known text of the story. These are the transition points from narrative to dialogue. The exercise was developed during rehearsals for Shared Experience's early show, *The First Arabian Night*. In this piece, as in many others by the company, the actor operates both as narrator of learned text and as improviser of action. The actor first has to find a personal way of narrating (creating his or her own text so that it bears the performer's personality). A way then has to be found of moving from narration into action.

Say the actor has text such as: 'When the prince heard this much from his royal sire, he was moved by youthful folly to reply, "Thou art great in age but small in wit".'[13]

Here the 'trampoline' word is *reply*. At that point he is going to change from narrator to actor. He has to be able to pitch right in to the scene at the correct energy level, that of the prince's youthful indignation,

> so he uses the previous sentence of the narration as a sort of run up, knowing that when he gets to the word 'reply' he has to gather all his forces to take off into the action; he literally has to bounce himself on that word and it gives him the time to change his focus from the audience to his partner in the scene.[14]

Once the transition has been made, improvisation takes over. The partner will respond as the prince's father and a scene will develop (in much the same way as a *commedia* scenario is fleshed out). The sections of learned narrative link the improvised passages together.

The audience's delight in the virtuosity of the actor becomes allied with its pleasure in the developing tale. The third-person narrative 'bounces' into the first-person improvisation, and whenever a scene is complete another narrator will take the thread. The action is never simply an *illustration* of the narrative. Often they have an ironic or an emotional relationship to each other. Sometimes the event seems to be randomly constructed, but the device of reincorporation, again, gives the piece its internal structure. The audience is lit throughout,[15] so that the narrators can make contact with them. That helps to engender a trusting relationship so that when a story is temporarily dropped, or new characters suddenly introduced, the audience suspends its judgement and simply waits for coherence to re-emerge. Then, as it perceives the complex structure of tale-within-tale, the audience responds with 'this wonderful reaction of "Oh, there it is!!" '[16]

Finally, there are other ways of using improvisation in the creation of a play. Group improvisation has been used by a number of professional playmakers for a long time. It can take the form of collaboration between writers and actors in the generation of an ultimately scripted play. Or it can lead to a play put together through improvisation in rehearsal – a play created entirely by the acting ensemble. Or it can be totally free, self-generating: the 'play' is entirely created in front of its audience.

In the first case, the writer/director can take a number of stances. He can supply the basic information (or organise its collation) and ask the actors to translate it into scenes via improvisation, which he will then take away and write up. Or he can take on the status of a recording mechanism, transcribing the improvised actions and polishing the (probably) clumsy dialogue that emerges. He might even use a tape-recorder or a video-camera to assist in this, although he runs the risk of inhibiting the actors in the process. Or he can play the *concertatore*, choosing the scenario and assigning the roles as he pleases, and drawing on the actors' skills to produce the finished result.

In the second case, working on an agreed subject, the whole company is the 'writer'. The director is the editor (and secretary) of a fully collaborative process; until, that is, the point is reached at which the work is to be scripted. At that point two things may happen. One is that some members of the cast will be mightily relieved to get back to something they feel secure with: a written script. The second is that the democratic process becomes again, by default, an autocratic one. The editorial voice becomes an authorial voice. This can be fine. It may be that the group wants this to happen. If it doesn't, then the only way to proceed is for the entire company to be involved in assembling the final script – a clumsy way of working sometimes, but often surprisingly fertile. Some writers are afraid of collaboration. It diminishes their sense of their own inviolably unique creativity. There is a very strong and pervasive myth that writing is a solitary vice (and, if you think that way, then that is what it becomes!). But theatre is a collaborative art.

The ultimate form of this is our third case, where the play is the result of a collaboration not just between the members of the acting ensemble before the public is admitted, but between the ensemble and the audience during performance.

This *may* be taken literally. The audience may be involved in shaping the play that it sees, offering suggestions, even taking roles. Or it may be left implicit, the collaboration one of mind and feelings as the actors shape their play in front of the audience, going along one pathway and abandoning others as they sense the mood of the spectators. Here the actors are truly creative, or

Table 1

EXERCISES AND ACTIVITIES

Preparation		Working together		Towards performance		Applied improvisation	
Activities	*Examples*	*Activities*	*Examples*	*Activities*	*Examples*	*Activities*	*Examples*
Relaxation	Tag Tai chi Yoga	Trust and respect	Trust circle Fish dives Blindfold	Senses	Blindfold Warm-up Massage	Who/where/what?	
					Trust games Journey	Objectives and Resistances	Intention Journey
Games and Body/think	With ball Fight in the Dark Grandma's Footsteps 'What are you doing?'	Group games Making a machine	Relay race Machine	Tenses	Presence	Point of concentration Memory	The party
		Showing and telling	Laughing snake Body sculptures Finding by sound Mime-stick			'Set'	
Space and movement	Laban Winearls	Entrances and exits		Objects	Naming Changing	Character	Previous circumstances
Concentration and attention	Circles of Attention Listening Observation	Meetings and greetings		Observation	Rhythms Gestures	Narrative	Stories Free association Lists Dreams Reincorporation
Impulses and directions	Starfish Change directions	'Blocking'	Use video Yes/yes but	Status	Master/servant		Trampoline words
				Masks	Neutral Expressive Larval *Commedia* Clown (red nose)		Collective writing

OBJECTIVES

Individual	Group		
Relax Tune-up Balance Feel Good Enjoy	Interactions Trust/support partners Encounter as dramatic structure Using anything	Confront inadequacies Extend body awareness Sharpen awareness of interaction Play with possibilities	Extend in time/space Incorporate/play/want Develop structures Link imagination and organisation Explore inner action Feel inner life
Begin individual 'unblocking'	Recognise mutual dependence	Discover performance dynamics	Develop organisational skills
Find mental/physical centredness	Extend sense of 'self'	Extend performance vocabulary	Work with complex structures
Establish self-confidence	Establish confidence in group		
Socialise	Overcome taboos	Liberate imagination	Build sequential performance

ACTIVE MEANINGS

Psychodynamics (individual)	Psychodynamics (group)	Text versus performance	Process of thinking
Play	Meaning as interchange	Signs and meanings	Hierarchies
Readiness/*Disponibilité*	Co-creativity	Multiplicity of possibility	
Mind/body relationship		Group creativity	Complex imaginative acts
Creativity	Form as process	Organic understanding	

rather *co-creative*. And here, truly, the improvised play becomes a paradigm of all theatrical experiences.

The skills and activities we have dealt with in this section promote qualities of focus, consistency and structure in both individual and communal improvised performance, and these qualities allow the performance to present character and narrative. At the same time it becomes clear that these are based on and emerge from the personal and group work outlined earlier, and can often profitably return to it. There is no fixed hierarchy in improvisation work, except in the sense that everything has to do with the enriching of *performance*: whether this is seen as individual realisation of action, expression and response; as a communal act of composition; as something shared with an audience; or as a celebration of the full resources of individual being and the ways they can be combined to create new patterns of significance.

Part III

Why? The Meaning(s) of Improvisation: Towards a Poetics

Introduction

We have looked at *who* improvises and at *what* they do. We need to understand the meaning of these acts for individuals, for performers and for society. Improvisation, like any physical or spoken act, necessarily produces meaning: indeed it may be said to be primarily a way of generating a plurality of meanings through performance. It can tell us a good deal about how we create meaning.

The practice of improvisation works initially to *free* the producer of meanings, both as an individual and in the network of relationships in which he or she operates, and to enable him or her to develop a larger 'vocabulary'. There are two main issues here: physical and psychological unblocking, which has both theatrical and paratheatrical implications for the quality of self, creativity, imagination and of relational acts between individuals and groups; and the acquisition of an enlarged range of communicative skills, which produce an extension of being, knowing and interacting.

Both these issues have important psychological, social and aesthetic implications for the nature of performative acts, the creation of form and the concept of 'play'.

Since meaning in improvisation is performative, we also need to consider the kinds of impact improvisation has upon the status of performance, its effects in terms of the relationship between performers, text and audience, and the possibility that it represents an 'alternative' theatrical tradition.

The sections which follow therefore examine how meanings are created, shifted, enriched or relocated through improvisation, and also reflect on the meaning of this process itself. They both implicitly and explicitly refer back to the examples of practitioners and practices presented in the preceding two parts.

Chapter 8

Enriching the Communication of Meaning

Communication involves a sender, a receiver and a message. If the message is to be as meaningful as possible, sender and receiver need to be as intelligent, sensitive, skilful and so on as possible. The basic requirement then is to unblock resistances, develop all kinds of responses and skills upon which personal and interpersonal behaviour depend. Many of the practices we have considered work to this effect. Their full implication can, however, be most usefully perceived in the light of paratheatrical and psychodramatic approaches. Developing the sender positively affects the quality of the message, and gives him more practical resources (verbal and physical imagination) in order to construct it. The vocabulary (sign-potential) of the communicative process is thus extended, as is its capacity to generate meaning.

Implications of psychodramatic and paratheatrical approaches

Improvisation activities help to discover, unblock, or tune up the psyche and the body, which evidently has implications for performance of any kind. Theatre can be a moral/political thermometer, or perhaps a tonic or an emetic: it is related to the health of a society, to the sense society makes of itself as an entity. The improvisatory act focuses on the gathering of energies, the freeing of possibilities of articulation, an alertness of giving and receiving, the establishment of connection. It, too, has to do with developing wholeness through developing the sense of self.

In psychotherapy, the 'protagonist' enacts his life-drama with or without the help of others, and may in the course of so doing reveal or give shape to fundamental situations, attitudes, complexes of which he or she may have been only dimly aware, or which taboos may have made it impossible to speak about directly.[1] This kind of activity can of course also be valuable in other, not specifically psychotherapeutic, contexts (for example, the use of role-play and simulation exercises in personal and professional development).

'Psychodrama' is related to a whole range of psychotherapeutic techniques which have as their aim the discovery, acknowledging and valuing of 'the whole person', of all aspects of the human being both individually and in all forms of relationship. There are generic similarities between psychodrama, mainly developed by J. L. Moreno, and, for instance, Jung's concept of 'integration', Maslow's 'self-actualisation' and Rogers's emphasis on 'client-centred' therapy. Therapy in general has become more eclectic, using techniques from a number of complementary approaches as appropriate, and one finds references to the same kinds of activity under different headings. Many approaches make considerable use of theatre games and impro exercises (for example, trust exercises, role-plays, mirroring) in addition to using active work with scenarios which involve the protagonist, and often the therapist as well, in 'improvising' his or others' roles in life-situations.

The formative historical link derives from Moreno, who adopted the Greek model of the protagonist aiming for catharsis through enactment. He constructed a number of theatres for the purpose: the first, built in Vienna in 1923, was called Das Stegreiftheater or Theatre of Spontaneity; he later opened an Impromptu Theater in Carnegie Hall, and his own Theater of Psychodrama at his Institute in Beaver, NY, in 1936.

To underline the link with improvisation it is sufficient to note that Moreno emphasised the following: play, sponta-neity, imagination, process, present moment, active relationship between 'protagonist' and 'audience'.[2] Psychodrama aims to enact psychological realities, including unexpressed and repressed material; movement, working through the body and unblocking are important features. The range of application stretches from mental and physical handicaps to personal and social dynamics.³

Psychodrama also represents a fascinating intercontextual area. Arising out of theatre work, it was developed as a form of group psychotherapeutic practice. Nowadays it is feeding back into theatre via drama training. Many drama schools and university drama departments include elements of psychodramatic technique in their training of the actor.

Impro and psychodrama are both about transforming what seems impossible, or inexpressible: disclosing it, not running away from it, releasing its negative or damming energy. The situations through which Grotowski or Johnstone or Lecoq take their 'players' are akin to the psychological (and maybe psychosocial) situation of not knowing who one is or how to go on. The aim is not necessarily the discovery of a single or stable self in the conventional sense; it may be more the activation of a range of possible roles and modes, the discovery of the ability to play with one's own life.

Bloński says of antagonism to Grotowski's theatre that it occurs because such a style of working 'opposes the ways of an age which prefers to change conditions rather than attitudes, circumstances rather than souls'.⁴ Improvisation, as it extends into the 'paratheatrical', may be a spearhead of methods of changing the environment from within, from the individual outwards.

But as well as the internal, psychological forms, the blockages or resistances have their external and political manifestations, as we shall see.

The censor's nightmare

The chief opponent of the improviser is not the writer of scripted drama; it is the censor. The antonym of 'improvisation' is 'censorship', because while improvisation represents the permission (and self-permission) for artistic expression, and the acceptance of one's own as well as others' creativity, censorship self-evidently stands for denial and refusal. This is true both literally and figuratively; and equally true whether the term refers to an external, political, public manifestation or to an internal, private and psychological process.

Impro has always been the censor's nightmare. The censor functions best when he deals with a precomposed, literary artefact

– ideally a manuscript. The censored manuscript of a poem or a novel can be delivered to the printer and the finished artwork disseminated in a controlled manner. Or it can be suppressed utterly, expunged from official culture (though it may appear in unofficial culture as samizdat).

But theatre has always been a problem area for the censors because of its immediacy and its dependence upon 'texts' other than those purely literary. (The insistence by some extreme critics of drama upon the primacy of the *literary* play-text plays into the hands of the censorious by denying theatre its flexibility, and its invaluable ability to *wriggle* out of tight corners.)

In fact, the 'text' of a play is rightly understood by the censor to include every word *and* every bit of business. The (mild, and often mildly absurd – if exasperating) censorship of British drama before 1968 is full of directives to cut stage business as well as the spoken part of the text (for example, 'there must be no scratching of private parts' – *Meals on Wheels*, Charles Wood; 'The statue of President Johnson must not be naked' – *Mrs Wilson's Diary*, Richard Ingrams and John Wells; 'It is understood that, wherever the word "shit" appears, it will be altered, in every case, to "it" ' – *Spare*, again by Charles Wood[5]). Thus the British censor (at that time, Lord Cobbold, the last Lord Chamberlain to act as censor) saw his function as extending to physical business, gestic props and scenery, and language.

The censor's nightmare is that, having licensed a play for performance, and thus given it official sanction, the performers will alter it in performance by improvising. They will make their own substitutions, deletions, insertions and restorations. Or they will introduce non-verbal elements which contradict the censor's intentions.

Joan Littlewood's Theatre Workshop, pioneer of improvisation, was singled out for prosecution in 1958 for the 'very wide divergence' between the text authorised by the Lord Chamberlain (at that time, the Earl of Scarbrough) and that actually experienced in the theatre. The prosecution (of *You Won't Always Be On Top*) succeeded, in that the company had to admit that, under the law, it was illegal to depart even in the slightest from the script as approved at St James's Palace, and, in fact, that whole new scenes and business had been added. The censor particularly objected to a new scene in which a mock opening ceremony was performed in a public lavatory, by an actor who vocally imitated

Sir Winston Churchill. (The censor's nightmare is made the more horrid by the awareness that even words that seem innocuous when read can be loaded in performance with satirical – even political – weight by the actor's choice of speech pattern.) In this case, the defendants pleaded guilty, and were given a nominal fine – less than £17 including costs. The case, in fact, gave Stratford East some good publicity, and brought the stupidity of the Lord Chamberlain's office to public notice:

> If the Lord Chamberlain's aim was to warn Joan Littlewood of the error of her ways – which included an impatient belief in improvisation as the basis of the actor's art – it is unlikely to have succeeded. . . . But under the Act (Theatres Act, 1843) which he is required to administer, improvisation is illegal; and the ban on it was spotlighted in 1962 when the cast of the American revue *The Premise* were discovered by the Chamberlain's Office to be acting unlicensed material every night and were ordered to stop – after they had been improvising (or, at any rate, had *announced* they were doing it) for four months.[6]

Richard Findlater obviously does not himself share Joan Littlewood's or *The Premise*'s belief in improvisation, but he does point out the difficulty here. Technically, improvisation has only been possible *on stage* in Britain since 1968 (though, of course, no such restrictions applied to rehearsals). This was another reinforcement of what we have called (in Part I above) the 'traditional' use of improvisation. But it's also true that the act of improvisation was seen by many as subversive in itself, and allied to subversive politics.

Littlewood's Theatre Workshop, which had grown out of the subsoil of early English political theatre (such as Unity Theatre, and before that the Manchester 'Red Megaphone' performances of Ewan MacColl), was avowedly left wing. There's nothing left or right wing about improvisation *per se*, but as a challenge to the dominant cultural assumptions about what is 'the basis of the actor's art', and an attack on received notions of the figure of 'the artist', the adoption of impro as a method of play creation becomes a political act in itself. It de-emphasises the individual writer, and privileges the creative ensemble – the workshop, with all its connotations of crafts and working-class skills.

The political climate that obtained in Britain in the aftermath of World War Two (the period which saw the downfall of the post-war Labour government of Attlee and the 'thirteen years of Tory mis-rule' up to 1964, with the Suez débâcle in 1956) was one of increasing disillusionment. The expansion of public education (in the wake of the Butler Act of 1944), allied to the growth of the new communication media, created a public increasingly at odds with its actual situation. Protest was in the air, especially young protest. The prime examples are the early Aldermaston marches. Protest had a literature, exemplified by writers such as Colin Wilson, Kingsley Amis, and the borrowed writings of Jack Kerouac and Allen Ginsberg. John Osborne gave it a dramatic literature. It found its own proper musical form. It found an affinity with the free, improvised art of jazz.

This was the British 'Jazz Age'. Jazz spoke to the condition of the time; it celebrated individual creativity under a mantle of technique worn so loosely as to seem invisible. It was 'free-form' – seemingly free, that is, of the restriction of externally imposed forms. It was suitably classless (or at least, not associated with ruling-class taste). It was American (when that was still good) and not stuffily British. It had energy, rhythm, beat – life. And a less intellectually pretentious form of jazz, skiffle, with its improvised instruments, brought out the beat in people who had hitherto never dreamed that they could make music – laying the foundations for the Dionysian explosion of rock music in the 1960s.

In the same way, theatrical improvisation can be assimilated to the same current of growing political discontent. Littlewood's work at Stratford East is exemplary. And the battle against censorship, which reached its climax at the Royal Court in the mid-1960s, was also the battle for the freedom to create appropriate artistic as well as political forms.

Keith Johnstone's Theatre Machine was born in that climate. Johnstone's *Clowning* show for the Royal Court Studio had to be presented officially as a lecture-demonstration. It could not *be* a play, because it was improvised and, as we have seen, that contravened official notions of what a play might be, as well as what it might be about. The Royal Court won the battle to allow Edward Bond's passionate political plays to be staged as their author intended: but the same victory equally made possible

Bond's mentor and friend Keith Johnstone's future creative development.

Under the censor, improvisation was condemned to remain a rehearsal device: as a performance tool, or even style, it was forced to remain an academic exercise – a lecture-demonstration not a play. Like other banned forms, an improvised play could have been put on in a theatre constituted as a private club. This loophole permitted censored plays to exist on the same terms – and with much the same status – as strip-tease acts in Soho. But it also meant that the creators of such works were forced to accept constraint upon their professional lives. The work could not transfer, could not make money, could not support the company. Under the censor, to commit oneself to a vision of a theatre based on improvisation was a remarkable act of faith.

In America, the process of censorship was different. Political censorship of the stage did not take the same form: the stage was controlled well enough without an overt censor. The Premise (a New York offshoot of Chicago's The Compass) might, indeed, have been freer to perform on Shaftesbury Avenue than on Broadway. Second City's first transfer to New York was aborted by the commercial management of the theatre. Improvised material, they feared, would never sell: or it might be scurrilous stuff which would alienate their traditional clientele – like Lenny Bruce's jokes. When they eventually realised that Chicago audiences had seen this material and not been corrupted, and that New York audiences also enjoyed it, then they were happy to tempt Mike Nichols and Elaine May away from Compass/Second City/Chicago to the Big Apple big-time. The triple censorships of trivialisation, commercialisation and assimilation naturally determined the shape of the material they would present.

At the other extreme, the recent experiences of Teatr Osmego Dnia (The Theatre of the Eighth Day) in Poland demonstrate that improvisation may be the best way for a company of artists to function in a repressive situation. Osmego Dnia began in Poznan in 1964, and at first modelled themselves on Grotowski's Laboratory work before finding their own distinctive style which, although still concerned with the exploration of theatre language, is more consciously political. Tadeusz Janiszewski, one of the actors, explains:

After 1976 we had more and more trouble from the security services. It was the year of the founding of KOR – the Committee
for the Defence of the Workers [punished for the riots in Radom
and Warsaw] – and we never tried to hide our sympathies.[7]

The theatre group was not allowed to disseminate information
about itself, to perform in some cities (especially Warsaw) or to
travel abroad. They were actively harassed by the security services,
and dragged for five years through the courts on trumped-up
fraud charges. Two members were imprisoned briefly. Their
1984 production *Absinthe* was based on the farcical but sinister
events of that period. By the end of the 1970s (and before the
upsurge of Solidarity in 1980), most other radical Polish groups
had either retreated into naturalism or abstracted themselves from
the political situation by doing laboratory research work. Osmego
Dnia were virtually the only company still involved in activist
theatre. Their relation to the censoring authorities is described
by Janiszewski:

> You have a special performance for one person, the censor.
> A scenario has to be submitted too. . . . But it is possible to
> outmanoeuvre the censor, particularly when there's consider-
> able improvisation. We've been developing our own creative
> method since 1973, based on improvisation.[8]

In Poland, the 'censoring authorities' can also include the
Catholic Church. When censorship is at its most repressive,
the theatre may have to abandon everything and return to the
improvising actor's starting place – the street and the crowd.

> [In August 1983] we predicted that we would not be able to
> get spaces for performing and started to think about working in
> the street. It's not easy in Poland, it can always be considered a
> demonstration, which is why we used the International Festival
> of Street Theatre in Jelenia Gora. . . . It gave us a chance to
> cheat censorship and play officially without police intervention.[9]

La disponibilité

Availability – openness – readiness – acceptance: the precon-
dition of creativity. It implies not resisting, but flowing *with*
the world and the self. It implies (to us) nakedness, but not

(strangely) defencelessness. The performer is without *armour*, but not without *weapons*: such as wit, agility, mobility and inventiveness. He or she is resource-full. *Disponibilité* is the state of 'armed neutrality' from which all movements are equally possible.

For Lecoq is is a state of calmness, of balance, in which the readiness is all. The performer (most pointedly in improvisation) is always ready, always aware and always able to respond: he or she is 'rendered open to what is happening in a situation, a gesture, a word . . . the imagination provoked to the invention of languages'.[10]

By 'open to what is happening' ('disponible à l'événement') we believe Lecoq infers open to all the processes which compose the situation, on all levels. It is a state in which the truth is revealed, not covered up by tricks. By 'the invention of languages' ('provoquant son imagination à inventer des langages') we understand him to mean that the actor is stimulated to create as many types of response to the truth of that situation, gesture or word as are appropriate. The 'languages' may be gestural, vocal or purely tactile, but they give truthful expression to the moment and whatever it holds.

Disponibilité sums up in a single term the condition improvisers aspire to. It offers a way of describing an almost intangible and nearly undefinable state of being: having at (or in) one's fingertips, and any other part of the body, the capacity to do and say what is appropriate, and to have the confidence to make the choice. It's a kind of total awareness, a sense of being at one with the context: script, if such there be, actors, audience, theatre space, oneself and one's body.

For Grotowski, technique is not abstract or external: it is how the body accedes to its own resources; how it discovers that it can be, say, do, understand and transmit – with and to anything and anyone. The bodily condition in which that capacity is touched is a tensed and balanced orderliness which – like an act of love, Grotowski says – is not closed off from anything.

Disponibilité is an appropriate word for this condition, for several reasons. It is an alien word, which means it is totally without misleading connotations in English. Just as, for example, Roger Caillois used Greek nouns to define the various types of play activity,[11] we feel we can usefully borrow this French word to suggest the *condition* the improviser seeks to discover and maintain.

Disponibilité suggests not just a theory but an experiential condition; a way of being which can be sought and found. It is a condition of being *centred* (in oneself) and balanced, ready to go in any appropriate direction. We might translate it as *neutrality*, but in English this has unfortunate connotations of asensuality and of being disengaged (like a car – idling, without purpose). *Disponibilité* suggests a charged and sensual state: Gide relates it to a process of coming-to-be-aware of the body. In this state the actor is fully inhabiting the world outside and the world within his body. He is 'neutral' only in the sense that he is *poised* between all possibilities. *Openness* might be a better English equivalent, but openness may also suggest passivity. *Disponibilité* doesn't suggest a passive, purely receptive state.[12] It is armed, pregnant with possibilities. If offers (especially in Gide's use of the term) the implication of sensory, even sensual, alertness. For Gide it is often related to the *puer* figure (a representation more of psychic adventurousness and youthfulness than a homoerotic ideal) and to the idea of awakening, of discovering a path in life.[13] It carries the sense of becoming aware of oneself and one's possibilities; aware of having *choice*. It represents the power to *dispose* of oneself and one's activity. As such, it is pre-eminently the condition of existentialism.

Disponible suggests, then, that the performer can dispose, can choose, can act. It suggests sensory alertness, even sensual alertness. The whole being is opened to the moment. And the moment of performance includes the audience. Stanislavsky enjoins the actor to keep his intentions 'this side of the footlights', and Grotowski, following Osterwa, warns against 'publicotropism'. But we are not talking of exhibitionism. That puts the audience into the role of unwilling voyeur – a sterile encounter. The improviser accepts (and shares creativity with) the audience. Like a flower turning towards the sun ('phototropism'), the performer naturally and organically includes the audience. The organism seeking to propagate itself seeks the condition in which creativity will come. And such a condition attracts stimuli to itself. By turning to the sun the flower not only absorbs warmth and light, but also become reflective: its pigmentation is enhanced by light, it glows and becomes visibly more present. That increases its chances of being selected by a bird or insect and hence increases its prospects of being fertilised. *Disponibilité* attracts creative impulses just as a flower attracts what it needs; a butterfly to be briefly ensnared and then released again into the commonwealth of flowers, bearing on its dusted wings the seeds of creation. As *art* it may be chancy, less certain of success than other methods; but it is close to the condition sought for by Rilke, a kind of tuning-in to organic form. As such, it may be the only way to arrive at genuinely new insights: it is less likely to leave anything out; it doesn't force the pace or the pattern; it has more chance of avoiding the trap of cliché. Emerson, Kleist and Rilke were all attracted by the notion of *falling* – an acceptance of natural law perhaps. (Curiously, German has *es fällt mir ein* – literally, 'it falls into me' – for what in English we might render as 'come to think of it', or 'it strikes me', or perhaps even 'I've got it!'). Being in that state includes the patience that can wait for the full emergence of the event. As Paul Valéry puts it:

> Chaque atome de silence
> Est la chance d'un fruit mûr!
> (Each atom of silence
> Is the chance of a ripe fruit!)[14]

Pregnant, the condition teems with creative possibilities. It is pregnant in the sense that it is the condition of wanting/waiting to give birth to something alive and new. It taps the creativity that is already there, dormant: not a passive 'waiting for something' but an active 'lying in wait'.[15]

It is a condition of relaxed awareness where one does not need to *impose* order on the external world or on the imagination: order is found *in* the world and in the imaginative response to others. One does not need to deny the ordering intelligence, the analytical self. Rather, that self takes its proper place. One does not need to subjugate the mind: the mind knows when not to dominate, and the body knows when to be still as well as when to move. For Lecoq (the body learning to think), *disponibilité* is a natural condition, harmoniously accepted; for Grotowski (the analytical brain learning to move) it is a condition sought through pain and denial. They are moving towards the same point; but they are coming from different worlds.

Disponibilité is a condition of responsiveness, but it isn't

passive reception. It implies *giving* as much as receiving.
Reciprocal giving between two or more *disponible* creators
(one is reminded here of the North American Indian custom of
potlatch in which individuals and whole communities compete in
giving) opens up a truly new form of artistic creativity. We have
seen how, for example, the clown gives to his partner on stage,
or how the improviser passes *élan* to his fellow actor in order
to make things possible for both of them, or how the failure
to do this destroys the possibility of creation. When the blocks
are removed, and when the giving is reciprocal, the result is a
creativity shared by both the performers and the audience. As
'art' it is unpredictable, momentary, unreflexive and dynamic. If
it descends into trickery – if it ceases to be true – then it closes
itself off and ceases to be *available* to all its potential creators. It
becomes privatised; it reverts to personal (rather than communal)
creativity which denies the possibility of *mutual* discovery. It
becomes transmission/reception; it reasserts the passivity of the
spectator, forcing him to relapse again into consumerism. That
is why the good theatre clown withholds his prepared routine
for as long as possible: once he begins to present his prepared
material he ceases to *play* with the audience, and reverts to the
role of hired entertainer. When the clown and the audience are
improvising together, stimulating each other, *encountering* one
another, the pleasure is doubled.

Transformation

Among her 'triggers of transformative experiences', Marilyn
Ferguson includes 'improvisational theater, with its requirement of
both total attention and spontaneity, [and] Psychodrama, because
it forces an awareness of roles and role-playing.'[16] This appears in
a list of 'psychotechnologies' which includes mental (meditative)
and physical (*Tai Chi Chuan*, Alexander) techniques, therapies,
self-help and mutual-help networks and programmes, and various
'shamanic and magical techniques'. The function of all these is to
shift awareness beyond Watts's 'skin-encapsulated ego'[17] to open
up new possibilities of being. Many of the methods she mentions
figure in drama school activities.

Abraham Maslow's list of the criteria for 'self-actualising'
people (in *Toward a Psychology of Being*[18]) includes the following:

- More efficient perception of reality. 'Self-actualised' people
  are not afraid of the unknown and can tolerate the doubt,
  uncertainty and tentativeness accompanying the perception
  of the new and unfamiliar.
- Acceptance of self, others and nature.
- Spontaneity. Freshness of appreciation.
- Problem-centring (that is, they attend to present business;
  they have a sense of responsibility).
- Autonomy.
- Empathy, sympathy, compassion.
- Unhostile sense of humour.

Many of these might be taken as goals for improvisation
work, and are developed through the games and exercises
discussed earlier. Like the 'new age' characteristics mentioned
above, they indicate a context to improvisation which extends
beyond the theatre. At its basis is a concern with development,
both personal and interpersonal.

Fritjof Capra points out that shamanism – which has much to
do with the origins of theatre – operates within a framework which
sees 'human beings as integral parts of an ordered system'.[19] The
distinction Capra notes between shamanism and psychotherapy
(the former treats *communities*, the latter helps people to
establish personal myths) is interestingly and profitably blurred
in improvisation and theatre work, which can thus be read as
means of relating wholeness to wholeness: individual to group
and context, actors to audience, imaginative evocation of myth
as personal and communal experience.

Improvisation frequently has to do with breaking down barriers.
Our conscious, rationalising ego operates within boundaries which
afford security of behaviour and identity, and are useful in many
contexts. But boundaries also inhibit, and the kind of 'lateral
thinking' which arrives at new insights is precisely an example
of the value of bypassing them and discovering a new shape to
knowledge and experience. Improvisation in one sense is about
'lateral being', if you like; about allowing and encouraging this
productive 'digression' with as much of the organism as possible.
One result is to permit subliminal or subconscious material to
surface, to make use of the sudden crazy idea, to allow a sequence
of action or speech to develop from a sensation or bodily position.
This can be both frighteningly insecure (the comfortable limits of

'who/what/why' are left behind – and frighteningly chaotic. But in profitable use it is both a discipline in itself and a means of exploring extra possibilities of synthesis. Jung and others suggest that the use and incorporation of subconscious psychic activity (dreams, fantasies and so on) is not irrelevant or narcissistic, but a way of drawing on a different and perhaps more extensive kind of knowing. Improvisation may also frequently work by sudden symbolic associations, or make logical leaps; and it often (like some kinds of comedy) appeals to an audience precisely because it stimulates the ability to function likewise. It becomes an exciting game, and in so doing it *makes sense* in another, not merely logico-rational way.

Grotowski, too, sensed that what is occurring in the intense work on the authenticity of self – which in his process has of necessity to be unscripted and non-externally directed – is an encounter with these at first dim, often uncomfortable and confusing forms of knowing and being. But the belief is that pursuing them can result in a more total and organic awareness and a freer capacity for action. As opposed to the behaviourist model, which may underlie ideas of 'building a character' (though it is clear that the best practice goes beyond this narrow version, see our comments on Stanislavsky and Leigh in Part I), we are here at root concerned with a 'humanistic' or post-Jungian framework which proposes that full human performance involves the acknowledgement of areas beyond the everyday scope of consciousness. Awakening these may require a passage through confusion and unknowing, and through a loss of identity as commonly conceived (as with Masks). It is no accident that theoretical and textual theatrical visions of recent decades (Artaud, Beckett) have aimed at a parallel exploration or explosion of the limits of language, self and their accepted configuration. Modernist and Post-Modernist art of all genres, plus associated theory, has often featured 'difficulty': paradox, lack of conventional plots and characters, frequent digressions. 'Reading' and understanding has become a challenging and perhaps dangerous business, precisely because the act of arriving at a new framework or symbolic nexus is – like reading metaphysical poetry and like the creating of works of art – one which involves a splitting apart and reconstituting of the self in its articulation as word and image. Learning to accept a feeling of loss is an essential part of the process.

This requires a different, and difficult, kind of discipline.

Grotowski and his actors have not drawn back from the demands, but the same assumption underlies the work of Copeau, Johnstone, Maude-Roxby, Lecoq and others. It again to some extent accounts for the slight messianic flavour, and from one angle one might say that they all regard their work both as education and as exploration. In this 'spiritual' or therapeutic context improvisation is part of the contemporary version of the myth of Quest (with a firmly internalised Grail). That is why, ultimately, performance for Grotowski is a sacrificial act, and why it must inevitably also lead beyond performance within the theatre. It means stripping away all pretence, all easily imitated forms of behaviour, all 'acting'. Grotowski also rejected the label 'improvisation' where it might be thought to equate with a lapse into a vague notion of spontaneity or the imitation of 'primitive' behaviour. He preferred to call his preparatory work 'studies' or 'sketches', and emphasised that they involved intense discipline and a concern for conscious realisation of structure; aiming at a blend, or *conjunctio oppositorum*, of spontaneity and discipline which to him seemed to fuse the best from the Stanislavskian and the Brechtian/Meyerholdian approaches. Grotowski is interested in identifying and confronting the situations in which we put up blockages, whereas a loose belief in spontaneity would fail to confront them and prefer the comfort of the known.

The boundaries of self, others and otherness begin to come into play here. For instance, R. D. Laing's gloss on Sartre's use of role, image and authenticity picks up the sense in which recognition of *another* is also acknowledgement of repressed (Freud) or 'shadow' (Jung) aspects of the self. We identify ourselves partly by contradistinction – I am *not* that – but to some extent this masks the reality that I am *also* that.

The 'recognition scene' is one of drama's stocks-in-trade – sometimes profound as in the moments of *anagnorisis* in Greek tragedy, often comic, but always involving a shock and relativisation of the notion of self. The shock is something like that in an 'Aha' experience: sudden conscious appreciation of something you 'knew' at a more intuitive level. It's an articulation of organic knowledge – another possible definition of theatre – which is experienced as a gasp, a gape or a gap: a momentary burst of just awareness, without as yet a clearly defined content to give it specific shape. You are blasted out of your mental set (which is what the blasted heath does to Macbeth!), no longer

what you thought you knew, but more a prelude to knowing –
like going down in a lift suddenly.

The recognition process, therefore, involves a *stopping* or
unseating, a prising-loose from former bounds of identity which
is uncomfortable, or puzzling, or exciting, or all three. It is
essentially a challenge and a proposal: a challenge to find the
context, the mental and physical resources, to cope with the new
situation; a proposal that the very gasp of recognition implies that
those resources are available, if as yet undefined.

Sartre's characters are often like reluctant improvisers who
spend all their time denying the possibility that they might
be different, preferring to hide behind a familiar and usually
flattering (or at least not too damaging) image which they try
to project. This image is always carefully preserved and yet
less consciously chosen than they like to think: it functions as
a protective screen for things they don't want others to reveal
to them, for *les autres* always serve as mirrors, although by no
means mirrors which don't lie, since they have reasons of their
own for what they reflect. This kind of hide-and-seek proposes
a whole web of inauthenticity, and its perpetrators are castigated
by Sartre as *salauds* – both cowardly and devious. Others are
a threat precisely because they represent this potential offer of
knowledge which one is desperate to barricade oneself against.
They are shunned or attacked because characters are unwilling to
take up the challenge to confront more of themselves. Excluding
the other or defining oneself against him/her is therefore a way
of denying the full possibility of self: role becomes a refuge for
the insecure (actor or person).

Improvisation, then, requires a courage which enables you
to get *out* of role – although you may then be able to get
back *into* it later – and discover other resources which you
didn't 'know' you had. That is never an easy option. One of
the most difficult improvisatory tasks for any actor is the basis of
Lecoq-style clowning as mediated by Clive Mendus. Coming on
stage as yourself, with no other resources available, is intensely
vulnerable, especially as any 'acting' is immediately 'drummed off'.
I Gelati's work with masks similarly transfixes any inauthenticity
(masks readily reveal discrepancies between body and gesture or
speech) by insisting on maintaining *presence* and input of energy.
Maude-Roxby's work, too, is about being fully present, working
off whatever is there, being prepared to respond and go with

whatever comes up. There's nowhere to hide in the face of this scrutiny of presence. Any slip into a familiar – learned or practised – response is a give-away.

Absence of strict form is here only apparent: it is a way of escaping from the fixed, the *a priori*, the already done, the dead and the repetitive. Accepting and *staying with* the state of not knowing 'who' or 'what' is a quite precise step towards activating a degree of present awareness, which is ready to sense and respond to a more coherent and extensive range of sensation, intuition and expression.

This is an authenticity of being which acknowledges that I am what I am in the present moment, and is prepared to keep that open for scrutiny rather than cloaked in a role. It acknowledges too that the present includes the full range of the 'past'; both in the historical/genealogical sense and in terms of 'buried' psychic material (for Grotowski this material is overtly that of the levels of collective consciousness of a community, nation or generation). I cannot be fully present unless I own that range of experience as fully as possible in my body.

There is a sense, then, in which memory is important in improvisation: not so much the deliberate memory of events (what Proust calls 'voluntary memory') as the memory of a bodily configuration, of the way something occurs and how it feels. This kind of memory is more sensory than intellectual, more an organic occurrence. Activating it means opening up the *faculty* of memory, the ability to remember process rather than event, the kind of total memory which Proust names 'involuntary'.

To be authentic is to be in touch with oneself in this extended sense, which is an opening to one's own life and to levels where it may touch on or merge with the life of others. That is why a great deal of creative energy can be liberated in this kind of work: energy which derives not from 'inspiration' in the clichéd sense of external aid, but from a breathing-in, a being in-tune with, one's own powers as a human being.

The openness of this condition is risky: risky to achieve, and risky in that it is always improvising – never static. Form is dynamic, the self in its articulation is always in the flow of change and needs to adjust to it. Stasis is death and stultification, in self-satisfaction at the 'right' action, word or image; what is crystallised soon becomes brittle. In Tom Stoppard's *Rosencrantz and Guildenstern are Dead* the Player says:

Why, we grow rusty and you catch us at the very point of decadence. By this time tomorrow night we might have forgotten everything we ever knew. That's a thought, isn't it. We'd be back where we started – improvising.[20]

Perhaps then, historically and essentially, improvisation is the basis of all theatre, and of the creation of a role or a life. 'Forgetting' at that 'point of decadence' may also be the very mechanics by which we gain access to 'everything we ever knew'.

What these perspectives have enabled us to discover is therefore a vital shift in the sense of self and in its function. They start with work which allows a freer sense of (*meaning for*) *self*; offer ways of 'unblocking', both in the personal and psychological sense, and in the social, political sense; move towards an awareness that *self is a capacity for generating* a plurality of *meaning*; and establish this as a directable *voluntary* operation through which self ceases to be merely the passive receptacle of deterministic influences and opinions and becomes a *productive agent*. By passing through the condition which Lecoq and Copeau identify as neutrality, Grotowski as disarmament, the self is prised free of its encrustation in habitual role, and becomes an active producer of its own meaning.

Under the influence of the improvisatory, self may thus begin to redefine itself: it is liberated both psychologically and semiotically. As it participates more effectively in the making of meaning, it is no longer so limited and closed off in solipsistic regard. It begins to operate as a generator of relationships; that is to say it becomes active in the context (environment), a vital part of processes of exchange. All of this can be seen as important for individual behaviour and for what happens in a theatre between actors and each other and actors and audience. This relocation of the self within the 'community' illustrates an important set of meanings for the 'wholeness' referred to earlier.

An extension of relating and communicating occurs through the medium of a sign system. The acquisitioon of extra sign-potential parallels the freeing of physical and mental capacities and is the means by which they are realised or actualised. In an important way, improvisatory practice enhances the languages available to the performer. Lecoq calls this 'provoking the imagination to invent languages'. If you can do things you couldn't (or daren't) do before, you can now *say* things thereby which you formerly could not articulate.

Since improvisation clearly has to do with the extension of knowledge of the self, and with the deploying of its resources in action, it is not surprising that it has found a place in education. Not merely in drama schools and on drama courses, where it can (though not always does) play a vital role, but also in 'Theatre in Education' (the use of drama, sometimes partly or wholly improvised, to bring to life any appropriate classroom study), in language learning and as a means of facilitating communicative skills. Its uses here have been dealt with by others, but it is worth pointing out that in these contexts, improvisation is not seen as something sloppy. It has a clearly understood contribution to make within certain parameters.

We have already indicated the kind of disciplined attention which Grotowski, Lecoq, Johnstone and others require. Improvisations can degenerate into loose and purposeless meandering or self-indulgence. But not if the participants are enabled to experience for themselves that what they are acquiring is the ability to use and direct the emergence of form. That means having a clear understanding and purpose to activity and maintaining critical alertness throughout. If the *process* is clearly understood (by teacher and/or participant, depending on the kind of activity and the stage it has reached) then there will be a framework which enables one to decide when to let things develop and when to intervene. Used in this way, improvisation can become a means of experiencing crucial processes of choice in the construction of any creative work.

Such a view is supported by the argument (an extension of the knowing-through-doing proposition) that drama in itself offers 'a complementary way of knowing'.[21] The view is advanced in slightly different ways by Keith Johnstone in *Impro* and John Hodgson and Ernest Richards in *Improvisation*. The theme in all cases is that improvisation in particular and drama in general can stimulate ways of experiencing, participating, analysing and understanding which more formal and conventional methods of teaching fail to arouse.

Jon Nixon, in an article in *New Theatre Quarterly*,[22] suggests that drama in education can be seen as *social interaction* (developing ways of exploring feelings, of imaginative insight into situations); as *discourse* (opening up ways of using language);

and as *cognition* (emphasising the *process* of knowing as a move through experiencing towards understanding). He gives examples of small and large group improvised activities which develop these aspects. Clearly, role-plays, scenarios, debates, various forms of historical and social reconstruction and so on are relevant: they are often used in classroom activity and form part of the repertoire of many TIE companies. In addition, improvisation, if it does extend knowing, does so because it unblocks inhibitions and prejudices, encourages participation and learning to take responsibility, enhances observation and body awareness, and develops verbal, tactile and other physical skills – it makes use of the whole body as a resource of channels of sensitivity and response, intelligence and insight, expression and articulation. Perhaps, even more than that, it is often fun, and it is rewarding because students experience doing something which makes sense of themselves in relation to an aspect of their world: it offers direct contextualisation of knowledge in a way which relates the individual to the environment and gives him a sense of beginning to come to terms with it.

All the functions of improvisation which have emerged from this discussion indicate that it has to do with the extension of being, knowing and communicating. None of these occurs entirely at random. The freeing, recognising and activating of personal resources requires a precise discipline.

As so often, Grotowski provides a way into one of the key problems concerned with the nature of improvisatory acts, both in and outside the theatre. He marked a crucial development in his career by a shift in style as director, becoming less *directive* and more responsive (this followed his third visit to India, from where he returned looking and dressing different). The Teatr Laboratorium's work became increasingly more exploratory and open ended after this point, less controlled by a strong directorial concept.

On one level this may appear to represent a move away from any kind of disciplined purpose, analogous to woolly ideas about the 'creative' value of so-called 'free improvisation' in educational theory of a certain era. However, as we have noted frequently both with reference to Grotowski and to other uses of improvisatory strategy (in Mask work, in Mike Leigh's controlled development of a script or in the highly alert interaction of therapist and client, for example), it is always the case that very intense discipline on the part of both guide and guided is integral to the process of exploration of these areas of awareness and performance, which are always new, and often very challenging or frightening. Improvisation is not for the feeble-hearted and it is not about avoiding challenges – certainly Grotowski and his company are the last people one could charge with that.

Indiscipline, both psychologically and aesthetically, represents a lack of respect for form. But form is neither preserved nor promoted by rigidifying or encapsulating it, because it is a dynamic occurrence. A more responsive attitude may be more responsible precisely because it recognises the growth potential of form.

In one sense, you can't train people to improvise. But you can train them to set up the conditions in which improvisation can begin; you can assist them to recognise what inhibits it and to have the courage to face up to those blocks; you can get them to play, to enjoy, to let go, and to learn to work with focused but not cramped attentiveness from that state. Such a form of training is most demanding and least coercive, because it leaves the responsibility for how far the process goes and for what emerges from it with the performer.

Chapter 9

Meaning and Performance

Improvisation promotes the capacity for creating meanings. Those meanings are created in performance, as a process occurring in the present moment. We now turn to some ways in which improvisation illuminates the nature of performative acts: how it amends, revises or interferes with the meanings they appear to offer, how it may interact with texts of various kinds, and how it may suggest alternative models or roles for performance (particularly of theatre) in the context of society.

Some aspects of meaning in performance

Improvisation underlies and underlines the fact that meaning is created in performance as the collision or negotiation of different sets of meaning: that, for instance, which appears to reside in the 'text' and that which individual performers perceive and/or mediate; that which the audience expects and that which they receive; and so on. Julian Hilton notes that performance involves (a) incarnation and transmutation, and (b) execution and origination.[1] All of these features are *processes*; that is to say, they are ongoing and open ended. They involve a change of state and the creation of something new. Improvisation contains all of them, but is particularly strong in terms of the second element of each pair. However, that element depends for its realisation upon the first, as for example Lecoq would stress that forms of play must be enacted physically. The integrative ('body-think') function of improvisation links the two terms in each pair, thus ensuring that performance is highly dynamic and rich in potential meanings. It articulates changes of statement through changes of the state of the performer. Since, as we have noted with reference to the 'message' content of communication, the quality and significance of the communicative act depends on the condition of the actor/communicator (and on that of the responder/receiver), the ability of improvisation work to produce a charged-up condition makes the communicative and performative act much more potentially resonant; it carries an increased capacity for meaning, which in effect means additional levels or possibilities of significance are opened up.

The integrative condition sought by impro work is an organic balance, an ease of performance ('free play' in both the mechanical and the aesthetic sense) which may indeed be 'natural', but is not at all 'everyday'. It represents a highly tuned level of activity which invites or stimulates the further integration of performer and audience.

Improvisation also points up another feature of performative acts, namely that each is quite *different* from every other. No two appearances wearing the red nose are the same, nor do they develop the same sequence of events.

Thus all improvised acts can be defined as *integrative*, yet each is also both *specific*, defining itself by its own parameters (for example, its own who/what/why?) and *polysemantic*. This curious and powerful combination may indicate why the experience of performance created in the present can have such wide-ranging effects.

The development of multiple significance is responsible for much of the richness which emerges from performance. One major way in which improvisation can affect this is through *interfering* with what appears to be the established sequence and expectation of meaning: not merely as occasional serendipity or brilliant ad-lib, but as a constant readiness to challenge 'the rules of the game'.

Texts, signs and meaning

The changing nature of 'text' is an important issue in the kind of meaning implied by the improvisatory style.

Partly because of the inability to record performance (even the act of recording, on film or videotape, crucially alters the nature of the original transaction and so alters its meaning), and partly because of the historically determined primacy of the written word in our culture, the play text, rather than performance, has become the focus of historical and critical speculation. Most of the theatrical events which give us the greatest pleasure and stimulation have begun as a written text, the personal creation of an individual mind. It is the basis upon which the actors, technicians and directors come together to work. After the completion of a production the published text can, of course, be used to generate new performances.

The written text, the script of the play, does not, however, always precede the performance. Nor can it convey half the complexity of the finished production: the multiplicity of signs which communicate[2] (though they need the active decoding of alert receivers). These include set, make-up, masks, movement, gesture, spatial relationships, vocal inflexion and so on.

The process of reading theatrical or *performance* text, however, is central to our understanding of how improvisation works. Semiotic analysis can illuminate difficult areas for us. It can remind us of two things: one, that the improvising performer is continuously and spontaneously generating information on many levels (much of which is unconscious); two, that the process does not only involve a 'sender' and a 'receiver' (an 'active' performer and a 'passive' spectator). The spectator is active, too – and more than usually so when watching something improvised. The act of decoding information implies the creation of new, often unsuspected or unintended meanings out of the signals received. The audience does not only 'read' the performance – in a very real sense it 'writes' it, too.[3]

The shamanic performer's Mask, for example, activates what Charles Sanders Peirce referred to as the 'triadic' system of signs. By being *there*, physically present amongst the audience, and by feeding the audience with simultaneous *iconic*, *indexical* and *symbolic* information, the Mask makes the dissolution of the boundary between the actual and the virtual possible. An 'icon' is a sign that is similar to what it represents (the masked actor looks like the imagined demon or god – colourful, impressive, larger than life, inhuman; the Mask purports to be, and is assumed to be, an image, a likeness of the spirit). An 'index' is a sign that points to other realities (the Mask points to the godliness of the performer). A 'symbol' is a sign bearing imputed, learned associations (the colour red stands for the demonic, for example, or green for heroism). The audience understands, or at least mentally operates on all three levels simultaneously. So the shamanic Mask enables the spectator to apprehend the intended meaning, and also to create that meaning. For, in truth, the performer has to do very little but to be there.[4] The spectator is the active partner: he is the one generating the meaning, the one 'writing' the play as it happens.[5]

The Mask is 'read from', and is also 'written to'. And, in primitive societies particularly, the meaning that is 'read' and 'written' in this way is of vital importance, for it concerns the belief system which underpins the whole community.

The information set supplied (meaning the totality of words, sounds, movements, colours, textures and proxemics) depends for its transmission upon there being a parallel set within the mind of the spectator. This second set is a matrix of language, associations, memories and images which enables the received information to be simultaneously contextualised and recontextualised. It is the interaction of these two complementary sets – their collision, or fusion perhaps, sometimes called by semioticians 'intertextuality' (Arthur Koestler refers to it as creative 'bisociation'[6]) – that creates both purpose and meaning, charging the event with significance.

What such semiotic investigations do is to indicate the complexity of a 'text', and of the processes by which is is 'read'. In recent times, the term 'text' has shifted its emphasis, and study of textual *variations* (a well-established academic activity) has become a means of appreciating the *relativity* of the text even in its written form: neither language nor its users are static. Much contemporary literary theory (deriving from linguistics) emphasises the arbitrary nature of linguistic acts, and a major theme in modern writing, including drama, is the impossibility of saying what you mean, or of saying anything meaningful at all (Pirandello, Beckett, Pinter, for example). Derrida says in one word (*'différence'*) that to write is to differ (be different from everything else) and to defer (not to say everything else).[7] In these emphases, 'text' comes to signify playing with meanings, or the play of meaning itself – the way meaning is created as a temporary and limited, but also highly suggestive and complex, interweaving of strands, contexts and possibilities. Here the term 'text' approaches the *ambiguity* or *hesitation* – themselves key terms in Russian Formalist views of the ways meaning can be shifted and extended in fantasy and other literature – which is found at the heart of improvisation, in the sense that 'anything can happen'.

Improvisation doesn't work entirely without a pre-existent 'text', any more than language or creativity do: but what it does is to operate with the ever-present possibility of reorganisation – of shaking the kaleidoscope again – which can keep you on your toes, on the edge of your seat or on the limits of your mental and physical world. It turns text into texturing, into the art of weaving new patterns, which indicates a strong link between the resurgence of improvisation (in theatre and in educational and psychiatric practice), and current critical and philosophical concerns about speech acts, the nature of meaning and the process of communication.

Co-creativity

An act of theatre has many sets of meaning. There is that which is created in the act of performance, and there is that which is re-created after the performance. The first is created *jointly* by the actor and his co-creator, the audience member; the second is created *privately* in the mind of either after the event is concluded and the partners in the original act have separated. And there is a third kind of meaning; the meaning of the whole event, which is apprehended by the whole group, the community which partakes in its creation. This is meaning*fulness*, where all participants experience the way meaning is made. It is an archetypal experience of theatre.

The meaning of a theatre event (unlike, say, the meaning of a novel) is not only experienced singly, but communally. This type of meaning derives not so much from the intention, but from the 'flavour' of the experience. Obvious examples might be the communal laughter shared during the performance of a successful farce, or the hushed stillness, when the communal heartbeat of the audience seems to race, during the performance of some terrifying stunt in the circus.

The spatial disposition of the audience, its relation to itself and to the actors, can have a profound effect upon this sort of experienced meaning. To take a single, modern example: when the Sheffield Crucible theatre was being planned, many notable actors condemned the thrust stage design (because it meant that they would have to share the same space as their audience, their role changed from dominance to willing co-operation). Most of the controversy raged over the stage shape. One seemingly trivial criticism of the design, however, was overlooked in the furore. The playwright David Rudkin asked that there be only one armrest between each pair of seats in the auditorium instead of the planned two. He wanted the audience to be subliminally, peripherally aware of itself, connected by touch – at the elbows if nowhere else. The seating contrived to isolate the participants in the drama (while the stage shape strove to unite them). The reinforcement of the audience's physical sense of itself was being denied, in the name of comfort. In 1987, Oleg Efremov, artistic director of the Moscow Art Theatre, made exactly the same point during a workshop in Oxford.[8] He looked forward to his company moving back into the refurbished *original* MAT, where the seats were harder and narrower, and where the spectators' elbows touched, 'completing the circle'.

The differentiation and isolation of audience members can be charted throughout modern theatre history. Its apotheosis belongs to the video age: the extreme being the masturbatory solipsism of video pornography with its squalid solo viewing cabins. But the process begins at least in the eighteenth century, in the vast opera-house-derived theatres of that period, and it reflects upon the decline of the improvised tradition.

The shaman's space is not enclosed. His theatre is the space around him, and his stage is his own body. The limits of that space are defined, as in all open-air performances, by the backs of the furthest attenders. There is an invisible boundary line behind the person furthest away from the performer who is still paying attention to him. The shaman can use an indoor space, his own hut for example (especially if he wishes to perform certain *coups de théâtre* to astonish his flock). For the most part, however, his space is open. Often he will use as a focal point a tree, or a stick planted upright in the ground, which serves both to point to the heavens, and to connect them to the earth. Down this vertical axis, the demons will travel.[9] The onlookers, sharers in the event, will crowd together around him, supplying him with the energy of their concentration and belief, and rhythmically reinforcing his act of transformation.

In the vast stone *theatron* of the Greek theatre, thousands of spectators sat, ate, watched together on the serried *kerkides* or wedges that made up the encircling bowl around the central dancing place. Across the *orchestra* the spectator was continually aware of his fellows throughout the daylit performance.

In the medieval 'rounds' the same was true; while in the processional dramas of Corpus Christi and around the booth stages of Europe, the crowds jostled and gaped, always as aware of themselves and of the *holiday* social value of the events they were creating as the attenders at an ancient mime in the Roman *fora* must have been.

In the Elizabethan outdoor theatres, too, the groundlings pressed together around the stage platform, so those in the galleries surrounding them were never able to isolate themselves completely. The audience was always part of the *meaning* of the event: its laughter, derision, rank breath, shuffling feet as much a part of the experience as Shakespeare's or Marlowe's poetry. In the indoor theatres of the Jacobean period, and in the tennis court theatres of the early Restoration, although the spatial arrangements of stage and auditorium had to alter to accommodate scenery, the intimacy of the building still compelled awareness of one's fellow participants (sometimes, as Pepys' *Diary* suggests, too strongly, so that the play was only the pretext for the audience's assembly in that place at that hour). The event *was* the audience, as much as it was the play and the player.

But, by the nineteenth century, the picture had altered drastically. The sense of community still obtained in the remote galleries, where the now despised mob still jostled and cat-called. But the inhabitants of the pit were different, and had learned to insist on silence and decorum. The play was regarded as being for each alone. Not for all together. The *interactive* audience was being suppressed. The change is coincidental with the rise of the novel, and the growth of the practice of solitary reading as opposed to communal experiencing.

The 1860s wooed the custom of the upper classes by providing a plushly carpeted 'stalls' area with armchairs in front of, and then in place of, the old 'pit'.[10] This quietened the audience, lessened the numbers (yet produced more income from a more affluent clientele) and attracted a 'better class of person' to the theatre. It made possible the rise of the quieter, more realistic English drama,[11] and effectively completed the segregation of the audience into economic classes. The upshot was the creation of the modern genteel theatre of the 'West End' (and, as compensation for the

poorer class, the rowdier East End music halls and melodrama
houses.[12]

But the improviser's stage cannot be decorous, in that sense.
He cannot be isolated from his co-creators, and they cannot be
isolated from each other. The event derives almost *all* of its
meaning from the experience in the theatre, and (compared with
the erudite written drama) relatively far less from the solipsistic
mental voyage after the experience is concluded. So much of it
is celebratory.[13] So much of it is momentary that it demands an
attentive but self-aware crowd within the actor's immediate space
– or the meaning and the value will be lost.

Practically, during improvised performances a lot of *small*
things happen. Being spontaneously created, there isn't time
for the actor to rehearse and selectively enlarge them. They
happen briefly and are then extinguished. The audience has to
be close enough to notice them, and to nudge itself in the ribs
to call attention to them. Often, the improvising actor will – in
the suddenness of discovery – forget other technicalities of the
traditional theatre, such as which way he's facing, or how loud
he's talking. Does this matter? Not for Grotowski, certainly:

> Can the theatre exist . . . without a text? Yes; the history
> of the theatre confirms this. In the evolution of the theatrical
> art the text was one of the last elements to be added. If we
> place some people on a stage with a scenario they themselves
> have put together, and let them improvise their parts as in the
> *Commedia dell'Arte*, the performance will be equally good even
> if the words are not articulated but simply muttered.[14]

But the audience needs, therefore, to be close enough to
see everything, and to hear everything.

The *ideal* space would permit the audience to respond actively,
physically – to become aware of itself not as passive 'audience'
but as equally responsible for the performance.

Increasingly fixed venues and performance codes parallel
the disappearance – or marginalisation to the 'fringe' – of
improvised theatre; this shift is connected to the 'closing' of social
borders. Theatre tends to become middle class and to segregate
its audience: in the late nineteenth and early twentieth century

the improvisatory resurfaces as music hall (for the 'uneducated') or cabaret (for the intellectuals); both are groups outside the prevailing cultural norm. Similarly, pressure from the church in earlier periods restricts the kinds of things permitted. In these senses theatre becomes more enclosed, less mobile, more an echo of the world-view of certain influential groups and less a public (celebratory, anarchic, rude, disruptive) occasion. Official theatre is more static, and it shuns the shiftiness, the moral ambiguity, the politically suspect nature of anything based around direct response and improvisation.

We can certainly observe a kind of Freudian volcanic upsurge of cabaret-type activity at crucial points in the twentieth century – in the 1920s and 1930s in Germany, for instance, or in the 1960s in Britain. Although not entirely improvised, much of this work used the methods of improvisation in its development (especially a direct, creative response to the immediate social and political context) and relied upon acute audience participation.

Names of theatre companies may tell us quite a lot about the way they see their role. Mainstream companies tend to be stuck to their venues or their sphere of operation: the Old Vic or the Royal Shakespeare Company, for instance. Fringe companies can express their identity (or their search for it) more inventively, particularly since they are almost by definition not required to function as mastheads for a fixed cultural or financial interest. Their method of funding (mainly from arts councils and civic authorities), if they are lucky enough to get any, pushes them into a peripatetic life-style, which may itself be conducive to a sense of continuous change. Certainly for them each run of performances is much more varied, simply in terms of physical location and kind of audience, than it can be for a resident company. They also have to rely on a relatively simple touring set, usually having to erect it themselves and accommodate it and the show to vastly different spaces. All of this, if it is not totally unsettling or exhausting, may generate a kind of excitement which helps to keep the performances fresh, responding to different contexts. There is, then, an important sense in which, financially and physically, as well as in terms of its development as a piece of theatre, each performance is built around improvisatory factors.

This is reflected in names like Hesitate and Demonstrate, or Research and Navigation (an experimental dance team, in fact); in the peripatetic flavour of Intercity Theatre and Mike Bradwell's original Hull Truck, or indeed of the concept of itinerant theatre presented by The Mediaeval Players, Trestle Theatre, Actors' Touring Company (ATC) and The Confederacy of Fools; or in the actor–audience relationship implied by Théâtre de Complicité or Shared Experience. Johnstone's Theatre Machine sums up all of this, giving the sense of theatre as a mobile entity producing all kinds of activity.

The relationship between theatre – both as institution and as event – and society is a complex and reciprocal one, but it can certainly be argued that forms of social change are at the least reflected, and possibly instigated or supported, in the form and content of drama. This implies that through improvisation the meaning of a theatre event is being shifted, or perhaps returned to what it may originally have been. Away from the comfortable and enclosed 'realism' of the conventional theatre, back towards something more disturbing, more immediate, but also more power-ful and rewarding.

Experiencing something communally depends very much on the degree of alertness or attentiveness one brings to it. Theatre shape and space conditions the meaning of such acts; perhaps largely because 'plush' theatre distances and lulls its audience, the quality of that meaning is less sharp: less directly experienced through the senses, less of a challenge to the intelligence. One major way in which improvisation is crucial to theatre is its emphasis upon honed attention. The psychological and sociological functions of theatre are determined in large measure by the alertness and par-ticipation which can be stimulated in the public.

Grotowski, too, came to recognise that the only really authentic participatory 'role' the audience can be offered is that of spec-tators – but spectators aware of what they are doing. In other words, their function and activity becomes conscious, they recog-nise it as defining their situation. In his later productions, the positions ascribed to the audience were those of voyeurs, judges, observers (as in *Apocalypsis cum figuris*, *Dr Faustus*) rather than expecting them to respond in some more ambitious way. What actually gives them a purpose is the recognition of their function as spectators, so that they may make that situation *active* rather than passive; this most closely parallels the actors' discipline of being where you are, cognisant of present feelings and giving them appropriate articulation, and also fully involved in the contextual situation (that is, the action of the performance and its physical, social and intellectual dimensions).

Gremlin's Theatre

So far we have spoken about the meaning created jointly by audience and performer – co-creation. To retain its value, however, this idea should not be oversold. It is obvious that there is also a more *directive* transmission of ideas from stage to auditorium. The writer, the director and the actor have their understanding of what a work means, and they seek to transmit it. An actor strives constantly to shape and direct the flow of information from the stage and, what is more, is empirically aware that the process of directing meaning works. If he changes the timing of a line, he changes its meaning for the audience, and he is directly aware of the change; he is aware of the effect he is having. Improvisation can seem like an abdication of the responsibility to transmit the agreed meaning of the piece.

What is patently true is that the actor can decide to narrow down the choices, from the many to the few. Put another way, theatrical semiosis can be decoded along the lines suggested by Roland Barthes: the (stage) image is perplexingly wide open, and what the theatre practitioners do is to narrow down the possibilities of meaning. This is done in a variety of ways. Barthes's model is drawn from the confrontation between text and image; and the playwright's text (including the actor's expression of any sub-textual clues) is the prime means of 'anchoring' the performance-text to a predetermined meaning.[15]

Barthes points out that this 'anchoring' – this reduction of the image to a very few predetermined possibilities of meaning – has ideological as well as aesthetic consequences. He describes it as a system for 'dispatching' us – in the sense of being shunted along predetermined tracks – towards a meaning chosen in advance.

Seen in this light, it becomes a question of attitude as to whether one decides that is a positive act of artistic intervention, or whether it is a reduction of the range of possible meanings available to the spectator. It becomes a question of whether the spectator is ever aware of those other myriad meanings, and appreciates the openness of choice, or whether the spectator demands direction from the artist.

What we have tried to indicate in this book is that alongside the directive technique of the actor there co-exists an infinite range of possibility – to which the act (or attitude) of improvisation is the gateway. The proof of this assertion lies in the pleasure we, the spectators, take in the *accidental*, in the *unrehearsable*, and our response to it.

Often directive meaning is changed, even contradicted, by accident. We mishear the words of a popular song, for example, and are disappointed when we later hear the correct version. Our 'original' version meant something personal to us; it was the way we sang that song. In the theatre, our neighbour coughs and we fail to hear a crucial piece of plot-setting; consequently we re- (as well as mis-) interpret the entire play. Or the gremlins intervene.

For example, in a workshop production of Strindberg's *The Father*, some years ago, the set fell down. It was a single large backflat, and its untimely collapse revealed the entire cast arrayed behind it. For a second they failed to realise that the flat had been removed! They were revealed in a variety of attitudes ranging from close aural attention to the action on stage to total indifference. The audience, of course, greeted this unexpected revelation with laughter that was at once an act of sympathy, and a hoot of derision. On stage, the actor playing 'The Captain' soldiered on bravely, while the cast behind swiftly collected themselves and, without panicking, picked up the flat – and the play continued, the audience (as audiences always will) choosing not to dwell on the moment of near-disaster.

The gremlins' intervention undermined the predetermined choice of meaning. For the actors here the event was about the nominal content of Strindberg's play, the 'psychic destruction' of a credibly portrayed character. After the incident with the flat, the play didn't cease to be about that, but it was *also* about other questions, of form as well as content. The meaning was enriched, even as the intended experience was debased. The accidental moment is a crucible in which precast meanings are melted down and reshaped. Improvisatory theatre advises us that such precast forms are always brittle. And its god, if it has one, is the gremlin.

Barthes's model, and the nature of such 'accidents', illustrate that we *choose* meaning, and that choice imposes limitations on the possible range of meanings available for any given act. Accidents can realign the choice, open up new directions, if – in tune with the improvising spirit – we go along with the unexpected. The improvising actor can deliberately offer this form of choice to the audience. Whereas a text, or an established performance style, implies certain rules (sequence or logic, for example), improvisation can challenge or revise the rules.

In this sense improvisation functions like a 'ludic' text, a form dear to Post-Modernist writers but equally to, say, Lawrence Sterne in *Tristram Shandy*. Here the text refuses to 'progress' according to the expected rules. Shandy sets out to write his life-story but never manages to get as far as his birth. Digressions become more important than chronological narrative. Similarly, accidents figure as incidents in several of Robbe-Grillet's novels and films, ranging from a flaw in an apparently perfect tomato to a car smash, and he, like Borges, Gombrowicz, Pynchon and others, makes frequent use of the Sternian digression. The flow of the text is interrupted, deflected: all sorts of other stories and speculations get in the way. Meanings proliferate: what is foregrounded is the *availability* of meaning; the fact that it can generate and regenerate from anywhere.

The improviser marks this possibility, defining as it were the extreme limit of play, the edge of the road before it drops over the precipice. If you dare, you can go right up to the edge. And once you know that, it affects the use you subsequently make of the road. We may view our life-scripts in a different way afterwards.

The improvisatory mode, as Jacques Lecoq and others have suggested, has frequently posed this challenge to orthodoxy. Its origins seem linked to a cultural matrix which the last few centuries have marginalised and reduced to 'alternative' status: the shamanistic, the clown, the carnival. Though its beginnings may be the beginning of theatre itself (Dionysiac rites, integrating community and environment, and centred on a state of being 'enthused', operating in a kind of psychic overdrive), many social orders have seen the need either to repress or to marginalise (by licensing in a strictly limited way) anything to do with the spirit of creative play. Individual creativity, from the point of view of order, is a dangerous and disruptive thing (as Keith Johnstone and Teatr Osmego Dnia strikingly record), and even more dangerous if it issues in communal ceremony and performance. The 'double' of society, anything to do with the liberation of instinct and feeling, has frequently been subjected to this kind of treatment.

Fo and Rame provide a contemporary example which the figure of the (sometimes 'divine') Fool extends through history in many cultures.

But the Fool survives, and continues to improvise his existence against the canvas of orthodoxy. He floats between classes, trammelled by none (the *Vidusaka* of ancient Indian theatre can be rude to gods and superhuman heroes, the *Phlyakes* burlesque the Greek gods, Shakespeare's fools outwit monarchs); sometimes between sexes, like Harlequin, or the Dada figure of Anna Blume; frequently between cultures. As Trickster he ridicules and upturns all conventions, from the moral to the linguistic: clowns are frequently rude and carnal, sometimes murderous, as in the Punch tradition. His space is in the interstices of all systems; he is there but not there as he acknowledges them only to mock and distort them. Although marginalised in 'polite' parlance, the improviser and the forms of his activity are powerful. Not merely because they stand outside the law; much more because he has the knowledge and the skills to fragment and reconstruct it. He operates at the limit of meaning, breaking and revitalising those systems of active signs which give personal and communal significance to life. Where a culture begins to seek out that point and those skills, it is on the verge of a transformation. In pursuing this, success may well depend on maintaining the Trickster ambivalence which refuses to be strait-jacketed by any orthodoxy, even a new one, and which keeps available all possible directions of movement.

The upsurge of energy that carnival, cabaret and, in one sense at least, the comic, all represent (and such forms are powerfully energetic in contrast to more staid respectability and status quo), may be seen as shaping an alternative tradition or mode, whose force is disruptive, acting as a banana-skin to 'official' mores. This tradition continually proposes alternative 'readings' of conventions and accepted norms of behaviour, often offering apparently bizarre or scandalous variants. It frequently links with popular forms of culture, acceptance of the down-to-earth and the (grossly) physical, and with scepticism towards official doctrines or ideologies. Improvisation, ad-libbing, verbal play, status-reversal and so on are frequent: they introduce a relativisation, a quizzical undermining, a series of shifting perspectives on class, role, accepted standards and codes.[16]

New combinations

The fear that the improviser experiences each time he or she is required to make the next move may be being reinstated in the communal experience of theatre. Certainly Samuel Beckett's work is concerned with making that stammering before speech or action part of the direct experience of the audience; other contemporary writers may be doing similar things. There is a paralysis before language that is due to excess rationalisation, and there is a paralysis within language in the inarticulateness of frustration. But there is another form of hesitation which is more a kind of sacred awe at words – because words *commit* an act of being which can never be fully adequate. At least learning to live with that kind of silence could be preferable to torrents of superficial explanation or 'entertainment': it brings home to us that we have a responsibility for what we are and what we present ourselves as. It takes a certain courage to participate fully in a Beckett play or an improvised production, whether as performer or as receiver; perhaps the fact that the experience is available in much contemporary theatre is a sign of increasing health.

Improvisation is about the creation of meaning, both for individuals and for communities. As such, it occurs within a framework of structures of meaning which somewhat aridly designated as intellectual history, represents the attempts of human civilisation to come to terms with its position. Parameters change: to major Western epistemologies encoded in Christian Hermeneutics, Renaissance Humanism and the Enlightenment, we may currently be in the process of adding another, whose contours include a Marxist view of history, a structuralist understanding (which would include anthropological, cybernetic and quantum-mechanical models) of how systems of behaviour and knowledge are encoded, and a feminist or psychodynamic model of social and personal relations. Improvisation may have a place, both in relation to these modes of understanding, and in so far as it represents one of the forces which are helping to generate a new vision.

Lecoq suggests that the improvisatory is characteristically found in phases of dissolution and re-formation – corresponding perhaps to what in physics would be called a 'phase transition' – thus indicating that it matches both with a diachronic model of development as well as with a synchronic focus on how processes of transformation occur. Improvisation in the practice of training actors and in its paratheatrical applications in education and psychotherapy is a way of locating and harnessing resources even in situations which may seem threatening, unfamiliar or chaotic; thus the improvisatory within the dynamic of history may unfold a similar potential. This potential is the richer because it is grounded in a holistic view of human life and because it includes basic insights into the mechanisms by which new structures arise.

Ilya Prigogine, awarded a Nobel Prize in Chemistry for work on the thermodynamics of non-equilibrium systems, entitles a recent book *Order Out of Chaos*;[17] similar concepts are frequent in many other treatments of current scientific thinking.[18] Beckett's 'I can't go on, I must go on' seems to be a feature of the universe as well as of individual existence. It is perhaps not too far-fetched to say that the universe improvises. And certainly the ability to do so is universal.

Perhaps what we (and whatever extension of our ecosystem we can manage to include) can most profitably improvise is an increased readiness to surprise ourselves. Being prepared to experience our limits is the only way in which we can both learn what they are and move beyond them. That may be not merely a challenge, but the prime necessity of our present condition.

Improvisation continually nibbles at meaning and nudges towards meanings. It highlights the way performance can be creative as well as normative, implying a dynamic model for the role of theatre and performance both for individuals and within society. It can assist in shifting the parameters by which we live. In bending the rules it proposes new forms: Lecoq's focus on 'the spirit of the play', found in many forms in improvisation work, picks up Schiller's sense that man is only fully human when he plays:[19] it is the 'will to play' (*Spieltrieb*) which produces new combinations of matter and form.

Roddy Maude-Roxby compiled a once-only show called *Willie No – in New Combinations*. 'Willie No', of course, did not exist in everyday life or even as a character in the show, and the 'new combinations' were derived from a delightful picture of two Chinese girls in old-fashioned bathing costumes which was used on the poster. From this bizarre absence emerged a performance combining the talents of actors, musicians and dancers, mask, movement and narration. Taking the risk produced a unique event which composed its own meaning as it progressed.

Julian Hilton speculates that performance in the contemporary situation requires a new code based on the 'discontinuous aesthetic' of television, which brings together 'structural discontinuity and perceptual continuity'.[20] The improvisatory mode foregrounds the dramatic (the creative and performative moment) as opposed to the narrative: its continuity is that of the creating subject, not of a pre-existent social or aesthetic model. It could offer a model by which all structures may be available to us in new combinations.

Notes

Notes to the Introduction

1. Cf., for example, Michael Gelb, *Body Learning: An Introduction to the Alexander Technique*. (London: Aurum Press, 1981) pp. 103ff.
2. Cf. Ernest Theodore Kirby, *Ur-Drama* (New York: New York University Press, 1975); and Rogan Taylor, *The Death and Resurrection Show: From Shaman to Superstar* (London: Anthony Blond, 1985).
3. Johan Huizinga, *Homo Ludens* (Leyden, 1938; trans. by the author, London: Paladin, 1970) pp. 141ff.
4. Antonin Artaud, 'Production and Metaphysics', in *The Theatre and its Double* (Paris, 1938; trans. Victor Corti, London: Calder & Boyars, 1970) p. 33.
5. John H, Towsen, *Clowns* (New York: Hawthorne Books, 1976) pp. 4–5
6. Ibid. Among the Hopi Indians, for example; or within the Burmese 'spirit-plays' or *nibhatkin*, where the clowns have the major roles, and have total freedom to improvise.
7. Ibid., p. 358 n. 9, Towsen cites J. Levine, 'Regression in Primitive Clowning', in *Psychoanalytical Quarterly*, 30 (1961); and see also Mel Gordon, '*Lazzi*: The Comic Routines of the *Commedia dell'Arte*', in *Performing Arts Resources*, vol. 7, ed. G. Cocuzza and B. Stratyner (New York: Theatre Library Association, 1981).
8. See Part I below, the section on Lecoq (p. 67ff.) for a further discussion of the semiotics of clowning.
9. William Shakespeare, *Hamlet*, III ii.ll. 40 ff. 'And let those that play your clowns speak no more than is set down for them.'
10. Towsen, *Clowns*, p. 37.
11. Allardyce Nicoll, *Masks, Mimes and Miracles* (London, 1931; reprinted New York: Cooper Square Publishers, 1963) p. 253.
12. Aristotle, 'The Poetics', *c.* 330 BC, Chap. III, in *Classical Literary Criticism*, trans. T. S. Dorsch (Harmondsworth, Middx: Penguin, 1965) p. 34. Aristotle acknowledges the historical primacy of the improviser (ibid., Cap. IV, p. 36).

13. W. Beare, *The Roman Stage* (London: Methuen, 1950, 3rd edn. 1964) p. 149; and see also N. Hammond and H. Scullard (eds), *Oxford Classical Dictionary* (Oxford: Oxford University Press, 1970, 2nd. edn.) p. 668 (entry on mimes).

14. 'He that schal pleye Belyal loke that he have gunne-powder brennynge In pypys in his handis & in his eris & in his ars whanne he gothe to battel.' From the fifteenth century *The Castell of Perseverance*, quoted in Richard Southern, *The Mediaeval Theatre in the Round* (London: Faber, 1957) p. 19. Not recommended for improvisers of a nervous or combustible constitution.

15. Mikhail Bakhtin, *Rabelais and His World* (Moscow, 1965; trans. Hélène Iswolsky, Cambridge, Mass.: MIT Press, 1968), cf. Chap. 5, 'The Grotesque Image of the Body and Its Sources', and especially p. 317. The account given by Bakhtin of the grotesque accords not only with ancient representations of the *mimi*, but also with Jacques Lecoq's *bouffonerie* (although Lecoq may be thought to shade out of the true grotesque into the fantastical). Cf. also n. 50 below.

16. Andrea Perrucci, *Dell'arte rappresentiva, premeditata e dall'improvviso* (Naples, 1699), trans. S. J. Castiglione, quoted in A. M. Nagler (ed.), *A Source Book in Theatrical History* (New York: Dover, 1952) p. 258.

17. Ibid. p. 259.

Notes to Chapter 1

1. Martha Graham, quoted in James Roose-Evans, *Experimental Theatre: From Stanislavsky to Today* (New York: Avon, 1970) p. 112.

2. Paul Gray, 'Stanislavsky and America: A Critical Chronology', in *Tulane Drama Review*, vol. 9, no. 2 (Winter 1964) p. 25.

3. Deirdre Hurst du Prey, interviewed July, 1978 by Peter Hulton, in 'The Training Sessions of Michael Chekhov', *Dartington Theatre Papers*, 3rd. series, no. 9 (1979–80) p. 13.

4. Edward Braun, *Meyerhold on Theatre* (New York: Hill & Wang, 1969) p. 115 (and see especially Meyerhold's essay 'The Fairground Booth' in the same volume, pp. 119–28). 'Doctor Dappertutto' is to be found in E. T. A. Hoffman's *Fantasiestücke in Callot's Manier*, part 2.

5. Cf. Nikolai A. Gorchakov, *The Theatre in Soviet Russia*, trans. Edgar Lehrman (New York: Columbia University Press, 1957) p. 68.

6. Jacques Copeau, *Registres* (Limon, 1916), quoted in Christopher D. Kirkland, 'The Golden Age, First Draft' (on Théâtre du Soleil's *L'Age d'Or*) in *The Drama Review*, vol. 19, no. 2 (T-66, June 1975, Political Theatre Issue) p. 58.

7. Albert Camus, quoted in Michel Saint-Denis, *Training for the Theatre, Premises and Promises*, ed. Suria Saint-Denis (New York: Theatre Arts Books, 1982) p. 32.

8. John Rudlin, *Jacques Copeau* (in the series 'Directors in

Perspective') (Cambridge: Cambridge University Press, 1986) preface, p. xiv.

9. Jacques Copeau, *Essai de Rénovation Dramatique* (Paris, 1913) p. 72 (our translation).

10. The second phase of this development was designed by Louis Jouvet, who was stage manager, leading man and part-time architect.

11. Saint-Denis, *Training for the Theatre*, p. 28.

12. Ibid., p. 32.

13. Mira Felner, *Apostles of Silence* (Toronto and London: Associated University Presses, 1985) p. 38. This excellent recent publication, though primarily concerned with the roots of modern mime-work, devotes a chapter to Lecoq, as well as one to Copeau.

14. Jacques Copeau, 'Notes sur l'éducation de l'acteur', in *Ecrits sur le théâtre* (Brient: Paris, 1955) pp. 47–53.

15. Rudlin, *Jacques Copeau*, p. 45. Meyerhold's view of the *cabotin* differs from Copeau's; for him 'The cabotin is a strolling player . . . a kinsman to the mime, the histrion, and the juggler . . . (who) keeps alive the tradition of the true art of acting' (in Braun, *Meyerhold on Theatre*, p. 122). Obviously there was no disagreement between them as to the qualities required for the new acting: what Copeau opposed was a style of acting made up of the conglomerated tricks of the *cabotin* – the shortcuts of the 'old pro' and 'ham-ateurism'.

16. Jacques Copeau; the prospectus is quoted at greater length by Rudlin (*Jacques Copeau*, pp. 43–4). We have added our own comments to his list; those we have retained are in quotation marks.

17. Jacques Copeau, ibid., p. 44.

18. Jacques Copeau, from a notebook in the Dasté collection, quoted in Rudlin, *Jacques Copeau*, p. 96.

19. Ibid., p. 26. This stage of the group's evolution was not without hiccups – financial, artistic and personal. They included an enforced move of headquarters and changes in personnel, acting in marquees in thunderstorms, and Copeau's own difficulties over his triple role of director, actor and writer.

20. Quoted in Rudlin, *Jacques Copeau*, pp. 102–3.

21. Michel Saint-Denis, *Training for the Theatre*, pp. 26–7.

22. It is worth noting that Lecoq, in our interview with him in Paris in April 1987, made a strong distinction between Copeau and les Copiaux: for him, it was the work of the latter during this period that laid the foundations of modern impro work. Léon Chancerel's 1935 Théâtre de l'Oncle Sebastien specialised in improvised work for children. Dasté and, of course, Saint-Denis expanded performance and training skills.

23. For example, the 'Genealogy of Modern French Mime' sketched out in Felner, *Apostles of Silence*, p. 49.

24. Adrian Kiernander, 'The Théâtre du Soleil, Part One: A Brief History', *New Theatre Quarterly*, vol. II, no. 7 (August 1986) p. 196.

25. Françoise Kourilsky and Leonora Champagne, 'Political Theatre in France Since 1968', *The Drama Review*, vol. 19, no. 2 (T-66, June 1975, Political Theatre Issue) p. 52.
26. Rudlin, *Jacques Copeau*, p. 60.
27. Michel Saint-Denis, *Training for the Theatre*, pp. 81–2.
28. Ibid.
29. Ibid., p. 48.
30. Ibid., pp. 86–99.
31. Ibid., p. 98.
32. Ibid., p. 82.
33. Paul Clements, *The Improvised Play: The Work of Mike Leigh* (London: Methuen Theatrefile, 1983) p. 7.
34. Ibid.
35. Mike Leigh, quoted in Clements, *Improvised Play*, p. 10.
36. Ibid., p. 11.
37. Mike Leigh, *An Account of the Development of My Improvised Plays 1965–69: An Application for the George Devine Award, 1969* (October 1969) (Leigh was the joint winner of this award in 1973); *Bleak Moments*, *Abigail's Party* and *Goose Pimples* have all won major awards. Leigh's account is quoted in Clements, *Improvised Play*, p. 15.
38. Mike Leigh, *Development of My Improvised Plays*, quoted in Clements, *Improvised Play*, p. 16.
39. *Abigail's Party* and *Goose Pimples*, devised by Mike Leigh (London: Penguin, 1983).
40. James Fenton, review of Phil Young's play *Crystal Clear*, in *The Sunday Times*, 12 December 1982 (quoted in Clements, *Improvised Play*, p. 57).
41. Cf. also Grotowski's method of 're-improvisation' (getting the actors to repeat certain movements or positions), which builds up an acting 'score' of signs developed from physical impulses.
42. Clements, *Improvised Play*, p. 21.
43. Ibid., p. 54.
44. Ibid., p. 63.
45. Ibid., p. 69.
46. Ronald A. Willis, 'The American Lab Theater', in *Tulane Drama Review*, vol. 9, no. 1 (Fall 1964) p. 113.
47. Ibid., p. 114.
48. Lee Strasberg, *A Dream of Passion*, ed. Evangeline Morphos (London: Bloomsbury, 1988) pp. 144ff.
49. Maurice Browne, *Too Late to Lament* (Bloomington, Ind., 1956) p. 165, quoted in Travis Bogard, *The Revels History of Drama in English*, vol. 8, 'American Drama' (London: Methuen, 1977) pp. 29–30.
50. Viola Spolin, *Improvisation for the Theatre: A Handbook of Teaching and Directing Techniques* (Evanston, Ill.: Northwestern University Press, 1963) p. xi.
51. Caldwell Cook's work was later continued by Douglas Brown:

cf. Christopher Parry, *English Through Drama* (Cambridge: Cambridge University Press, 1972).

52. Neva L. Boyd, *Handbook of Recreational Games* (Chicago, 1945; re-pub. New York: Dover, 1973) p. 6. Neva Boyd just *may* have been influenced by Suzanne Bing's work. Bing and Copeau worked in the United States from 1917 to 1919 with the Vieux-Colombier Company, and Bing in particular taught movement and acting via animal improvisation and games. Had Boyd perhaps seen/heard of/been involved in Bing's workshops?

53. Spolin, *Improvisation for the Theatre*, p. xi.

54. Ibid., p. 383.

55. Jeffery Sweet, *Something Wonderful Right Away* (New York: Avon, 1978; Limelight edition, 1987) p. 46.

56. Paul Sills, interviewed by Charles Mee, 'The Celebratory Occasion', *Tulane Drama Review*, vol. 9, no. 2 (Winter 1964) p. 174; and cf. also Jeffery Sweet, *Something Wonderful*. Main offshoots of the original Compass idea: Second City, Chicago, founded 1959 by Sills and still going; The Premise, founded New York by Theodore J. Flicker, 1960–4; The Committee, founded San Francisco by Alan Myerson, 1963–73. In 1955, Sills had been on a Fulbright scholarship to Bristol University, where he taught improvisation.

57. Paul Sills, interviewed by Charles Mee, *The Celebratory Occasion*, p. 175. All employees at Second City are offered free improvisation classes. The actress Betty Thomas (best known for *Hill Street Blues*) waitressed there, loved the workshops, went on tour with one of Second City's companies, then spent two years with the main Chicago company, among whom were Gilda Radner, Bill Murray and Dan Aykroyd. Thomas has since gone on to run women's workshops with a number of groups in Los Angeles (for example, The Public Works, Funny You Should Ask and Best All Women's Improv Group). One 'busboy' who also took advantage of these free classes was the leading playwright David Mamet.

58. Sweet, *Something Wonderful*, pp. 18–19.

Notes to Chapter 2

1. Programme for a Theatre Machine event at Wells, Norfolk, 1987. Written by Ben Benison, Roddy Maude-Roxby, Ric Morgan and John Muirhead.

2. Loose personnel structure, too: Justin Case (an English Lecoq graduate) has worked with Maude-Roxby in Canada under the Theatre Machine umbrella with two American actors. In fact, it's now as much an *idea* as a company. Keith Johnstone (*Impro* (London: Methuen, 1981) p. 27) says they were 'the only pure improvisation group I knew, in that we prepared nothing, and everything was like a jazzed-up drama class. . . . It's weird to wake up knowing you'll be on stage in twelve hours, and that there's absolutely nothing you can do to ensure success.'

3.   'Impro-Olympics' (and 'Theatre Sports' generally) are booming: for example, the radio and television improvisation game *Whose Line Is It Anyway?* Games (which also make useful exercises) include 'Authors' (impro on an audience-suggested subject in a given literary style); 'Every Other Line' (one partner reads from a classic play, the other improvises an unrelated scene); and 'Improvising a Rap' (improvising rhyme and rhythm).

4.   And, of course, Johnstone himself was very much involved in that programme to develop new writers.

5.   Terry Browne, *Playwrights' Theatre* (London: Pitman, 1975) pp. 46–7; and see also Philip Roberts, *The Royal Court Theatre 1965–1972* (London: Routledge & Kegan Paul, 1986) pp. 24–5.

6.   Quoted by Irving Wardle in his Introduction to Johnstone's book *Impro*, p. 9. Johnstone currently lives in Canada: the cover of his book shows a photograph of his Loose Moose Theatre Company, in Calgary, Alberta. Roddy Maude-Roxby lives in Norfolk, acts, teaches Mask and drama workshops and runs community projects.

7.   Theatre Machine programme cited above.

8.   Ibid.

9.   Ibid.

10. See below, pp. 61ff: the section on Lecoq.

11. Also, to Grotowski, 'the actor' means 'an individual in action, who aims not at acting, but at acting less than in daily life and who draws others to the simplest, the most human, the most direct actions' (Talk on Polish Radio October 1979, in J. Kumiega, *The Theatre of Grotowski* (London: Methuen, 1985) p. 236.

12. Susanne Langer, *Feeling and Form* (London: Routledge & Kegan Paul, 1959).

13. Jacques Lecoq, interviewed by Jim Hiley, 'Moving Heaven and Earth', *Observer* (20 March 1988) p. 40.

14. Ibid., and most recently at the Queen Elizabeth Hall, London, in March 1988.

15. Most quotations by Lecoq in this section are derived from brochures published by the École Jacques Lecoq, 57 rue du Faubourg Saint-Denis, Paris (unless otherwise attributed). These are supplemented by information provided by M. and Mme Lecoq themselves during an interview with the authors in Paris in April 1987.

16. Jacques Lecoq (ed.), *Théâtre du Geste* (Paris: Bordas, 1987) p. 17.

17. The systematisation of space in Lecoq's analytical work parallels that of Laban, at least in its recognition that 'There's a link, a reverberation between inner and outer space. If I make a physical action – pulling or pushing – it's analogous to internal emotion, love or hate. An oblique gesture can be sentimental, melodramatic. A vertical gesture is tragic. I indicate passions in space' (Jacques Lecoq, interviewed by Hiley, 'Moving Heaven and Earth').

18. Lecoq's students are often surprised, at least initially, to discover how much time is taken up by the *auto-cours* – and about how much they are expected to teach themselves. But many of the groups

stemming from Lecoq first worked together and first discovered common interests in the *auto-cours* sessions.

19. Jacques Lecoq, *Théâtre du Geste*, p. 17.

20. The 'vocabulary' of Indian dance is primarily pantomimic in Lecoq's sense, or denotational: it draws upon an established and highly stylised code. Lecoq, as we indicate below, is intent on a more Artaudian exploration of movement and sound *prior* to linguistic formulation.

21. Marivaux's theatre derives from *commedia* and is highly quizzical towards received social and sexual mores, implying that people are much more human when they 'let themselves go' or adopt an improvisatory stance. This is signalled also in Schiller's idea that man is most a man when he plays (discussed in Julian Hilton's *Performance* (London: Macmillan, 1988) p. 45) and in Huizinga's notion of 'Playing Man' – *Homo ludens*.

22. Tony Mitchell, *Dario Fo: People's Court Jester* (London: Methuen, 1984, 2nd rev. edn, 1986) makes the distinction between *pantomime blanche* (white mime – the silent mime of Marceau, for example) and *pantomime noire* (black mime, which includes verbal language). Perhaps more useful distinctions, though, are Lecoq's own. He distinguishes between his own *mime naturel*, *mime de fond* ('mime') and the *mime statuaire*, *mime de forme* ('pantomime') of Decroux (cf. Felner, *Apostles of Silence* (Toronto and London: Associated University Presses, 1985) p. 149). Interestingly, Lecoq is primarily regarded in England and Germany (when he is regarded at all) as a teacher of mime: as we have seen, this is true – but only in the sense that 'mime' embraces the whole realm of physical theatre. His status as a teacher of improvisation is totally unknown. There is also virtually nothing written on Lecoq in English, though Felner's *Apostles of Silence* (referred to above) has an excellent chapter on Lecoq as a mime.

23. See Part II below, section on masks, for further details about Lecoq's work with various types of mask.

24. Felner, *Apostles of Silence*, p. 148.

25. Ibid., p. 153.

26. Not so far from Grotowski's *via negativa* perhaps, and certainly related to Copeau's use of stillness (which is itself connected to work in modern dance – particularly that of teachers like Jooss and Leeder, and Jane Winearls).

27. Jacques Lecoq, 'Le Mouvement et le théâtre', *ATAC Informations*, no. 13 (December 1967).

28. See S. Eldredge and H. Huston, 'Actor Training in the Neutral Mask', *The Drama Review*, vol. 22, no. 4 (December 1978, Workshop Issue) pp. 20–1. And see also Part II below.

29. Lecoq calls it 'a state of unknowing, a state of openness and availability for the rediscovery of the elemental', 'L'Ecole Jacques Lecoq au Théâtre de la Ville, *Journal du Théâtre de la Ville* (January 1972) p. 41.

30. We are especially indebted here to Clive Mendus, formerly

of the Mediaeval Players, both for his account of training at Lecoq's school and for his excellent workshops on improvisation and clowning based on Lecoq's method. Much of Lecoq's clowning work has been developed in practice by some of his early graduates who have returned to teach at the school; in particular, Philippe Gaulier.

31. Charles Sanders Peirce, *Collected Papers*, 8 vols (Harvard University Press, 1931–58). And see also Keir Elam, *The Semiotics of Drama and Theatre* (London: Methuen, 1980) pp. 21–7.

32. Jacques Lecoq, 'Mime – Movement – Theater', *Yale Theater*, vol. 4, no. 1 (Winter 1973) pp. 119–20. Quoted in John H. Towsen, *Clowns* (New York: Hawthorne, 1976) pp. 353–4.

33. Lecoq always requires the 'refutation of the recipe' (interview with Lecoq, Paris 1971, cited in Felner, *Apostles of Silence*, p. 156): no reliance on cliché or established routine. He regards the *pantomime* of, for example, Decroux and Marceau, as falling into this category, and thus his own training highlights instead those debunkers of tradition the clown and the grotesque *bouffon* (cf. n. 52 below).

34. There is a Grotowskian note here, of course, and a link with paratheatre and psychodrama; archetypal impro situations highlight the nakedness of performance and are always vulnerable.

35. Lecoq concurs with this view. See Felner, *Apostles of Silence*, p. 168.

36. Samuel Beckett, *The Beckett Trilogy* (London: Calder, 1959). (This edition London: Picador, 1979 pp. 381–2.)

37. Lecoq, *Théâtre du Geste*.

38. From the Brochure of L'Ecole Jacques Lecoq.

39. 'Seriously, I want to be a classic, and just like the classic writers, I try to do things that are ephemeral. The Greeks used to write tragedies to be performed only a few times. They were produced to be destroyed . . . and burned the day they were performed. Shakespeare didn't write for posterity, no way'. Dario Fo, in *Arena*, 'The Theatre of Dario Fo', BBC television documentary by Dennis Marks, first broadcast 28 February 1984.

40. Dario Fo, in *Playboy* (Italian Issue, December 1974) trans. in Mitchell, *Dario Fo*, p. 58.

41. Dario Fo, from *Mistero buffo: Giullarata popolare, nuova edizione aggiornata nei testi e nelle note* (Verona: Bertoni, 1977) p. vii: trans. in Mitchell, *Dario Fo*, p. 18. An English translation of *Mistero buffo* has appeared during the writing of this book (trans. Ed Emery, Methuen, 1988).

42. Stuart Hood, Introduction to Dario Fo and Franca Rame, *Female Parts*, trans. Margaret Kunzle, adapted Olwen Wymark (London: Pluto Press, 1981) p. iv.

43. 'In my show, because I've worked on it, and especially because I've worked on it with audiences, I get a thousand or so laughs.

Here it's a couple of hundred, because they've cut the translation, chucked out what they don't understand, and distorted the overtly political aspects', Franca Rame, from an interview in the Italian theatre magazine *Sipario* (September 1983) p. 37; trans. in Mitchell, *Dario Fo*, p. 115.

44.   Mitchell, *Dario Fo*, p. 36.
45.   Ibid., p. 11.
46.   Dario Fo, Programme of the Washington Arena Stage production of *Accidental Death of an Anarchist*, 1984: quoted in Mitchell, *Dario Fo*, p. 121.
47.   Fo's *Grammelot* is, of course, generically related to Saint-Denis's *Grummelotage*.
48.   Mitchell, *Dario Fo*, p. 40.
49.   'Franca Rame belongs to a family of travelling players which even under fascism performed in the small towns and villages of Italy. It was in this hard school that she learnt the art of improvisation (at which she excels), of working with a minimum of sets and props, and of making a major contribution to a company in which everyone shares in the organisation of a performance' (Stuart Hood, Introduction to *Female Parts*, p. iv).
50.   See David L. Hirst, *Dario Fo and Franca Rame*, to be published by Macmillan (1989). Our grateful thanks are due to the author for letting us read the manuscript in advance of publication.
51.   Stuart Hood, Introduction to *Female Parts*, p. iii.
52.   This is perhaps related to Lecoq's fascination with the grotesque figure of the *Bouffon*. In *bouffonerie*, the grotesque (but not masked) character comments ironically and satirically on the supposedly normal world around him. The *Bouffon* figure is less well-known in the UK than in Europe.
53.   *Arena*, 'The Theatre of Dario Fo', and see also Part II below, section on masks.
54.   Mitchell, *Dario Fo*, p. 21.
55.   Ibid.
56.   Hirst, *Dario Fo and Franca Rame*, p. 15.
57.   Dario Fo, quoted in Mitchell, *Dario Fo*, p. 21.
58.   Martin Buber, *I and Thou*, trans. Walter Kaufmann (Edinburgh: T. & T. Clark, 1970).

Notes to Chapter 3

1.   One of the most profound influences on Grotowski's work was the example of the earlier Polish director Juliusz Osterwa (1887–1949) who founded the Reduta theatre studio in 1919. This was one of the first theatre *communities*: it was a theatre, an acting workshop, a school, based on the idea of communal sharing. There have been many such experiments: Osterwa at the Reduta; Copeau at Pernand-Vergelesses; Michel Saint-Denis and Charles Dullin both tried to set up theatrical communities; Stanislavsky's Studio

experiments at Eupatoria (on the shores of the Black Sea, where each of the actors built his own house and lived in it, sharing all communal tasks) is another famous attempt; the Group Theatre in the USA tried it in the 1930s, and the Becks' Living Theatre and Peter Schumann's Bread and Puppet Theatre tried it in the 1960s. All these are precedents and examples for Grotowski's later work at Brzezinka.

2. Jennifer Kumiega, *The Theatre of Grotowski* (London: Methuen, 1985) pp. 11–12.
3. Ludwig Flaszen, *Cyrograf* (Cracow, 1974) p. 110, trans. Kumiega, *Theatre of Grotowski*, p. 12.
4. Cf. Kumiega, *Theatre of Grotowski*, pp. 17ff.
5. For example, in *Faustus* the audience was seated at refectory tables, partaking in Faust's last supper, while the actors used the table tops as their stages; in *Kordian* the spectators sat on the beds of the asylum in which Grotowski set the play; in *The Constant Prince* the audience surrounded the action and looked down on the martyrdom below with the detachment/involvement of observers at a medical operation; and in *Akropolis* they sat on platforms in the midst of the concentration camp – by the end of the play they were hemmed in by metal junk, suggesting oppression and, ultimately, the crematorium.
6. Jerzy Grotowski, 'The Actor Bared', in *Teatr*, no. 17 (1965), cited in Tadeusz Burzyński and Zbigniew Osiński, *Grotowski's Laboratory* (Warsaw: Interpress, 1979) p. 36.
7. Jerzy Grotowski, *Towards a Poor Theatre*, ed. Eugenio Barba (Copenhagen: Odin Teatrets Forlag, 1961) p. 21.
8. Jerzy Grotowski, 'Holiday', *The Drama Review*, vol. 17, no. 2 (T-58, June 1973) p. 121.
9. Cited in Kumiega, *Theatre of Grotowski*, p. 113.
10. Grotowski, 'Holiday', p. 121.
11. Richard Fowler, 'The Four Theatres of Jerzy Grotowski: An Introductory Assessment', *New Theatre Quarterly*, vol. 1, no. 2 (May 1985) p. 173. Fowler's four phases are: Theatre of Performance (1959–69); Theatre of Participation (1969–75); Theatre of Sources (1976–82); and Objective Drama (from 1983).
12. Grotowski in the programme for *Theatre of Nations* (Warsaw, 1975), cited in Fowler, *The Four Theatres*, p. 176.
13. Ibid.
14. Grotowski, 'Holiday', pp. 115 and 119.
15. Cited in Kumiega, *Theatre of Grotowski*, p. 144.
16. Grotowski, 'Holiday', p. 119.
17. Programme for *Polish Thanatos*, trans. Kumiega, *Theatre of Grotowski*, p. 208.
18. Grotowski, 'Holiday', p. 115.
19. A final point, made by Tadeusz Burzyński, is that nearly all of Grotowski's theoretical statements are, themselves, improvisations: 'Grotowski has a special way of speaking, very much his own. He always improvises, inspired by questions. His books are simply

transcripts of his public appearances.' (*Grotowski's Laboratory*, p. 108).

Notes to Chapter 4

1. Clive Barker, *Theatre Games: A New Approach to Drama Training* (London: Methuen, 1977) p. 68.
2. Ibid., p. 29
3. Jacques Lecoq, interviewed by J. Hiley, 'Moving Heaven and Earth', *Observer*, 20 March 1988, p. 40.
4. Constantin Stanislavsky, *An Actor Prepares*, trans. Elizabeth Reynolds Hapgood (London: Geoffrey Bles, 1937) p. 78.

Notes to Chapter 5

1. Clive Barker, *Theatre Games: A New Approach to Drama Training* (London: Methuen, 1977) p. 124.
2. Keith Johnstone, *Impro: Improvisation and the Theatre* (London: Methuen, 1981) pp. 94–5.

Notes to Chapter 6

1. Barker, *Theatre Games: A New Approach to Drama Training* (London: Methuen, 1977) p. 162. The understanding of the tenses of acting derives from Brecht; it is a primary method in achieving the *Verfremdungseffekt*.
2. Ibid., pp. 89–90. Grotowski makes a similar point in *Towards a Poor Theatre* (p. 192): 'Next I want to advise you never in the performance to seek for spontaneity without a score. In the exercises it is a different thing altogether. . . . Today . . . I will create these details and you can try to find their different variations and justifications. This will give you an authentic improvisation – otherwise you will be building without foundations.'
3. Jiri Veltrusky, 'Man and Object in the Theater' (Prague, 1940), quoted in Keir Elam, *The Semiotics of Theatre and Drama* (London: New Accents series, Methuen, 1980) p. 7. The whole article is translated in Paul L. Garvin (ed.), *A Prague School Reader on Esthetics, Literary Structure and Style* (Washington: Georgetown University Press, 1964) pp. 83–91. Veltrusky's central statement is 'All that is on the stage is a sign.' We shall make further reference to this idea in Part III.
4. Johnstone, *Impro*, p. 36.
5. Ibid., p. 47.
6. Ibid., pp. 62ff. Theatre Machine's 'Sir and Perkins' plays were built on this principle.
7. See also section on Lecoq in Part I, pp. 61ff.
8. Jacques Lecoq, notes from *Stage d'été* (1971), cited in Mira Felner, *Apostles of Silence* (Toronto and London: Associated University Presses, 1985) p. 158.

9. Felner, *Apostles of Silence*, p. 158.
10. Ibid.
11. Jacques Lecoq, 'L'Ecole Jacques Lecoq au Théâtre de la Ville', *Journal du Théâtre de la Ville* (January 1972) p. 41.
12. Felner, *Apostles of Silence*, p. 164.
13. Jacques Lecoq, notes from *Stage d'été* (1971), cited in Felner, *Apostles of Silence*, p. 166.
14. 'It's true that an actor can wear a mask casually, and just pretend to be another person, but [William] Gaskill and myself were absolutely clear that we were trying to induce *trance* states. The reason why one automatically talks and writes of Masks with a capital "M" is that one really feels that the genuine Mask actor is inhabited by a spirit. Nonsense, perhaps, but that's what the experience is like, and has always been like' (Johnstone, *Impro*, pp. 143–4).
15. Ibid., p. 170.
16. The Tunisian Lassaad Saide, the chief exponent of this teaching method, was an associate of Lecoq for ten years – first as a student, later as a fellow teacher – before leaving to establish his own school in Belgium. His work is taught in Britain by, especially, the I Gelati group (whose name is a pun on the famous *commedia* troupe, I Gelosi) led by James MacDonald and Malcolm Tulip.
17. The danger is always of 'introversion' – closing out the spectator in the search for truthful contact with the other performers, or one's imagination. To inculcate the habit of extroversion for later performance, 'sideline coaching' during workshops often has to be powerfully intrusive, keeping the performer's attention *up* and *out*. This accounts for the sometimes belligerent style of teaching by Saide and I Gelati. Another technique we have found useful is to imagine a scene as a double-act by two cross-talk comedians who have to talk to each other via the audience, standing shoulder to shoulder but looking away from each other, so that the focus is always outwards.
18. The idea of Il Magnifico (Pantalone) as a rooster was first suggested by Pierre Duchartre (*The Italian Comedy* [Paris: 1924; trans. R. T. Weaver, 1929; re-published New York: Dover, 1966]), and eagerly seized upon by Copeau, who played Pantalone and from whom the modern tradition stems. (Amusingly, Lecoq – whose name implies a rooster – also specialises in the Mask of Pantalone! And Dario Fo brilliantly demonstrates the chicken walk and scratchy voice of the Magnifico in his Umbrian Summer schools). Cf. also Carlo Mazzone-Clementi, '*Commedia* and the Actor', *The Drama Review*, vol. 18, no. 1 (T-61, Popular Entertainments Issue, March 1974) p. 59.

Notes to Chapter 7

1. Viola Spolin, *Improvisation for the Theatre* (Evanston, Ill.: Northwestern University Press, 1963; London: Pitman, 1973).

2. Keith Johnstone, *Impro: Improvisation and the Theatre* (London: Methuen, 1981) p. 27.

3. Spolin, *Improvisation for the Theatre*, p. 77.

4. Andrea Perrucci, *Dell'arte rappresentiva, premeditata e dall'improvviso* (Naples, 1699; trans. S. J. Castiglione), quoted in A. M. Nagler (ed.), *A Source Book in Theatrical History* (New York: Dover, 1952) p. 258.

5. See also mnemonic games devised as learning strategies in Tony Buzan's *Use Your Head* (London: BBC Publications, 1974), which are used in the context of an organic learning method.

6. R. Natadze, 'On the Psychological Nature of Stage Impersonation', in *British Journal of Psychology*, vol. 53, part 4 (November 1962) pp. 421 ff.

7. Ibid.

8. Ibid.

9. Constantin Stanislavsky, *Creating a Role*, trans. Elizabeth Reynolds Hapgood (London: Geoffrey Bles, 1963) p. 182.

10. Clive Barker, *Theatre Games: A New Approach to Drama Training* (London: Eyre Methuen, 1977) p. 167.

11. Johnstone, *Impro*, p. 116.

12. Mike Alfreds, *A Shared Experience: The Actor as Story-teller*, an interview with Peter Hulton, London (June 1979). Published as *Dartington Theatre Papers*, 3rd series, no. 6 (1979–80) p. 15.

13. Ibid.

14. Ibid.

15. The convention of darkening the auditorium only dates from Wagner's practice at Bayreuth. Brecht was, perhaps, the first to challenge the notion, and Shared Experience is one of a number of contemporary groups to insist on visually including the audience in the performance event. The Mediaeval Players, for example, fit-up a small trestle stage indoors or out. If it is indoors, they leave the auditorium lights on so that the actors can achieve direct eye-contact with the audience, enabling the 'public' and presentational acting style required by their material.

16. Mike Alfreds, *Shared Experience*, p. 10. (Also 'And sometimes you were just ahead of them': Theatre Machine Programme quoted in Part I.)

Notes to Chapter 8

1. Jerzy Grotowski, 'The individual indeed may be their own improvisation', from a talk to schools on Polish Radio, cited in Jennifer Kumiega, *The Theatre of Grotowski* (London: Methuen, 1985) p. 237.

2. Howard Blatner, *Psychodrama, Role-Playing and Action Methods: Theory and Practice* (private publication, 1970) table 4, p. 131. See also John Hodgson, *The Uses of Drama*; Eric Bentley, *The Theatre of War*; and, of course, Moreno's own books, *Psychodrama, I* (1946) and *Psychodrama, II* (1959).

3.　Cf. Keith Yon, 'Communication Therapy with Mentally-handicapped Adults', *Dartington Theatre Papers*, 3rd series, no. 4
(1979–80) p. 42.
4.　Cited in Kumiega, *Theatre of Grotowski*, p. 53.
5.　Cf. Richard Findlater, *Banned!: A Review of Theatrical Censorship
in Britain* (London: MacGibbon & Kee, 1967).
6.　Ibid., p. 175.
7.　Tadeusz Janiszewski, quoted in Tony Howard, ' "A Piece of Our
Life": The Theatre of the Eighth Day', *New Theatre Quarterly*, vol.
II, no. 8 (November 1986) p. 296.
8.　Ibid., p. 297.
9.　Ibid., pp. 300–2.
10.　From the brochure of L'Ecole Jacques Lecoq (our translation).
11.　Cf. Roger Caillois, *Man, Play and Games* (London: Thames
& Hudson, 1962).
12.　This relates clearly to an emergent notion of 'active reception': it
fits more with an interactive ('computing') model of reception than
with the active/passive (consumerist) model of 'radio reception' (the
notion of transmitter and receiver, wherein the 'receiver's' activity
is merely to 'decode' the 'signal' sent by the artist).
13.　Cf. Bernard in *Les Faux Monnayeurs*, who 'n'a plus rien: tout est
à lui' (Andre Gide, *Les Faux Monnayeurs* (Paris: Gallimard, 1925)
p. 59. And: 'toute sensation est d'une *présence* infinie' (p. 23); 'que
chaque attente, en toi, ne soit même pas un désir, mais simplement
une disposition à l'accueil' (p. 29). Both from Gide, *Les Nourritures
Terrestres* (Paris: Gallimard, 1917–36).
14.　Paul Valéry, 'Palme', in *Poésies* (Paris: Gallimard, 1968)
pp. 112–13.
15.　It might also be thought of as an expectant 'lying in'; and cf. F. L.
Lucas's description of 'wise passiveness' as 'how to catch the ideas
that creep forth in the stillness, like magic mice, from their holes',
in *Style* (London: Cassell, 1955) p. 262.
16.　Marilyn Ferguson, *The Aquarian Conspiracy* (Los Angeles: J. P.
Tarcher, 1980) p. 90.
17.　Alan Watts, *The Book: On the Taboo Against Knowing Who
You Are* (New York: Random House, 1972).
18.　Abraham Maslow, *Towards a Psychology of Being* (New York:
Van Nostrand Reinhold, 1968).
19.　Fritjof Capra, *The Turning Point* (New York: Simon & Schuster,
1982) p. 337.
20.　Tom Stoppard, *Rosencrantz and Guildenstern are Dead* (London:
Faber & Faber, 1967) p. 16.
21.　The phrase appears on the contents page of *New Theatre
Quarterly*, vol. III, no. 9 (February 1987) in summary of the
article cited in n. 22 below. Gavin Bolton (*Drama as Education:
An Argument for Placing Drama at the Centre of the Curriculum*
[Harlow: Longman, 1984] p. 142) argues that imaginative acts (of
which drama is the paradigm) reconstruct 'habits of conception and
perception' directly.

22.   Jon Nixon, 'The Dimensions of Drama: The Case for Cross-curricular Planning', *New Theatre Quarterly*, vol. III, no. 9 (February 1987) pp. 71–81.

Notes to Chapter 9

1.   Julian Hilton, *Performance* (London: Macmillan, 1988) pp. 4–5.
2.   Roland Barthes thought of theatre as a paradigm for semiological analysis; so dense and rich are its signs that they offer 'a real informational polyphony' that often daunts the analyst – who retreats into textual study (Roland Barthes, 'Literature and Signification', in *Essais critiques* (Paris: Seuil, 1964) trans. Richard Howard, as *Critical Essays* (Evanston, Ill.: Northwestern University Press, 1972) p. 262; and cf. Keir Elam, *The Semiotics of Theatre and Drama* (London: Methuen, 1980) p. 19.
3.   The terms 'read from' and 'written to' are, of course, borrowed from the language of computing. They are used here to stress the 'inter-active' nature of the way in which meaning (information interchange and *use*) is created in theatre.
4.   A good example of the process of 'writing to' the performance (as well as 'reading from' it) comes from the Indian *Ramlila*. The child actor playing Rama is often described (by outsiders) as passive and immobile. To the Western way of thinking, the signs transmitted are mostly those of the actor's 'inadequacies'. To us, this inhibits belief – we have culturally learned to demand technical proficiency before we will surrender wholly to the event. Not so the Indian spectator. To the devotee, the child is holy – Shiva incarnated. As such he does not need to *do* anything. He has only to be there. His presence provides the necessary visual focus for the act of devotion. At such times, we might say that the traditional Western notion of the 'actor' (the word implies one who *does* things) has been turned on its head. It is the spectator who is active and the actor who is passive: the boy player is the blank slate upon which the spectator 'writes' the real drama of the event.
5.   A very complex illustration of how the audience creates the drama rather than the actor is provided by those Roman 'mythological dramas' in the arenas in which the chief 'actors' were condemned criminals. They represented, for example, Orpheus taming the beasts with his lyre – until a wild bear appeared who actually tore the performer to pieces. In truth, these victims were not acting at all – they were *being*. The audience (fusing and confusing the principles of actuality and virtuality) imaginatively superscribed the heroic character onto the tablet of the 'actor's' body – which it then allowed to be wholly erased. The 'play' existed only in the mind of the audience. For the poor 'player', existence itself ceased after one brief, necessarily improvised, death scene. (Cf. Roland Auguet, *Cruauté et Civilisation: Les Jeux Romains* (Paris, Flammarion, 1970), trans. as *The Roman Games* (St Albans: Panther, 1975) pp. 104ff.)

6. Arthur Koestler, *The Act of Creation* (London: Hutchinson, 1964; rev. Danube edn: London, 1969): 'When two independent matrices of perception or reasoning interact with each other the result . . . is either a *collision* ending in laughter, or their *fusion* in a new intellectual synthesis, or their *confrontation* in an aesthetic experience. The bisociative patterns found in any domain of creative activity are trivalent: that is to say, the same pair of matrices can produce comic, tragic, or intellectually challenging effects' (p. 45).

7. Jacques Derrida, *L'Ecriture et la Différence* (Paris, Seuil, 1967), trans. A. Bass, *Writing and Difference* (London: Routledge & Kegan Paul, 1978).

8. 'A Visit from Vanya', broadcast on BBC 2, 21 October 1987, in the *Bookmark* series.

9. The shaman's 'vertical axis' occurs in many forms. Among many examples, we could cite the Shiva *lingam* of Indian theatre (creative energy of manifestation, power that structures the world of forms), or the Amerindian 'totem pole'– even the European 'May pole'. See also Ernest Kirby, *Ur-Drama: The Origins of Theatre* (New York: New York University Press, 1975) pp. 44–8.

10. Introduced by Sir Squire Bancroft and his wife Mary Wilton first at the Strand Theatre, later at the Prince of Wales and the Haymarket.

11. For example, Tom Robertson's drawing-room ('cup-and-saucer') plays like *Society* (1865) and *Caste* (1867).

12. For example, the Britannia Theatre, Hoxton (1841) and the Canterbury Music Hall, Lambeth (1851).

13. Cf. Peter Brook's three stages: to make concrete the idea that everything is possible; to make the invisible appear; and to celebrate that. (Taken from Georges Banu, 'Peter Brook's Six Days', trans. Susan Bassnet, *New Theatre Quarterly*, vol. III, no. 10 (May 1987) pp. 99–106.)

14. Jerzy Grotowski, 'The Theatre's New Testament'. An interview with Eugenio Barba, trans. Jörgen Andersen and Judy Barba, in *Towards a Poor Theatre* (Denmark, 1968; London: Methuen, 1969) p. 32.

15. Cf. Roland Barthes, 'The Rhetoric of the Image', in *Image/Music/Text*, trans. Stephen Heath (New York: Hill & Wang, 1977) esp. pp. 38–40.

16. Aristotle's description of the origins of comedy with 'the leaders of the phallic songs' hints at a Greek carnival tradition (*Poetics*, Chap. 4); while Mikhail Bakhtin's *Rabelais and His World* (trans. Hélène Iswolsky, Cambridge, Mass: MIT Press, 1968) discusses popular festive forms, and the grotesque body. See also Tony Gash's chapter on *Carnival and Reversal* in the introductory volume of this series: *New Directions in Theatre*, ed. Julian Hilton (London: Macmillan, forthcoming).

17. Ilya Prigogine and Isabelle Stengers, *Order Out of Chaos* (London: Flamingo, Fontana, 1985).

18. For example, J. Briggs and F. D. Peat, *Looking Glass Universe*

(London: Fontana, 1985), which has the subtitle *The Emerging Science of Wholeness*; D. Bohm, *Wholeness and the Implicate Order* (London: Routledge, 1983); Fritjof Capra, *The Tao of Physics* (London: Fontana, 1976) and *The Turning Point* (London: Fontana, 1983).

19.   Friedrich Schiller, *Aesthetic Letters*, discussed in Hilton, *Performance*, pp. 45–6.

20.   Julian Hilton, *Performance*, p. 153.

Bibliography

Alfreds, Mike, *A Shared Experience: The Actor as Story Teller*, an interview with Peter Hulton, London (June, 1979). Published as *Dartington Theatre Papers*, 3rd series, no. 6 (1979–80).

ARENA, The Theatre of Dario Fo, BBC TV documentary by Dennis Marks; first broadcast 28 February 1984.

Aristotle, 'The Poetics', *c.* 330 BC, in *Classical Literary Criticism*, trans. T. S. Dorsch (Harmondsworth, Middx.: Penguin, 1965).

Artaud, Antonin, 'Production and Metaphysics' and 'On the Balinese Theatre', in *Le Théâtre et son Double* (Paris, 1938), trans. Victor Corti as *The Theatre and its Double* (London: Calder & Boyars, 1970).

Auguet, Roland, *Cruauté et Civilisation: Les Jeux Romains* (Paris: Flammarion, 1970), trans. as *Cruelty and Civilisation: The Roman Games* (London: George Allen & Unwin, 1972) and as *The Roman Games* (St Albans: Panther, 1975).

Bakhtin, Mikhail, *Rabelais and His World* (Moscow, 1965; trans. Hélène Iswolsky, Cambridge, Mass.: MIT Press, 1968).

Banu, Georges, 'Peter Brook's Six Days', trans. Susan Bassnett, *New Theatre Quarterly*, vol. III, no. 10 (May 1987).

Barker, Clive, *Theatre Games: A New Approach to Drama Training* (London: Eyre Methuen, 1977).

Barthes, Roland, 'Literature and Signification', in *Essais Critiques* (Paris: Seuil, 1964), trans. Richard Howard as *Critical Essays* (Evanston, Ill.: Northwestern University Press, 1972) pp. 261–7.

Barthes, Roland, *Image/Music/Text* (London: Fontana, 1977).

Barthes, Roland, *S/Z* (Paris: Seuil, 1970; trans. Richard Miller, London: Cape, 1975).

Beare, W., *The Roman Stage* (London: Methuen, 1950, 3rd edn 1964).

Beckett, Samuel, *'Proust' and 'Three Dialogues with Georges Duthuit'* (originally published in *Transition*, 1949) (London: John Calder, 1965).

Beckett, Samuel, *The Beckett Trilogy* (comprising *Molloy, Malone Dies* and *The Unnamable*; first published together London: Calder, 1959; London: Picador, 1979).

Bentley, Eric, 'Epilogue: Theatre and Therapy', in *Theatre of War: Modern Drama from Ibsen to Brecht* (originally published 1969 in

New American Review, this edn, New York: Viking Press, 1973) pp. 213–29.

Blatner, Howard, *Psychodrama, Role-Playing and Action Methods: Theory and Practice* (private publication, 1970) see esp. table 4.

Bogard, Travis, 'American Drama', in *The Revels History of Drama in English*, vol. 8 (London: Methuen, 1977).

Bohm, David, *Wholeness and the Implicate Order* (London: Routledge, 1983).

Bolton, Gavin, *Drama as Education: An Argument for Placing Drama at the Centre of the Curriculum* (Harlow: Longman, 1984).

BOOKMARK, A Visit from Vanya, BBC TV documentary, produced by Richard Denton. First broadcast 21 October 1987. Oleg Efremov, with actresses Anastasia Vertinskaya and Valentina Yakunina; introduced by David Jones.

Boyd, Neva L., *Handbook of Recreational Games* (Chicago, Ill.: Fitzsimmons, 1945; reprinted New York: Dover, 1975).

Braun, Edward, *Meyerhold on Theatre* (New York: Hill & Wang, 1969).

Briggs, J. and Peat, F. D., *Looking Glass Universe: The Emerging Science of Wholeness* (London: Fontana, 1985).

Brown, Maurice, *Too Late to Lament* (Bloomington, Ind., 1956).

Browne, Terry, *Playwrights' Theatre* (London: Pitman, 1975).

Buber, Martin, *Ich und Du* (1923, 2nd edn, Jerusalem, 1957), trans. Walter Kaufman as *I and Thou* (Edinburgh: T. & T. Clark, 1970).

Burzyński, Tadeusz, 'Away from Theatre', in T. Burzyński and Z. Osiński, *Grotowski's Laboratory* (Warsaw: Interpress, 1979).

Buzan, Tony, *Use Your Head* (London: BBC Publications, 1974).

Caillois, Roger, *Man, Play and Games* (London: Thames & Hudson, 1962).

Capra, Fritjof, *The Tao of Physics* (London: Fontana, 1976).

Capra, Fritjof, *The Turning Point* (New York: Simon & Schuster, 1982; London: Fontana, 1983).

Clements, Paul, *The Improvised Play: The Work of Mike Leigh* (London: Methuen Theatrefile, 1983).

Copeau, Jacques, *Essai de Rénovation Dramatique* (Paris, 1913), trans. and cited in Roose-Evans, *Experimental Theatre*.

Copeau, Jacques, Prospectus or *Brochure* of ideal training school, quoted at length in Rudlin, *Jacques Copeau*, pp. 43–4.

Copeau, Jacques, *Registres*, vol. I (Limon, 1916) quoted in Kirkland, 'Golden Age'.

Copeau, Jacques, *A Notebook* in the Dasté Collection, cited in Rudlin, *Jacques Copeau*.

Copeau, Jacques, 'Notes sur l'education de l'acteur', in *Ecrits sur le Théâtre* (Paris: Brient, 1955).

Courtney, Richard, *Play, Drama and Thought: The Intellectual Background to Drama in Education* (London: Cassell & Collier Macmillan, 1968; 3rd. rev. and enlarged edn 1974).

Derrida, Jacques, *L'Ecriture et la Différence* (Paris: Seuil, 1978), trans. A. Bass as *Writing and Difference* (London: Routledge and Kegan Paul, 1979).

Duchartre, P. L., *La Comédie italienne* (Paris, 1929), trans. R. T. Weaver as *The Italian Comedy: The Improvisation Scenarios, Lives, Attributes, Portraits and Masks of the Illustrious Characters of the Commedia dell'Arte* (republished New York: Dover, 1966).

Elam, Keir, *The Semiotics of Theatre and Drama* (London: Methuen 'New Accents' series, 1980).

Eldredge, S. and Huston, H., 'Actor Training in the Neutral Mask', *The Drama Review* vol. 22, no. 4, T-80 December 1978, Worskshop Issue.

Felner, Mira, *Apostles of Silence* (Toronto and London: Associated University Presses, 1985). This contains chapters on both Copeau and Lecoq.

Fenton, James, a review of Phil Young's improvised play *Crystal Clear*, *The Sunday Times* (12 December, 1982), cited in Clements, *Improvised Play*.

Ferguson, Marilyn, *The Aquarian Conspiracy* (Los Angeles: J. P. Tarcher, 1980).

Findlater, Richard, *Banned!: A Review of Theatrical Censorship in Britain* (London: MacGibbon & Kee, 1967).

Flaszen, Ludwik, *Cyrograf* ('The Bond') (Cracow: 2nd edn 1974) cited in Kumiega, *Theatre of Grotowski*.

Fo, Dario, interview in *Playboy* (Italian issue, December 1974), cited in Mitchell, *Dario Fo*.

Fo, Dario, *Mistero buffo; Giullarata popolare nuova edizione aggiornata nei testi e nelle note*, 1969 on (Verona: Bertoni, 1977).

Fo, Dario, *Mistero buffo – Comic Mysteries*, trans. Ed Emery (London: Methuen, 1988).

Fo, Dario, programme of the Washington Arena Stage production of *Accidental Death of an Anarchist* (1984), cited in Mitchell, *Dario Fo*.

Fo, Dario and Rame, Franca, *Theatre Workshops at Riverside Studios, London* (London: Red Notes, 1983).

Fowler, Richard, 'The Four Theatres of Jerzy Grotowski: An Introductory Assessment', *New Theatre Quarterly*, vol. 1, no. 2 (May 1985) pp. 173–8.

Garvin, Paul L., (ed.) *A Prague School Reader on Esthetics, Literary Structure and Style* (Washington: Georgetown University Press, 1964). (Contains a translation of, *inter alia*, Veltrusky.)

Gash, Anthony, 'Carnival and Reversal', in *New Directions in Theatre*, ed. Julian Hilton (London: Macmillan, 1989).

Gelb, Michael, *Body Learning: An Introduction to the Alexander Technique* (London: Aurum Press, 1981).

Gide, André, *Les Nourritures Terrestres* (Paris: Gallimard, 1917–36).

Gide, André, *Les Faux Monnayeurs (Paris: Gallimard, 1925).*

Goldberg, RoseLee, *Performance Art: From Futurism to the Present* (London: Thames & Hudson, 1979; rev. edn 1988).

Gorchakov, Nikolai, *The Theatre in Soviet Russia*, trans. Edgar Lehrman (New York: Columbia University Press, 1957).

Gordon, Mel, '*Lazzi*: The Comic Routines of the *Commedia dell'Arte*', in

Performing Arts Resources, vol.7., ed. Ginnine Cocuzza and Barbara Naomi Cohen Stratyner (New York: Theatre Library Association, 1981).

Gozzi, Carlo, *Opere*, iv, 35, cited in Duchartre *La Comédie italienne*.

Gray, Paul, 'Stanislavsky and America: A Critical Chronology', *Tulane Drama Review*, vol. 9, no. 2 (Winter 1964).

Grotowski, Jerzy, 'Aktor ogolocony' ('The actor bared'), *Teatr*, no. 17 (1965), cited in Burzyński and Osiński, *Grotowski's Laboratory*.

Grotowski, Jerzy, *et al.*, *Towards a Poor Theatre*, ed. Eugenio Barba (Copenhagen: Odin Teatrets Forlag, 1968; trans. various, London: Eyre Methuen, 1969).

Grotowski, Jerzy, 'The Theatre's New Testament', an interview with Eugenio Barba, trans. Jörgen Andersen and Judy Barba, in *Towards a Poor Theatre*.

Grotowski, Jerzy, 'Holiday', *The Drama Review*, vol. 17, no. 2 (T-58, June 1973, Visual Performance Issue).

Hammond, N. G. L. and Scullard, H. H. (eds) *Oxford Classical Dictionary* (2nd edn, Oxford: Oxford University Press, 1970).

Hilton, Julian, (ed.) *New Directions in Theatre* (London: Macmillan, forthcoming).

Hilton, Julian, *Performance* (London: Macmillan, 1988).

Hirst, David, L., *Dario Fo and Franca Rame*, MS of forthcoming volume to be published by Macmillan, London, kindly lent by the author.

Hodgson, J. (ed.), *The Uses of Drama: Sources Giving a Background to Acting as a Social and Educational Force* (London: Eyre Methuen, 1972).

Hodgson, J. and Richards, E., *Improvisation* (London: Methuen, 1966; 2nd edn 1974).

Hood, Stuart, Introduction to Dario Fo and Franca Rame's *Female Parts*, trans. Margaret Kunzle, adapted by Olwen Wymark (London: Pluto Press, 1981).

Hood, Stuart, Introduction to Dario Fo, *Mistero buffo*, trans. Ed Emery (London: Methuen, 1988).

Howard, Tony, ' "A Piece of Our Life" ': The Theatre of the Eighth Day', *New Theatre Quarterly*, vol. II, no. 8 (November 1986).

Huizinga, Johan, *Homo Ludens* (Leyden, 1938; trans. by the author; re-published London: Paladin, 1970).

Hunt, Albert, *Hopes for Great Happenings: Alternatives in Education and Theatre* (London: Eyre Methuen, 1976).

Hurst, Deirdre, 'The Training Session of Michael Chekhov', an interview with Deirdre Hurst du Prey by Peter Hulton, July 1978, *Dartington Theatre Papers*, 3rd series, no. 9 (1979–80).

Johnstone, Keith, *Impro: Improvisation and the Theatre* (London: Methuen, 1981).

Kiernander, Adrian, 'The Théâtre du Soleil, Part One: A Brief History of the Company', *New Theatre Quarterly*, vol. II, no. 7 (August 1986).

Kirby, Ernest T., *Ur-Drama: The Origins of Theatre* (New York: New York University Press, 1975).

Kirkland, C. D., 'The Golden Age, First Draft', *The Drama Review*, vol. 19, no. 2 (T-66, June 1975, Political Theatre Issue).

Koestler, Arthur, *The Act of Creation* (London: Hutchinson, 1964; rev. Danube edn , 1969).

Kourilsky, F. and Champagne, L., 'Political Theatre in France Since 1968', *The Drama Review*, vol. 19, no. 2 (T-66, June 1975, Political Theatre Issue).

Kumiega, Jennifer, *The Theatre of Grotowski* (London: Methuen, 1985).

Langer, Susanne, *Feeling and Form* (London: Routledge & Kegan Paul, 1959).

Lea, Kathleen M., *Italian Popular Comedy: A Study in the Commedia dell'Arte, 1560–1620, with Special Reference to the English Stage* (London, 1934, 2 vols, reprinted New York: Russell & Russell, 1962).

Lecoq, Jacques, *Le role de l'improvisation dans l'enseignement de l'art dramatique*, transcript of a lecture-demonstration by Lecoq at the Institut International du Théâtre, Bucharest, 1964, p. 136, cited in Felner, *Apostles of Silence*.

Lecoq, Jacques, 'Le mouvement et le théâtre, *ATAC Informations*, no. 13 (December 1967).

Lecoq, Jacques, *Stage d'été* (Paris: Brochure, 1971), cited in Felner, *Apostles of Silence*.

Lecoq, Jacques, 'L'Ecole Jacques Lecoq au Théâtre de la Ville', *Journal du Théâtre de la Ville* (January 1972).

Lecoq, Jacques, 'Mime – Movement – Theater', *Yale Theatre*, vol. 4, no. 1 (Winter 1973) cited in Towsen, *Clowns*.

Lecoq, Jacques, *Brochure* of L'Ecole Jacques Lecoq, 57 rue du Faubourg Saint-Denis, Paris. All translations by R. Yarrow (1987).

Lecoq, Jacques, (ed.) *Le Théâtre du Geste* (Paris: Bordas, 1987).

Lecoq, Jacques, 'Moving Heaven and Earth', interview with Jim Hiley in the *Observer* (20 March 1988) p. 40.

Leigh, Mike, *An Account of the Development of My Improvised Plays 1965–69. An Application for the George Devine Award, 1969*, cited in Clements, *Improvised Play*.

Leigh, Mike, *Abigail's Party* and *Goose Pimples* (plays devised from scratch through improvisation) (Harmondsworth, Middx.: Penguin, 1983).

Leigh, Mike, *Abigail's Party* and *Nuts in May* (BBC Video releases, 1988).

Levine, Jacob, 'Regression in Primitive Clowning', *Psychoanalytical Quarterly*, 30 (1961).

Lucas, F. L., *Style* (London: Cassell, 1955).

Maslow, Abraham, *Toward a Psychology of Being* (New York: Van Nostrand Reinhold, 1968).

Mazzone-Clementi, C., '*Commedia* and the Actor', *The Drama Review*, vol. 18, no. 1 (T-61, March 1974, Popular Entertainments Issue) p. 59.

Meyerhold, Vsevolod, 'The Fairground Booth', in Braun, *Meyerhold on Theatre*, pp. 119–28.

Mitchell, Tony, *Dario Fo: People's Court Jester* (London: Methuen, 1984; 2nd revised edn 1986).

Moreno, Jacob Levy, *Psychodrama, I* (New York: Beacon House, 1946).
Moreno, Jacob Levy, *Psychodrama, II* (New York: Beacon House, 1959).
Nagler, A. M., (ed.) *A Source Book in Theatrical History* (New York: Dover, 1952).
Natadze, R., 'On the Psychological Nature of Stage Impersonation', in *British Journal of Psychology*, ed. Boris Semeonoff, vol. 53, part 4 (Cambridge: Cambridge University Press, November 1972) pp. 412 ff.
Nicoll, Allardyce, *Masks, Mimes and Miracles: Studies in the Popular Theatre* (London, 1931; reprinted New York: Cooper Square Publishers, 1963).
Nicoll, Allardyce, *The World of Harlequin: A Critical Study of the Commedia dell'Arte* (Cambridge: Cambridge University Press, 1963).
Nixon, Jon, 'The Dimensions of Drama: The Case for Cross-Curricular Planning', *New Theatre Quarterly*, vol. III, no. 9 (February 1987).
Oreglia, Giacomo, *The Commedia dell'Arte* (Italian version, Stockholm, 1961; rev. Swedish edn Stockholm, 1964) trans. Lovett F. Edwards (London: Methuen, 1968).
Osiński, Zbigniew, 'In the Theatre', in T. Burzyński and Z. Osiński, *Grotowski's Laboratory* (Warsaw: Interpress, 1979).
Parry, Christopher, *English Through Drama* (Cambridge: Cambridge University Press, 1972).
Perrucci, Andrea, *Dell'arte rappresentativa, premeditata e dall'improvviso* (Naples, 1699) trans. S. J. Castiglione, cited in Nagler, *Source Book in Theatrical History*.
Prigogine, Ilya, and Stengers, Isabelle, *Order Out of Chaos* (London: Flamingo, Fontana, 1985).
Rame, Franca, Interview in *Sipario* (Italian Theatre magazine), (September 1983) cited in Mitchell, *Dario Fo*.
Rame, Franca, and Fo, Dario, *Female Parts*, trans. Margaret Kunzle, adapted by Olwen Wymark (London: Pluto Press, 1981).
Rame, Franca, and Fo, Dario, *Theatre Workshops at Riverside Studios, London* (London: Red Notes, 1983).
Roberts, Philip, *The Royal Court Theatre 1965–72* (London: Routledge, 1986).
Roose-Evans, James, *Experimental Theatre: From Stanislavsky to Today* (New York: Avon Books, 1970).
Rudlin, John, *Jacques Copeau* (Cambridge: Cambridge University Press, 'Directors in Perspective' Series, 1986).
Saint-Denis, Michel, *Training for the Theatre: Premises and Promises*, ed. Suria Saint-Denis (New York: Theatre Arts Books, 1982).
Schiller, Friedrich, *Aesthetic Letters*, discussed in Hilton, *Performance*, pp. 45–6.
Sills, Paul, 'The Celebratory Occasion', interview by Charles Mee Jr, *Tulane Drama Review*, vol. 9, no. 2 (Winter 1964).
Smith, Winifred, *The Commedia dell'Arte: A Study of Italian Popular Comedy* (originally published New York, 1912; reprint New York: Benjamin Blom, 1964).

Southern, Richard, *The Mediaeval Theatre in the Round* (London: Faber, 1957).

Spolin, Viola, *Improvisation for the Theater* (Evanston, Ill.: Northwestern University Press, 1963; London: Pitman, 1973).

Stanislavsky, C., *An Actor Prepares*, trans. Elizabeth Reynolds Hapgood (London: Geoffrey Bles, 1937).

Stanislavsky, C., *Creating a Role*, trans. Elizabeth Reynolds Hapgood (London: Geoffrey Bles, 1963).

Stoppard, Tom, *Rosencrantz and Guildenstern are Dead* (London: Faber & Faber, 1967).

Strasberg, Lee, *A Dream of Passion*, ed. Evangeline Morphos (London: Bloomsbury, 1988).

Sweet, Jeffrey, *Something Wonderful Right Away* (New York: Avon Books, 1978; 2nd Limelight edn 1987).

Taylor, Rogan, *The Death and Resurrection Show: From Shaman to Superstar* (London: Antony Blond, 1985).

Towsen, John H., *Clowns* (New York, Hawthorne Books, 1976).

Valéry, Paul, 'Palme', in *Poésies* (Paris: Gallimard, 1968).

Veltrusky, Jiri, 'Man and Object in the Theatre' (Prague, 1940), cited in Elam, *Semiotics of Theatre*, trans. in Garvin, *Prague School Reader*.

Wardle, Irving, Introduction to Johnstone's *Impro*.

Watts, Alan, *The Book: On the Taboo Against Knowing Who You Are* (New York: Random House, 1972).

Willis, Ronald A., 'The American Lab Theater', *Tulane Drama Review*, vol. 9, no. 1 (Fall 1964).

Winearls, Jane, *Modern Dance: The Jooss-Leeder Method* (London: Adam & Charles Black, 1958; 2nd edn, 1968).

Yarrow, Ralph, ' "Neutral" consciousness in the experience of theatre', *Mosaic*, vol. XIX, no. 3 (Summer 1986) pp. 1–14.

Yon, Keith, 'Communication Therapy with Mentally-Handicapped Adults', *Dartington Theatre Papers*, 3rd series, no. 4 (1979–80).

Index

1789, 30

Abigail's Party, 41
Absinthe, 151
Accidental Death of an Anarchist, 74, 75, 76–7
accidents, 176–7
acrobatics, 6, 26
active meanings, 96, 138–9
'active metaphysics', 5
Activity Therapy Program, 49
actor, 4–5
 as creator, 34
 as improviser, 33
 as interpreter, 33
 actor's gift of himself, 86
 actor–spectator relationship, 85
Actors' Studio, 47–8
Actors' Touring Company (ATC), 174
Adler, Stella, 47
Adventure on New Year's Eve, 19
Aesthetic Letters, 65
Age d'or, L', 30–1
Aix-en-Provence, 28
Akropolis, 84
Albahaca, Elizabeth, 84
Alda, Alan, 53
Alexander technique, 97, 155
Alexander, Andrew, 53
Alexandrinsky, Imperial
 theatre, 18
Alfreds, Mike, 135
alienation effect, 118
Alk, Howard, 52
American Laboratory Theatre (the Lab), 46–7
A Minute Too Late, 72
An Actor Prepares, 15, 102
anagnorisis, 158
Anderson, Sara Pia, 41
Anthropologie du geste, 63
Antoine, André, 21–2
Apocalypsis cum Figuris, 84, 89, 174
Appia, Adolphe, 21
Arabian Nights, 55
Arden, John, 56

Arena, documentary on Dario Fo, 80
Aristotle, 6
Arkin, Alan, 53
Arlecchino, 8, 26–7, 121, 123
Artaud, Antonin, 5, 15, 23, 66, 84, 86, 157
Arts Council of Great Britain, 32
Asian drama, modern, 6
Asner, Edward, 51
Association Théâtrale des Etudiants de Paris (ATEP), 30
Association Travail et Culture (TEC), 61
Atelier, L', 23
Athens, 6
attention, 102, 113, 126, 128
audience, 50–2, 153, 169–74
auteur, 9, 84
auto-cours, 63–4, 188 (n. 18)
autokabdaloi, 6
avanspettacolo, 77
Avner the Eccentric, 72
Aykroyd, Dan 53

Babies Grow Old, 41
backward roll exercise, 87–8, 103
balaganschik, 19, 31
balance, 98, 100
Barba, Eugenio, 84
Barker, Clive, 50, 97–8, 109, 113–14, 132
Barrault, Jean-Louis, 23, 45, 61, 90
Barthes, Roland, 90, 175–6, 196 (n. 2)
Beckett, Samuel, 15, 38, 70–1, 157, 168, 179–80
Belushi, John, 53
Benison, Ben, 55
Benny, Jack, 69
Berkoff, Stephen, 72
Berliner Ensemble, 37
Berman, Shelley, 53
Bing, Suzanne, 22–4, 26–7, 50, 83, 117, 186 (n. 52)
bio-mechanics, 19
bird of paradise exercise, 122
bisociation, 168

Blair, Les, 41
Blake, William, 57
Blanchot, Maurice, 64
Bleak Moments, 41
Blin, Roger, 61
blocking, 110–11, 127
Bloński, Jan, 146
Blume, Anna, 178
body-sculptures, 111
body/think, 98, 100, 114, 165
Boleslavsky, Richard, 17, 45–7
Bond, Edward, 56–7, 149–50
Borges, Jorge Luis, 117
Borge, Victor, 69
Boston Toy Theatre, 49
bouffonerie, 79, 183 (n. 15), 190 (n. 52)
boulevard theatre, 21
Boverio, Auguste, 26–7
Box Play, The, 38, 41
Boyd, Neva, 49–50, 53, 186 (n. 52)
Bradwell, Mike, 41, 173
'breakthrough', personal, 88
Brecht, Bertolt, 35–6, 43–4, 51, 54, 62,
    72, 77, 86, 113, 123, 158, 194 (n. 15)
Brighella, 8
Bristol Old Vic Theatre School, 14
Brixham Regatta, 55
Brook, Peter, 38, 43, 72, 90, 197 (n. 13)
Browne, Maurice, 48–9
Browne, Terry, 56
Bruce, Lenny, 53, 150
Brzezinka, 89
Buber, Martin, 82
Building a Character, 15
Burgundy, 26–7, 32
Burmese 'spirit plays', 182 (n. 6)

carbaret, 51, 173, 178
cabotin, 19, 23, 31, 78, 184 (n. 15)
Caillois, Roger, 152
Callot, Jacques, 19
Camus, Albert, 20
canovacci, 8, 77, 79
Can't Pay? Won't Pay!, 74
Capra, Fritjof, 156
Cardinal Sins of
    Improvisation, 108, 110
carnival, 7, 79, 177–8
Case, Justin, 186 (n. 2)
Cassavetes, John, 37
catharsis, 145
'Célestine', 27
censorship, 6, 52, 77, 111, 134, 146–51
'César', 27
Cévennes, 31

Chagrin, Claude, 56
Chancerel, Léon, 26–7, 184 (n. 22)
Chaplin, Charles, 115
character, 16, 18–19, 26, 35–6, 39–42,
    44, 46–7, 78, 85–6, 109–10, 113, 118,
    126, 131–3, 140, 157, 176
Chekhov, Anton, 34
Chekhov, Mikhail, 17, 45
Cherry Orchard, The, 16
Chicago Little Theatre, 49
Chicago style, 45, 48–53
Chicago Training School for Playground
    Workers, 49
Chronegk, Ludwig, 16, 20
Cieślak, Ryszard, 84, 91
circles of attention exercise, 102
circus, 30, 70, 72, 169
Claudel, Paul, 28
Clements Paul, 40–1, 43
clown, 4–8, 23–4, 59, 67–71, 81, 118,
    155, 159, 177–8
Clowning, 55–7, 149
Clowns, Les, 30
Clurman, Harold, 47
co-creation, 58, 125, 140, 169, 172, 175
cognition, 163
collectivity, 42–4
Columbine's Scarf, 18
combinations, 60–1, 179–81
Comédie Française, 21–3, 62
comédie nouvelle, la, 25–7, 29, 31–2, 39
comedian, 81
comic, 5, 53, 56
comici dell'arte, 7, 19, 76, 77, 81
commedia dell'arte, 5, 7–9, 19–20, 25–9,
    31, 51–2, 57, 61, 62, 65, 72, 76, 77,
    79–80, 89, 109, 117–18, 123, 136, 172
Committee, The, 52
communication, 54, 144, 166, 169
community theatre, 20, 29, 31
Compagnia Fo-Rame, 78
Compagnie des Comédiens, 61
Compagnie des Quinze, 23, 28, 31–3
Compass, The, 51–2, 150
Comune, la, 79
concentration, 101–3, 128
concertatore, 8–9, 20, 137
Confederacy of Fools, The, 174
conjuror, 5
Constant Prince, The, 84, 89
Cook, Caldwell, 49
Copeau, Jacques, 3, 20–32, 39, 49, 59,
    62, 83, 90–1, 101, 116–18, 158, 161
Copeau, Pascal, 26
Copeau, Marie-Hélène, 26

Copiaux, les, 26–9, 73, 184 (n. 22)
counselling, 92
Craig, Edward Gordon, 21, 25
Creating a Role, 15
creativity, 2, 9, 22, 32, 48, 57, 65, 125–6, 143, 153–5, 177
Crucible Theatre, Sheffield, 169
Crystal Clear, 41
cube, 101
Cynkutis, Zbigniew, 84

Dance, 24, 26, 46
Danse de la Ville et des Champs, 27, 32
'Dappertutto, Doctor', 19
Dartington, 17
Dasté, Jean, 23, 26–7, 61–2
deconditioning, 87
Decroux, Etienne, 23, 62, 83
deikeliktai, 6, 8
Dell'arte rappresentiva, premeditata, e dall'improvviso, 8
Derrida, Jacques, 168
Devine, George, 33, 56
Diderot, Denis, 130
Dionysos, 4, 7, 177
director, 8–9, 18, 21, 33, 35, 37, 39, 43, 92, 133, 137, 163
disarmament, 15, 87, 161
discorsi, 79
discourse, 162
disponibilité, 65–6, 151–5
disposable drama, 58, 75
Dito nell'occhio, Il, 77
Doctor Faustus, 84, 174
Don Juan, 28
Dorian Mime, 6
Dottore, 8
'double', 5, 19
draining exercise, 97
Dramagraph, 38
drama schools, 33–5, 37, 42, 146, 162
Dullin, Charles, 25, 61, 83
Duncan, Andrew, 51
Duncan, Isadora, 31
Durano, Giustino, 77
Dziady, 84

Earth Project, 89
Ecole Internationale de Mime et de Théâtre, 62
Ecole Jacques Lecoq, L', 78
Ecole Supérieure d'Art Dramatique, Strasbourg, 34
Ecstasy, 41
education, 15, 24, 180

Education par le Jeu Dramatique (EPJD), 61
Education physique de l'entrainement complet par la méthode naturelle, L', 24
Efremov, Oleg, 170
Elizabethan outdoor theatres, 171
Emerson, Ralph Waldo, 154
emotional recall, 112
encounter, 70, 85–6, 90, 109–1
end-stage,
English music hall tradition, 57, 172
English Stage Company, 33, 56
ensemble, 20, 22, 26–7, 46, 59, 148
entheos, 4
entrances and exits, 108–9
environmental theatre, 85
Essai de Rénovation Dramatique, 21
étude, improvisational, 47
'eunuch/pauper' game, 88, 99–100, 112
eurhythmics, 24, 46
exercises, 97ff.
existentialism, 153
eye contact, 123, 135

fabulatori, 76–8
fairground booth-player, 19
fairy-tale, 56
fantasy, 60
farce, 24, 77
Father, The, 176
Federal Theatre Project, 52
Felner, Mira, 184 (n. 13)
Female Parts, 74
fencing, 24, 46
Ferguson, Marilyn, 155
Fergusson, Francis, 47
fiabe, 19
fight in the dark, 99–100, 112
Findlater, Richard, 148
Finger in the Eye, A, 77, 78
First Arabian Night, The, 135
Flaszen, Ludwik, 84
Flicker, Ted, 52, 186 (n. 56)
Fly, lazzo of the, 8
Fo, Dario, 3, 6, 8, 58, 61–3, 72–81, 123, 178
Fool, 5, 178
Footsbarn Theatre, 72
Forefather's Eve, 84
Fowler, Richard, 89
Fratellini Brothers, the, 24
free association exercises, 134
French system of physical education, 24

Freud, Sigmund, 158, 173
'fringe' companies, 173
Futurism, 20

Game of Hurt, The, 52
games, 20, 23–4, 29, 33, 43, 49–50,
  53, 97–8, 100, 116, 129, 132, 145
Game Theatre, 53
Gaskill, William, 56–7
Gaulier, Philippe, 189 (n. 30)
gestus, 36, 123
Gide, André, 66, 153
Ginsberg, Allen, 149
GITIS (Moscow drama school), 83
giullari, 7, 9, 76–8, 80–1
given circumstances, 47, 115
glee-maiden, 7
gleeman, 7
Goldoni, Carlo, 8, 19
Gombrowicz, Witold, 177
Good Hope, The, 46
Good Person of Szechwan, The, 72
Goose Pimples, 41
Gorky, Maxim, 16
Gozzi, Carlo, 8, 19
Graham, Martha, 13
grammelot, 77–8, 80
Grammelot dello Zanni, Il, 80
Grassi, Paolo, 62
Gray, Paul, 17
Greek chorus, 117
Greek tragedy, 62
Gremlin's Theatre, 175ff.
Grotowski, Jerzy, 4, 15, 23, 29, 54,
  56, 59, 70, 83–9, 91, 103, 146, 150,
  152–4, 157–8, 160–4, 172, 174, 191
  (n. 5, n. 11), 192 (n. 19, n. 2)
group creation, 30
  improvisation, 136
  process, 44
  work, 105, 140
Group Theatre, The, 30, 47
grummelotage, 28, 72, 79

half-mask, 133
Halliwell, David, 37
Hall, Peter, 38
Hamlet, 6
Hamlet Study, The, 84
Hapgood, Elizabeth Reynolds, 17
Harlequin, 18, 31, 178
Harris, Barbara, 53
Hauptmann, Gerhart, 18
healer, 5
Hébert, Georges, 24

Herakles, 7
Hesitate and Demonstrate, 173
High Hopes, 41
Hilton, Julian, 165, 181
Hirst, David, 78
Hoffmann, E. T. A., 18–19
'Holiday', 89, 171
Hollywood, 47, 50
Home Sweet Home, 41
Homo Ludens, 65
Hood, Stuart, 75
Hopi indians, 182 (n. 6)
Huizinga, Johan, 4, 65
Hull Truck, 41, 173
Hunt, Albert, 50
hypokrités, 4, 54

I and Thou, 82
icon, 67, 71, 167
I Dritti, 77
I Gelati, 72, 159, 193 (n. 16)
Illusion, L', 32
impersonation, 130
Impro, 1, 55, 114, 131, 162
Impromptu Theater, 145
Impro Olympics, 54, 56, 187 (n. 3)
Improvisation, 162
Improvisation for the Theatre, 51
improvisation (selected topics in):
  applied, 45, 96, 126, 131, 133
  definition(s), 1–3
  free, 163
  in alternative drama, 55
  in American drama, 45
  in creation of a play, 136
  in education, 44
  in traditional drama, 35
  professional, 8
  proto, 16
  pure, 15, 101, 131, 133
  small group, 46
  solo, 133
  strands in twentieth-century, 15
  'total', 57
  'traditional' use of, 148
improvs, 36, 53, 131
impulses, 103, 106
index, 67, 167
Indian folk theatre, 111
Ingrams, Richard, 147
Intercity Theatre, 173
Interlude House, 18–19
International Festival of Street
  Theatre, 151
intertextuality, 85–6, 168

Jacobean indoor theatres, 171
Jacques-Dalcroze, Émile, 24
Jaholkowski, Antoni, 83
Janiszewski, Tadeusz, 150–1
Jarry, Alfred, 15
jazz, 13, 149
'Jean Bourgignon', 27
Jeanetta Cochrane Theatre, 56
jester, 81
Jeu de l'Amour et du Hasard, Le, 65
jeu de styles, 71
jeu du masque, 59
Johnstone, Keith, 1, 55–7, 59, 66, 91,
    110–11, 114–15, 119–21, 126–7, 129,
    134, 146, 149, 158, 162, 174, 177, 186
    (n. 2), 187 (n. 6)
jongleur, 7, 19
journey exercise, 113
Jouvet, Louis, 23, 184 (n. 10)
juggling, 2, 6–7
Julliard School, 34, 45
Jung, Carl Gustav, 90, 145, 157–8

Kamerny Theatre, 20
Kathakali, 64
Kelley, Sheila, 41
Kerouac, Jack, 149
kinaesthetic sense, 98
Kleist, Heinrich von, 154
Knipper, Olga, 17
Koestler, Arthur, 168, 197 (n. 6)
Komisarzhevskaya Theatre, 19
Kootiyattam, 67
Kordian, 84
Kumiega, Jennifer, 84
Kuzmin, Mikhail, 19

Laban, Rudolf, 63, 97, 101
Laing, R. D., 158
Langer, Susanne, 61
language learning, 92, 162
larval mask, 72, 118
'laughing snake' exercise, 106
Lawrence, D. H., 14
lazzi, 8, 25, 57, 77, 79
Lecoq, Jacques, 3, 8, 14, 23, 56, 59,
    61–7, 69, 71–3, 78, 81–2, 89, 91,
    101, 113, 116–18, 146, 152, 154,
    158–9, 161–2, 165, 177, 179–80,
    187 (n. 17), 188 (n. 20, n. 22), 189
    (n. 33)
Leigh, Mike, 3, 14, 18, 37–45, 48, 157,
    163
life drawing class, 37
life-mask, the, 86

*Little Malcolm and his Struggle Against
    the Eunuchs*, 37
Little Theatre Movement, 49
Littlewood, Joan, 37, 147–9
Living Theatre, the, 57
London Film School, 37
London Theatre Studio
    (LTS), 33–4
Look Back in Anger, 37, 56
Loose Moose Theatre
    Company, 187 (n. 6)
Lord Chamberlain, 57, 147–8
'Lord Quick', 27
Lowenfeld, Margaret, 50
Lower Depths, The, 16
ludic text, 177
lumpen-bourgeoisie, 51

MacColl, Ewan, 148
Mactatio Abel (Wakefield), 81
Maeterlinck, Maurice, 18
Magarshack, David, 17
'magical language', 119
'magic If', 130
Magnifico, il (Pantalone), 77, 123, 193
    (n. 18)
Mahabharata, 6
mainstream theatre, 32
Maistre, Aman, 26
make-up, 46, 167
making a machine exercise, 106
Marat-Sade, 38
Marceau, Marcel, 23, 83
Marinetti, Filippo, 20
Marivaux, Pierre Carlet de Chamblain
    de, 8, 65
Marlowe, Christopher, 171
Martian, The, 55
Martin, Claude, 61
Martin, Robert, 50
mask, 6, 8–9, 19–20, 22–3, 25–7, 29,
    31, 33–4, 39, 56–7, 65–7, 77, 80,
    85, 87, 109, 114, 116–17, 118–25,
    157, 159, 163, 167
    larval, 65, 120
    neutral, 63, 65, 66–7, 71, 87, 102,
    116–18
    red nose, 67–8, 71, 118, 166
Maslow, Abraham, 145, 155
master–servant, 8, 116
master–slave comedies, 8
Maude–Roxby, Roddy, 50, 55–6,
    59–60, 66, 91, 107, 116, 119,
    121, 158–9, 180
Mayakovsky, Vladimir, 84

May, Elaine, 51–2, 150
McCarthyism, 51
McGrath, John, 81
McNally, Gerald, 40
Meals on Wheels, 147
meaning, 143, 161, 166, 169, 175,
    179–80
  and performance, 165
  in novel, 169
Mediaeval Players, 174, 194 (n. 15)
medieval trestle stage, 29
  mystery plays, 7
  rounds, 171
  theatre, 79
meeting, 89–91, 109–10
Megara, 6
melodrama, 63, 65
memory, 129, 160
  games, 129
  involuntary, 112
  voluntary, 160
Mendus, Clive, 159, 189 (n. 30)
mental warm-ups, 129
Method, The, 17, 48, 115
Meyerhold, Vsevolod, 18–20, 30–31,
    83, 158
Mickiewicz, Adam, 84
Midland Arts Centre for Young
    People, 38
mime, 6, 9, 19, 20, 23, 25–6, 28–9, 33,
    43, 46, 56, 62, 65–6, 72–73, 107–8,
    118, 124, 188 (n. 22)
mimes, the, 7–9, 19, 76
minnesinger, 7
minstrelsy, 7
Mirecka, Rena, 83, 86–7, 103
mirrors, 119
Mistero buffo, 75–6, 78–81
Mitchell, Tony, 76
Mnouchkine, Ariane, 30–1, 72
Moby Dick, 55
moi permanent, 112
Molière, Jean Baptiste Poquelin de, 8
Molik, Zygmunt, 83
Monteith, John, 52
Moreno, Jacob Levy, 145
Morgan, Ric, 55
Mort de Tintagiles, La, 18
Moscow Art Theatre
    (MAT), 16–18, 20, 45–6, 170
Moskvin, Ivan, 17
Mountain Project, 89
mountebanks, 7–8
Moving Picture Mime Show, 72, 118
Mrs Wilson's Diary, 147

Muirhead, John, 55
Mummenschanz, 118
music-hall, 172
Myerson, Alan, 52, 186 (n. 56)
My Parents Have Gone to Carlisle, 38
Mystery-Bouffe, 84
'mythological dramas',
    Roman, 196 (n. 5)

narrative, 5, 56, 60, 134–6, 140
Nascita del giullare, La, 80
Natadze, R., 130–1
National Revue Co., 43
National Theatre (NT), 33
National Theatre School of Canada, 34
naturalism, 16, 18, 39, 53
Nelson, Ruth, 47
Nemirovich-Danchenko,
    Vladimir, 19
NENAA, 9–40
neutrality, 22, 63, 65–6, 70, 87, 99,
    103, 152–3, 161
neutral mask, 63, 65, 66–7, 71, 87,
    102, 116–18
new age, 156
New Deal, the, 50
New Improvised Comedy, 25, 32
New Theatre Quarterly, 162
New York style, the, 47–8, 51
nibhatkin, 182 (n. 6)
Nichols, Mike, 51–2, 150
Nixon, Jon, 162
Noah, 28
Noh theatre, 26
'no position', 99
not acting, 59
Nuts in May, 41

Obey, André, 28, 32
'Objective Drama', 91
objectives, 96, 128
objects, 39, 46, 60, 85, 115
obscenities, 5
observation, 34, 42, 46, 63, 72, 106,
    115, 163
obstruction exercises, 87
Odin Teatret, 84
Old Vic Theatre, 173
Old Vic Theatre School, 34
Olivier, Laurence, 48
one-minute plays, 46
opening the pelvis exercise, 98
Order out of Chaos, 180
Origin of the Giullare, The, 80
Osborne, John, 56, 149

'Oscar Knie', 27
Osterwa, Juliusz, 83, 153, 190 (n. 1)
Ouspenskaya, Maria, 17, 46–7

Pacquebot SS Tenacity, Le, 21
Pantalone, 8, 26–7, 31, 77, 123, 193 (n. 18)
Paradoxe sur l'Acteur, 130
paratheatre, 4, 15, 29, 54, 56, 83, 85, 89, 91, 143–4, 146, 180
Parenti, Franco, 77
Paris Conservatoire, 23
parodic impulse, the, 7
Pedrolino, 27
Peirce, Charles Sanders, 67, 167
Peking Opera, 99
Pepys, Samuel, 171
performance, 1, 29, 89, 91, 140, 167
Pernand-Vergelesses, 26–7, 32
Perrucci, Andrea, 8, 129
Perse School, the, 49
phase transition, 180
phlyakes, 178
Piaget, Jean, 50
Piccolo Teatro (della Città) di Milano, 30, 62, 77
Pinter, Harold, 168
Pirandello, Luigi, 117, 168
Piscator, Erwin, 61
planoi, 6
platt, 52
play, 59, 63–5, 69–70, 90, 100, 143, 155, 177
play instinct, 5, 24
play of styles, 63
play of the signifier, 60, 64
'Play Way', 49
Playwrights' Theatre, 56
Playwrights' Theatre Club, 51
plot, 109
poet, 5
poétique de l'espace, 63
point fixe, le, 124
point of concentration, 128
point of observation, 128
Polish State Theatre School, 83
Polish Thanatos, 91
politics and the activist, 75
  and censorship, 6, 146–51
  and clowning, 81
  and improvised American theatre, 52
  and the satirist, 6
poor theatre, 85–6
popular theatre, 28, 30
potlatch, 155

Prakrit, 6
pre-commedia actors, 9, 76
Premise, The, 52, 148, 150
preparation, 95, 104
pre-rehearsals, 39
presence, 100–1, 113, 159
present moment, art of the, 45
previous circumstances, 131
priest, 4–5
Prigogine, Ilya, 180
private moment exercise, 48
proletarian theatre forms, 54
proscenium arch, 21
'protagonist', 145
protest literature, 149
Proust, Marcel, 112, 160
proxemics, 168
psychodrama, 9, 48, 92, 111, 144–5, 155
Psychodrama, Theater of, 145
psychotechnologies, 155
psychotherapy, 15, 44, 145, 156, 180
Pulcinella, 26
Punch, 178
Pynchon, Thomas, 177

RADA, 37
Radner, Gilda, 53
Ramayana, 6
Rame, Franca, 58, 62, 73–6, 77–9, 178, 190 (n. 43, n. 49)
Ramlila, 196 (n. 4)
Rand, Suzanne, 52
recognition scene, 158
Red Megaphones, 148
red nose, 67–8, 71, 118, 166
Reduta Theatre Studio, 190 (n. 1)
re-enactment, 113–14
Registres, 31
re-improvisation, Grotowski's, 185 (n. 41)
reincorporation, 69, 134–6
relaxation, 97, 100, 102
research, 44, 63
Research and Navigation, 173
resistances, 87, 128, 144, 146
Restoration theatre, 34, 171
rhythm, 63, 68, 70, 72, 75, 106, 117, 133
Rilke, Rainer Maria, 154
ritual, 5
Rivers, Joan, 53
Robbe-Grillet, Alain, 177
Robinson Crusoe, 55
Rocca, Peter, 40
rock music, 149
Rogers, Carl, 145

rôle-play, 92, 145, 155
*Rosencrantz and Guildenstern are
    Dead*, 160
Royal Court Studio, 149
    Theatre, 33, 55–6
Royal Shakespeare Company
    (RSC), 33, 38–9, 62, 73,
    173
Rudkin, David, 169
Rudlin, John, 20, 23, 25, 32
Russian Formalism, 168

Sahlins, Bernie, 52–3
Sahl, Mort, 53
Saide, Lassaad, 193 (n. 16)
Saint-Denis, Michel, 21–3, 26–8, 30–8,
    45, 54, 56, 59, 62
samizdat, 147
San Francisco, 52
Sanskrit, 6
Sartori, Amleto, 123
Sartre, Jean-Paul, 86, 158–9
satire, 81, 148
Saxe-Meiningen, Duke of, 16
scenario, 8, 19, 25–6, 52, 66, 80, 136–7,
    151, 163
Schepkin, Alexander, 16
Schiller, Friedrich, 65, 180
Schiller Theater, 62
Schluck und Jau, 18
Schnitzler, Arthur, 18
Scierski, Stanislaw, 84
scop, 7
Seagull, The, 16
'Sebastien Congré', 27
Second City, Chicago, 45, 52–3, 150
Second City, Toronto, 53
self-actualisation, 44, 54, 155
semiotics, 60–1, 67, 85, 167, 175
sensation memory, 112
senses, 112
'set', 107, 123–4, 126, 130–2, 158, 168
sexuality and scatology, 5, 19
sexual politics, 31, 79
Shakespeare, William, 8, 72, 124, 171,
    178
Shakuntala, 84
shamanism, 4–6, 8–9, 91, 120, 155–6,
    167, 170, 177
Shared Experience, 135, 174
Shaw, Glen Byam, 33
Sheffield Crucible Theatre, 169
Shepherd, David, 51, 54
showing, 107–8, 133
sign-potential, 144, 161, 167

Sills, Paul, 51–4
Sills, Rachel, 53
simulation exercises, 145
singing, 24, 26
Sir and Perkins plays, 55
*Six Characters in Search of an
    Author*, 117
Skazka Theatre, 18
skiffle, 149
skomorokhi, 7, 19
Slowacki, Juliusz, 83
socialist realism, 30
soggetto, 8
Solidarity, 151
Spare, 147
Special Projects, 89
spieltrieb, 180
spirit world, the, 4
Spolin, Viola, 49–51, 53–4, 126, 128–9,
    134
Spontaneity, Theatre of, 145
stage combat training, 35
Stanislavsky, Constantin, 14–21, 30,
    34–6, 39, 46–8, 51, 83, 102, 112,
    128, 130–1, 153, 157–8
starfish exercise, 103
status, 114–16, 126, 178
Stegreiftheater, Das, 145
stereotypes, 118
Sterne, Lawrence, 177
stock masks, 8
Stoddard, Eunice, 47
Stoppard, Tom, 160
story-telling, 4, 49, 76
Story Theatre, 53
Strasberg, Lee, 47–8
street entertainers, 7, 19, 79
Strehler, Giorgio, 30, 62, 73, 77–8
Strindberg, August, 176
structuralism, 60–1, 64
Sulerzhitsky, Leopold
    Antonovich, 17, 46
symbolic, 67, 71, 167
symbolism, 61
Synthetic Theatre, 20
S/Z, 90

tactile inhibitions, 106
'tag', game of, 97
Tai Chi Chuan, 97, 155
Taïrov, Alexander, 20
Tbilisi Theatrical Institute, 130
Teatr Laboratorium, 83–4, 88, 91, 163
Teatr Osmego Dnia, 150–1, 177
television plays, 43

telling, 107–8, 133
Tennis court theatres, 171
'tenses of acting', 113
'text', 85, 147, 165–6, 168
Theatre and its Double, The, 5
theatre as communion, 20, 28–9
theatre as direct intervention, 79
theatre communities, 83, 190 (n. 1)
Théâtre de Complicité, 43, 72, 174
Théâtre de l'Oncle Sebastian, 184
  (n. 22)
Théâtre des Champs-Elysées, 23
théâtre digestif, le, 79
Théâtre du Soleil, 30–1
Theatre Games, 97
Theatre Guild, 30
Theatre-in-Education
  (TIE), 162–3
Théâtre Libre, 21–2
Theatre Machine, 55–60, 74, 149, 174
Théâtre Nationale Populaire (TNP), 62
'Theatre of Participation', 89
'Theatre of Performance', 89
'Theatre of Sources', 91
Theatre of the Eighth Day, *see* Teatr
  Osmego Dnia
Theatre of the Thirteen Rows, 83–4
Theatre Act (1843), 148
theatre sports, 54, 187 (n. 3)
Theatre Workshop, 147–8
therapy, 48, 50, 92
'third act', the, 75, 81
Thomas, Betty, 53
thrust stage, 169
Time Machine 55
timing, 68, 72
Tout Bouge, 62
Toward a Psychology of Being, 155
Towards a Poor Theatre, 85
Towsen, John, 6
training, 14, 31, 33, 35, 37, 49, 56,
  59, 73, 85, 95, 98, 130, 133, 146,
  164
Training for the Theatre, 34
trampoline words, 136
trance, 4–5, 27, 119, 125, 193 (n. 14)
transformation, 4, 9, 34, 78, 91, 120,
  155, 170, 178
translation, 75
Trestle Theatre Company, 120, 174
Trickster Theatre Company, 120
trickster figure, 178
Tristram Shandy, 71, 177
trouvère, 7
trust exercises, 88, 105, 145

Unity Theatre, 148
University of California, Irvine, 91
University of Chicago, 51
University of Paris, 62
'University of Research', the, 90

Vakhtangov, Yevgeni, 19, 83
Valéry, Paul, 154
vatic poet, 4
Veil of Pierrette, The, 18
Veltrusky, Jiri, 192 (n. 3)
Venetian mountebanks, the, 7–8
via negative, 86, 116
video, 110, 137, 166, 170
Vidusaka, 5–6, 178
Vieux-Colombier, 20–1, 23, 25, 26, 28,
  32, 49
Vilar, Jean, 73, 83
Vildrac, Charles, 21
Villard-Gilles, Jean, 32
Viol de Lucrèce, Le, 28
Vita, 6
Volkenberg, Ellen Van, 48

Waiting for Godot, 70
'waking-up' exercise, 66, 117
Watts, Alan, 155
Weaver, Fritz, 51
Weiss, Peter, 38
Wells, John, 147
whole-body awareness, 122
Whose Line Is It Anyway?, 5, 187 (n. 3)
who/where/what exercise, 126–7
Willie No – in New Combinations, 180
Wilson, Colin, 149
Witkiewicz, Stanislaw, 83
Wood, Charles, 147
Works Progress Administration
  (WPA), 50
Writer's Group, 56
writers-in-residence, 20

Yakshagana, 111
Yavin, Naftali, 50
'yes/yes, but' exercise, 111
yoga, 86, 97
Young Actors' Company, 50
Young, Phil, 41
'Your turn to play', 70
You Won't Always Be On Top, 147

zanni, 8, 80
Zanni's Grammelot, 80